The young generation expects a worse fate than the war generation of 1939-45, if we don't fight back. Fate has a name: Transhumanism & 5G.

Everything described in this book is real:
- Artificial intelligence,
- Transhumanism,
- Mind control,
- Weather manipulation,
- Chemtrails,
- HAARP,
- Bioweapons,
- Morgellons,
- 5G .

A justiciable processing of this
"Weapons Against Humanity"
has already begun.
It is reflected in the indictment of representatives of the
Deep State,
Case No: '19CV2407CAB AHG ,
filed at the Supreme Court in California on 16 December
2019.
The charges are:
(1) MISUSE OF ARTIFICIAL INTELLIGENCE,
CYBERNETICS, ROBOTICS, BIOMETRICS,
BIOENGINEERING, 5G, AND QUANTUM COMPUTER
TECHNOLOGY
(2) ENDANGERMENT THE HUMAN RACE WITH THE
MISUSE OF ARTIFICIAL INTELLIGENCE
TECHNOLOGY
(11) BRAINWASHING HUMANITY WITH A.I. CODING
& ALGORITHM BIAS
(12) CULTURAL GENOCIDE BY MISUSE OF
ARTIFICIAL INTELLIGENCE
(and 22 other charges[1])

Dr. Joachim Sonntag

2025

The Endgame
or
The coup from above

3th edition, extended sand updated
Translation from German

3th edition, extended and updated
Published by the author himself

www.sonntag-physik.de
https://joachim.jugnw.org.uk/

Translated from German

The original German title (ISBN 9783751936330)
„2025 – Das Endspiel *oder* Der Putsch von oben"

This book is also available in translation in the languages:
Français: „2025 – Fin de partie …"   ISBN 9783751935708
Русский: „2025 – финальная игра …"   ISBN 9783751935548
Español: „2025 – El Final juego …"   ISBN 9783751935586

ISBN 9783751930024

Production and publishing: BoD- Books on Demand, D-
Norderstedt

Bibliographic information from the Deutsche
Nationalbibliothek: The German National Library lists this
publication in the Deutsche Nationalbibliografie. Detailed
bibliographic data is available on the internet via dnb.dnb.de

"Divide and conquer."

—

When there was still time to turn things around, people fought:
Right against left,
"Young against old",
Patriots versus do-gooders,
Natives against migrants,
Muslims against Christians and Jews,
poor against rich,
Vaccination advocates against vaccination opponents,
Conspiracy theorists against mainstream believers.

Is it still possible to escape a hellish world without hope?

About the author (JS)
Dr. Joachim Sonntag studied physics at the Technical University of Dresden. From 1972 until 1989 he worked at the Central Institute for Solid State Physics and Materials Research, specializing in electron structure in metallic alloys. He then moved to Dortmund and worked for HL-Planartechnik GmbH as a developer for temperature and radiation sensors. He specializes in radiation physics, multi-phase alloys and nanomaterials, for which he has published a number of fundamental works in leading international journals. From him came the formulas / theory on thermoelectric force (2005; 2017), on the Hall effect and Giant Hall effect (2016) and on electron redistribution in composites (1989) (details: *www.sonntag-physik.de*). At the beginning of 2019, together with two other colleagues, he published his last specialist article, a review article with the title: *"Electronic Transport in Alloys with Phase Separation (Composites)"*. [2]

Stephen Philp, (SP)
[proofreader for the English translation of the book]
Stephen Philp is an author and presenter of poetry workshops. From 1977 to 1986 he was the English editor for EGIS (Environmental Groups Information Services) and EGIS Education.
Stephen Philp has a degree in Archaeology and worked at the University of Liverpool in the Planning, Physics and Biology departments. Prior to his retirement he was Director of a Liverpool charity (2015 to 2018) which focused on the needs of war veterans. Additions to the text by Stephen Philp are identified by.

"All in all, I would say that your book has helped to keep me sane during the Coronavirus horror, and for that I will always be grateful to you." (SP)

Contents   Page

The sections in italics are new compared to the German 1st edition 2019.

Prologue – The Road to Tyranny

What is it all about? It's about profit, power, and enslavement. It is nothing less than the abolition of democracy and the establishment of a new slave-owning society.

To achieve these long-term objectives the élite or Deep State have planned some intermediate steps: destroying the nation states, uprooting the people, dividing the population, destroying family cohesion and the family itself, lowering the level of education, creating fear (of terror, climatic disaster, corona etc), creating mass migration, racial mixing[3,4,*], land and property expropriation, total control of all people, introducing the abolition of cash, dissolving the differences between men and women[†], reducing world population to 500 million, and undermining the health of survivors. Such claims obviously need to be proven. For this trilogy with the overarching title **Agenda 2025** the title of the first part, *2025 – The penultimate act*, was already published in April 2019 (there is a short summary of it at the end of this book). The third part, now in preparation, has the working title *2025 – The final act*. Who or what embodies the élite and the Deep State is discussed in the epilogue.

Central theme of this 2nd part of the trilogy are the "Weapons Against Humanity" and how they are used by the powerful of this earth with the aim to bring mankind into its total dependence. They make use of the latest developments in the fields of artificial intelligence, transhumanism, mind control, weather manipulation,

---

[*] Nicolas Sarkozy (2008): *The Goal is Racial Mixing*. In German, *Das Ziel ist die Rassenvermischung!*

[†] That might sound absurd to you and me; however, that is the project's ultimate aim. In German, *Das klingt absurd; das ist jedoch das Endziel des Projekts* (See Gender Mainstreaming and Transhumanism, chapter 5, 3)

chemtrails, HAARP, bioweapons, morgellons, 5G. With the help of these "tools" they are planning:
1) the genetic modification of the human being,
2) whose total control and
3) Reduction of the world population to 500 million.
Transhumanism and 5G play a key role in these "weapons against humanity" listed here, topic of chapter "5th Mind Control and Transhumanism".

For the sake of maintaining power, the world population will be reduced to a minimum. This will be achieved by means of artificially created illnesses, with bioweapons de-clarified as epidemics; but also by means of targeted famines and wars. The reason stems from the realization that once most people can no longer finance their own diet the rich will be forced to provide relief measures or risk a hugely dangerous potential for conflict.[5,6]
This is point 10 of Carl Friedrich von Weizsäcker's 12 prophecies[7] about future trends in the world.[‡] As noted in a blog[§] on May 1, 2018, this quote and the associated 12 prophecies came not from Carl Friedrich von Weizsäcker directly but from an unknown author probably writing in the year 2007. However, I have become very careful in my research, especially with regard to fact-check portals like CORRECTIC or MIMIKAMA, but also Wikipedia,[8] which in my experience are not independent, as well as the public media. For example, the peace researcher Daniele Ganser is called a "conspiracy theorist"[9] by Wikipedia in order to make him appear implausible. Even the "New World Order" is still called a "conspiracy theory" on Wikipedia and its credibility is questioned.[10] And Mimikama states in contradiction to a mass of available evidence: *The chemtrail conspiracy theory has existed for more than 20 years. – And to this day there is not a single piece of*

[‡] Carl Friedrich von Weizsäcker (1912-2007), German physicist and philosopher, was the longest-surviving member of Werner Heisenberg's nuclear research team of World War Two. An authority on nuclear fusion as well as solar activity and planetary formation in the solar system, in later years he became a Christian pacifist interested in Eastern mysticism and the environment (https://en.wikipedia.org/wiki/Carl_Friedrich_von_Weizs%C3%A4cker) [SP]
[§] falsezitate.blogspot.com

credible evidence. (For details of the evidence see Chemtrails – The Chemical Soup in the Sky, chapter 4, 2). Sadly, most people presumably believe in these media.

My distrust of institutional politics, the media, and the websites that allegedly check facts arose in connection with the one-sided reporting of 9/11, which swept the obvious main contradiction under the carpet: How could three skyscrapers have been destroyed by two airplanes? Instead the media unswervingly adheres to the official version of 9/11 that a conspiratorial team of Islamic suicide bombers planned and carried out the attack. Contradictions between the official version and the accepted facts[11] are still not discussed openly.

Then there are the wars in the Near and Middle East and the slander campaigns and denunciations of the Alternative for Germany party (Alternative für Deutschland, or AfD) by politicians of the mainstream parties and the media, along with systematic brainwashing in TV news programmes, talk shows and analyses. To summarize my impressions in an exaggerated way: The lie becomes the truth and the truth becomes a lie.

Back to the quote. Even if this quotation does not come from Carl Friedrich von Weizsäcker the question arises: to what extent do these 12 prophecies[12] describe the reality of life and future developments in the world? If we consider this point alone, we must realize that the quasi-Weizsäcker quote already rings some frightening bells. For decades, military and intelligence labs have been working to develop *bioweapons*, and it looks as if these weapons have already left the lab, leading to the death and misery of many people throughout the world. (More about that in Biological Warfare, chapter 6). *Famines and wars* appear to be an inextricable part of our reality today. If the politicians in the rich industrialized nations actually had an interest in preventing the world's children from starving, these problems would have been solved (or seriously mitigated) already by meaningful economic aid (including clean-water programmes and food redistribution). And the problem of overpopulation could be solved in a humane way, through better education and a movement away from the practice of free trade agreements that make Third World countries even poorer than they already are. Instead, Third-World markets are flooded with the cheap products of rich industrialized countries and their resources are exploited.

In terms of foreshadowing or of contemporary description the other 11 quotes also have a frightening reality. Anyone who follows the social development of the West with critical alertness will recognize the harbingers that point precisely in the direction these forecasts address. This book is about these harbingers, which prophesy a bitter reality for us all.

As you read the following chapters, you should always remember the contents of this Prologue, especially if common sense suggests that something is simply not possible or is opposed to the humanistic ideal. Or that (surely) people could not and cannot be doing this to other people?! Note that are dealing here with psychopaths who are alien to empathy.

After completing the book and then checking a number of quotations, I found that some of them were no longer accessible, in short had been deleted. Some have fallen victim to censorship, which unfortunately seems to be becoming more and more intensive. Censorship of so-called unwanted content has been legitimized by new laws passed recently, for example the so-called Network Enforcement Act (NetzDG), which came into force on October 1, 2017. Attorney Steinhöfel calls it the 'Freedom of Opinion Combating Act'.[13] Indeed, *we are faced with a drastic interference by the political and media élite in one of our most important fundamental rights, namely through a legislative proposal that is unconstitutional, unlawful under European law and simply unnecessary.*[**] Under this law, critics of the government parties are not only to be fought, defamed and ridiculed, they are supposed to be silenced.

[**] The video by Steinhöfel cited here is also no longer available: *This video is no longer available because the YouTube account linked to this video has been terminated* - a gagging formula frequently used as a reason.

There may be readers who will place the contents of this book in the conspiracy theory corner and judge, for example, the quoting of YouTube videos as unscientific. Though readers should remember I am a scientist by profession, this book is not a scientific treatise, but a warning about what the élite have been planning for us for a long time, and what they intend to do by 2025. My hope is that the majority of people will wake up, come out of their comfort zone and fight back. If you want to get to know my scientific papers, I recommend that you visit my website.[††] There the reader will also find the opportunity to call up directly the complete list of sources for the book.

If you think that what is described here in this book is exaggerated and unimaginable, then mentally put yourself in the time before 9/11. Could you have imagined then that the government would send thousands of its own people into an inferno and all media would offer suspiciously similar and inaccurate versions of 9/11?[14,15]

[††] *www.sonntag-physik.de*

1. Agenda 2025

Through its very incredibility, truth eludes recognition.
(Heraclitus of Ephesus around 500 BC)

Three Documents with identical end goal "2025"

The destruction was so great that this weapon was banned by the United Nations in 76–77. An agreement has been reached (ENMOD convention[‡‡]) that air-conditioning weapons should not be used for armed conflicts. But in fact it (sic) is still used. What can you do and what can you not do with this weapon? With this weapon you can generate rain, storms, clouds, lightning, thunderstorms anywhere in the world or the opposite, you can dissolve rain fronts, stop the hail and snowfall and also create drought. What is happening? Whoever owns this climate control weapon[§§] has absolute control over the world's treasured resources. Especially food. So in plain language: when a country has this technology it controls the world's water tap. Do what you are told and you will get water, and if you resist your country will be under-supplied with water, the clouds will be destroyed, and an extended drought will be the consequence, leading to an inability to feed the people of that country. Result: famine. It [the technology] does exist. There are countries that have this technology, and in the United States it has become part of foreign policy. A report by the North American Air Force means – watch out for the title! - **'Weather as force multiplier: Owning the**

[‡‡] *Convention on the Prohibition of Military or Any Other Hostile Use of* **Environmental Modification Techniques** is an international treaty drafted by the United Nations Disarmament Commission prohibiting military or other hostile use of environmental technologies (Wikipedia).

[§§] Although this translation (from Spanish) speaks of *climate, climate weapons,* and *climate control,* the terms *weather, weather weapon,* and *weather control* seem to characterize the facts more accurately in English (and also German) usage (JS, SP).

weather in 2025' *(see Figure 1). This self-explanatory title leaves us speechless and breathless. The fact that one can be so presumptuous as to want to control the tap of the world, is hard to get one's head round. This report also states that climate change is part of American foreign policy, whether the world wants it or not. And this policy is enforced, with bilateral agreements, by organizations such as NATO, which are responsible to us; or by the United Nations. In fact, in the last General Assembly of the United Nations, section D of the 5th Climate Change Report (IPCC) more or less legitimized what is called geoengineering.*[16]

Just as people today are stigmatized as 'conspiracy theorists' when they say that geoengineering sprays thousands of tons of poisons from airplanes overhead, so are people who claim that the weather is manipulated by the military, intelligence agencies, or other forces, or that droughts, floods, earthquakes, hurricanes, tsunamis can be artificially disrupted or induced. Because this stigmatization is supported and fuelled by so-called experts via the media, these stigmatized 'conspiracy theorists' are not believed. But precisely because humanity was technically capable of triggering such natural disasters as early as the 1970s, the world community took this opportunity to create the ENMOD Convention. The interpretation agreement on the ENMOD Convention clearly states that the issue is the use of meteorological weapons, explicitly speaking of tsunamis, earthquakes and shifting the ecological balance. This means that the technique of weather manipulation was state of the art even before 1976 (details in HAARP – The Food Slicer in the Sky, chapter 4, 5).

The year 2025 in the title of this book is borrowed from the document mentioned in the above quote (Figure 1) whose title reads in the original text: **Weather as a Force Multiplier: Owning the Weather in 2025**[17,18], hereinafter referred to as the Weather War Document. Figure 1 shows the document's cover page.

Weather as a Force Multiplier: Owning the Weather in 2025

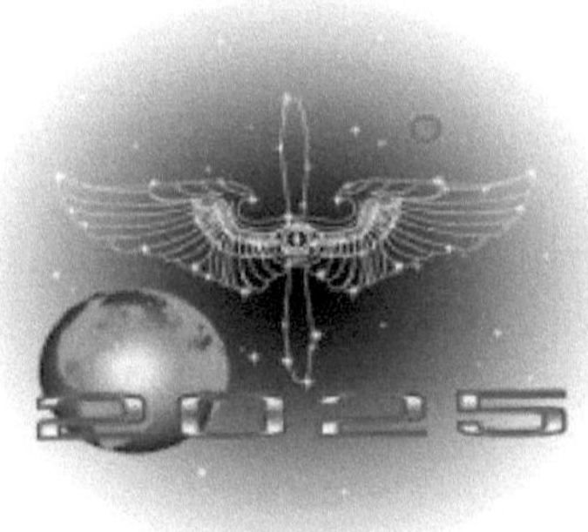

A Research Paper
Presented To

Air Force *2025*

by

Col Tamzy J. House
Lt Col James B. Near, Jr.
LTC William B. Shields (USA)
Maj Ronald J. Celentano
Maj David M. Husband
Maj Ann E. Mercer
Maj James E. Pugh

August 1996

Figure 1: Cover page of the weather war document 'Weather as a Force Multiplier: Owning the Weather in 2025'

This Weather War document, prepared by the US Department of Defense, was submitted on June 17, 1996. It means:[19] *In 2025, U.S. aerospace forces can control the weather by benefiting from new technologies and by focusing on developing those technologies for warfare. Such a capability provides the armed forces with tools to design the combat area in a way never before possible. Current technologies that will mature in the next 30 years will offer anyone with the necessary resources the opportunity to change weather conditions and the associated effects, at least locally. The current demographic, economic and ecological trends will lead to global tensions that give many countries or groups the necessary impetus to convert this ability to change the weather into practical action.* This proramme for developing meteorological weapons raises the following important questions:

1) Is there a connection to the document 'Future Strategic Issues / Future Warfare [Circa 2025]' (see Figure 2)? Is there a common agenda behind both documents? This question is obvious, since both documents give the identical date 2025 as their basis. What is the consequence?

2) To what extent have these developments, as described in the Weather War document, progressed to the present day? What weather-influencing capabilities does the military have today, and are they already being used?
The first question implies another question:

3) Is the Weather War Document part of the élite project that characterizes the transition from the creeping process of globalization to global empowerment?[20]

Question 3) is very likely to be answered in the affirmative. Because there is a third document with the corner point 2025. In this document, a dramatic population reduction in the western world is predicted for the year 2025. This document (Figure 5 shows an excerpt in which population figures for the year 2025 are predicted) comes from the company Deagel,[21] which deals with information of a military nature obtained directly from the CIA, FBI, NSA, US Army, Mossad, NATO, EU (for details, see Reduction of the world Population, chapter 2, 2).

Therefore, obviously there is a plan, an agenda – let's call it **Agenda 2025** – which aims at the collapse of the Western world, the great crisis on whose rubble it is intended to establish the New World Order (NWO), in the spirit of David Rockefeller's statement: *We are on the brink of global transformation, all we need is the right all-encompassing crisis and the nations will agree to the new world order.*[***]

The NASA document, Figure 2, outlines the plan for transitioning from the creeping process of globalization (in which we are now) to the global empowerment of the élite. For this plan to work, and for the expected resistance from the populations not to threaten the plan, the élite need this 'right all-encompassing crisis'. The number 2025 stands as a synonym for the day X, on which the power takeover is to take place. And this takeover will take place simultaneously in the USA, Germany and the other EU countries.[22]

Already in 1961, former US President Eisenhower and US President Kennedy had warned of the dangers of an increasingly powerful shadow government, established by the military-industrial complex.[23] Kennedy said in his historic and programmatic speech on April 27, 1961: *We are dealing with a monolithic and nefarious global conspiracy that spreads its influence by covert means: infiltration instead of invasion, overthrow instead of elections, intimidation rather than self-determination, with guerrilla fighters at night instead of armies by day. It is a system that has built with huge human and material resources a complex and efficient machinery that combines military, diplomatic, intelligence, economic, scientific and political operations. Their plans are not published but hidden, their failures are buried, not published. Dissenters are not praised, but silenced* ... [24] Because Kennedy announced that he would disclose the machinations of the élite, he was murdered.[25]

[***] 1994 on the Economic Committee of the United Nations (UN Business Council). (https://wahrheitinside.wordpress.com/2017/04/19/zitate-zur-neuen-weltordnung/)

Future Strategic Issues/Future Warfare [Circa 2025]

The Future Is Now!

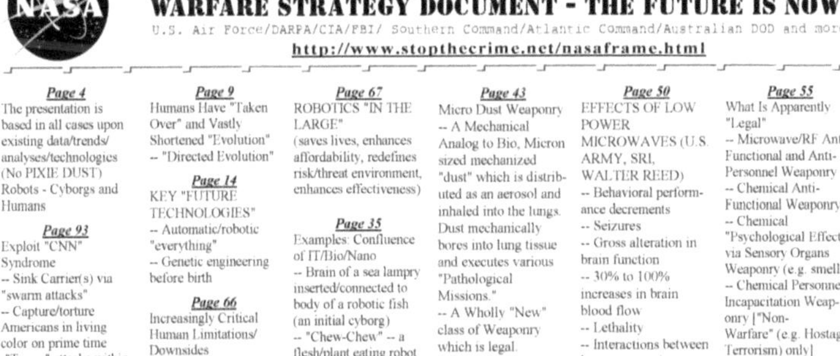

Dennis Bushnell, Chief Scientist – NASA Langley Research Center

WARFARE STRATEGY DOCUMENT - THE FUTURE IS NOW!

U.S. Air Force/DARPA/CIA/FBI/ Southern Command/Atlantic Command/Australian DOD and more

http://www.stopthecrime.net/nasaframe.html

Page 4
The presentation is based in all cases upon existing data/trends/analyses/technologies (No PIXIE DUST) Robots - Cyborgs and Humans

Page 93
Exploit "CNN" Syndrome
-- Sink Carrier(s) via "swarm attacks"
-- Capture/torture Americans in living color on prime time
-"Terror" attacks within CONUS (binary bio, critical Infrastructure "takedown, " IO/IW, EMP, RF against Brain, etc.)
-- Serious "Psywar" (collateral damage exploitation, etc.)

Page 9
Humans Have "Taken Over" and Vastly Shortened "Evolution"
-- "Directed Evolution"

Page 14
KEY "FUTURE TECHNOLOGIES"
-- Automatic/robotic "everything"
-- Genetic engineering before birth

Page 66
Increasingly Critical Human Limitations/Downsides
-- Large
-- Heavy
-- Tender
-- Slow (physically, mentally)
-- Require Huge Logistic Train(s) i.e., Humans have rapidly decreasing-to-negative "Value Added"

Page 67
ROBOTICS "IN THE LARGE"
(saves lives, enhances affordability, redefines risk/threat environment, enhances effectiveness)

Page 35
Examples: Confluence of IT/Bio/Nano
-- Brain of a sea lampry inserted/connected to body of a robotic fish (an initial cyborg)
-- "Chew-Chew" -- a flesh/plant eating robot that hunts/bio-digests "natural foods" to "live off the land"
(Chew-Chew robot inventor: Stuart Wilkinson expresses concern about the dangers of the robots eating humans)

Page 43
Micro Dust Weaponry
-- A Mechanical Analog to Bio, Micron sized mechanized "dust" which is distributed as an aerosol and inhaled into the lungs. Dust mechanically bores into lung tissue and executes various "Pathological Missions."
-- A Wholly "New" class of Weaponry which is legal.

Page 45
Beam Weapons Increasingly Prevalent

Page 50
EFFECTS OF LOW POWER MICROWAVES (U.S. ARMY, SRI, WALTER REED)
-- Behavioral performance decrements
-- Seizures
-- Gross alteration in brain function
-- 30% to 100% increases in brain blood flow
-- Lethality
-- Interactions between low power (microwatts per sq. cm./.4 to 3 GHz) MW and brain function

Page 55
What Is Apparently "Legal"
-- Microwave/RF Anti-Functional and Anti-Personnel Weaponry
-- Chemical Anti-Functional Weaponry
-- Chemical "Psychological Effects" via Sensory Organs Weaponry (e.g. smell)
-- Chemical Personnel Incapacitation Weaponry ["Non-Warfare" (e.g. Hostage Terrorism) only]
-- PSYWAR
-- Acoustic Weaponry
-- Mechnical Micro Dust

THESE ARE JUST A FEW EXAMPLES OF WHAT IS IN THE N.A.S.A. DOCUMENT THAT ARE HAPPENING NOW !
www.StopTheCrime.net/nasaframe.html

Figure 2: NASA Document from 2001 (Cover Page) On Future Warfare, authorized by NASA, the US Air Force, CIA, FBI …[26].

Some websites 'sneer at and ridicule those who take the US Air Force programme Owning the Weather 2025 seriously. We are – as usually claimed – conspiracy theorists. Hence this statement by former US Secretary of State Cohen:[27] Others (terrorists) are even *engaging in an eco-type of terrorism whereby they can alter the climate, set off earthquakes, volcanoes remotely through the use of electromagnetic waves ... So there are plenty of ingenious minds out there that are at work finding ways in which they can wreak terror upon other nations ... It's real, and that's the reason why we have to intensify our efforts.* And these efforts combine in a programme formulated in the Weather War document, Figure 1.

Just like the Weather War document, the NASA document[28] (Figure 2) – also information from the company Deagel (DEAGEL.com) – are doubted or ridiculed from different sides. However, taking into account the research done by the authors of the YouTube video[29], we would do well to pay close attention to Deagel.com information.

This **Agenda 2025**, a long-term project with the aim of a global takeover of power by the élite, has been adopted many decades earlier, visible for example in the document **Silent Weapons for Quiet Wars**[30], dating from 1986, whose genesis should go back to the year 1954, the year in which the Bilderberg Group was founded.[31] So answering the third question with YES might mean that *day X, when ... the global takeover of power by the élite takes place*[32] will not only be confined to the western sphere of elitist influence, but also encompass the rest of the world. Because the weather-changing techniques described in the weather war document are already so matured that their effects can reach any point on earth with devastating consequences for the respective country (details in Destroying our living conditions, chapter 2), a global weather war suddenly seems more likely than a worldwide nuclear war. After all, a nuclear war would leave a planet contaminated for everyone (including the élites) for an unthinkably long time.

In parallel with this geoengineering programme, the development of new biological weapons and of new beam weapons, whose devastating effects on humanity will be gigantic, will be carried out in parallel with international agreements.

These meteorological weapons, biological and beam weapons belong to the plan, which aims at the reduction of the earth's human population to a level below 500 million[†††]. In addition, there will be an inevitable impairment of the survivors' health as well as the manipulation of thinking and emotions to be able to control survivors safely. (Details in Biological Warfare, chapter 6)

Nanochips and dust particles (Smart Dust) can be introduced into our bodies in various ways without our being aware of it, made possible by the intelligent IoT (Internet of Things) grid, directed specifically to the brain of each person selected, with certain states of consciousness impressed and controllable from the outside.[33] In addition, a completely new category of life forms, called Morgellons fibres[34], has been created with the help of synthetic biology ... which replicate themselves and can be used as transmitters and receivers of foreign signals or information, by which people's thoughts, feelings and bodily functions cannot only be registered but can also be controlled remotely.

To remotely manipulate and control populations by over-writing, re-programming, and controlling the thoughts, feelings and actions of the masses would be the ultimate endgame. Because that sounds like an unbelievable conspiracy theory, it has to be proven. Hence this book.

If you look at the existing technological possibilities of the military, the problems

Depletion of our raw materials
Littering of the seas
Rainforest deforestation

have so far clearly been neglected by governments and must therefore be considered by them to be of subordinate importance. For these problems would obviously be solvable if the will to

---

[†††] *Be not a cancer on the earth – leave room for nature – maintain humanity under 500,000,000 in perpetual balance with nature* (Inscribed on the Georgia Guide Stones)

resolve them finally prevailed at the highest level. But how do those responsible in politics and business respond to these threats? Even if individual governments appear superficially to take on the problem (the keyword being sustainability), the depletion of our raw materials continues, as well as the pollution of the oceans, the deforestation of the rainforests, the exploitation of the 3rd world, perennial world hunger and perpetual wars (see Figures 3 and 4). Today the military, especially the military of the US Empire, is the world's largest polluter. *The gigantic war machine is the world's largest consumer of petroleum products. Officially, 320,000 barrels of oil are used daily at the 7,000 military bases worldwide. It [the military] causes most of the so-called greenhouse gas emissions and hurls millions of toxic substances into the environment every day. But the Pentagon is exempt from all international climate and environmental agreements. The Pentagon produces more highly toxic waste than the five largest American chemical companies combined. Among the toxic substances are pesticides, lead or radioactive materials from weapons production, to name but a few. For example, during both invasions, Iraq was bombarded with depleted uranium ... Until today, large parts of Vietnam are contaminated with dioxin.*[35]

With regard to Figure 3: *This bar is very worrisome right here. Although US troops are being withdrawn from Syria and Afghanistan, which should bring significant cost savings, the US has increased its military budget for 2019 as dramatically as in the past six years. The question is, is money being made available here for a major war? Maybe even for a war against the SCO [Shanghai Cooperation Organization]?*[36]

Weighted equally seriously in terms of environmental degradation are the at least 2200 destructive nuclear weapons tests since 1945, which had a total explosive force at least 6000 times larger than the Hiroshima atomic bomb.[37] These atomic bomb tests are likely to have had a much more lasting impact on the global climate than all civilian influences put together: cow exhaust, car exhaust, aircraft, ships, coal-fired power plants.

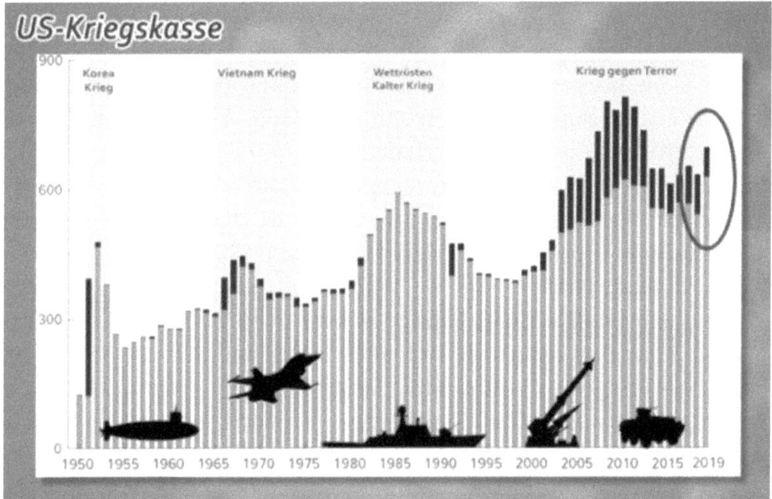

Figure 3: Developments in the US military budget (in US $ bn).[38] The maximums correlate with the Korean War and the Vietnam War as well as with the arms race/Cold War and the War on Terror.

Figure 4: SCO (Shanghai Cooperation Organization), an association of green marked countries founded in 2001, encircled by the US military and NATO, illustrated by the deep blue symbols.[39]

Wars are waged for raw materials and power; free trade agreements are concluded with third world countries that make them even poorer and prevent those countries from developing economically, supporting corruption instead. The deforestation of the rainforests continues,[40] driven by the pursuit of profit, and the littering of the seas is not stopped. Instead of solving these problems, those responsible are trying to draw attention to an artificially and propagandistically inflated problem called 'human-made climate change'. As we will see in the following chapters, this human-made climate change is both a destructive weapon and a huge hoax that makes the rich even richer and the rest poorer. By 'destructive weapon' I mean the Geoengineering program, which is to be tried – so the official view goes – to stop global warming, but in reality a gigantic program is being implemented for the manipulation of climate, weather, and ionosphere and for the production of artificial earthquakes. These so-called weather weapons will dominate future warfare, but are already used today. This geoengineering program is mainly driven by the military and intelligence services and financed by taxpayers' money as well as donations from private investors: a group of super rich people, who I refer to as the élite.

Anyone who wants to get an idea of what geoengineering means can get information on the homepage of the Bundeswehr's planning office.[41] Geoengineering is presented there as a technology of the future that aims to combat global warming. However, geoengineering has been used for decades, by the Military generally and in Germany by the US military; though to prevent lawsuts against the resultant environmental destruction this is not officially confirmed, because in the event of pollution charges being made these would have to be proved beyond doubt. Such proof is all the more difficult to obtain if the application of geoengineering is officially denied. On the homepage of the Bundeswehr (German Armed Forces)[42] planning office it is clearly stated that geoengineering is a *future* technology. The headline reads: 'Geoengineering – a security perspective,' and one of the subheadings, still more explicit in its futuristic construction, reads:

'How *could* geoengineering be used?' (rather than 'How *is* geoengineering used?')

On one website[‡‡‡] you can read[43]: *Since the US Navy and Airforce launched the programme, 'Owning the Weather by 2025' in 1996, our sky is not the same: littered with toxic chemtrails and HAARP washboard clouds – and 'our' ideological meteorologists are constantly trying to educate us on non-existent manmade global warming.*

The Role of the EU in the globalization process

The year 2025 also appears in another context: the abolition of the European nation states – more precisely, the EU member states. On December 7, 2017, Martin Schulz, the leader of the Sozialdemokratische Partei Deutschlands (Social Democratic Party, or SPD), calling for the United States of Europe to be established by 2025, recommended a resolution to that effect by the European nation states.[44] Therefore the sovereignty of the German state would come to an end in that (fateful) year. ***The day will come when governments will be forced to admit that an integrated Europe is an accomplished fact, without saying anything in terms of defining its foundations. All that would then be left for them to do is to merge all of their autonomous institutions into a single federal administration and then proclaim the United States of Europe.***[45] Germany will then be merging *"with a democratically illegitimate, lobbyist-controlled bureaucratic Monster called the EU ... that is the end of a free and democratic Europe..."*[46] This will be the same year in which, according to the plans of the globalists, the New World Order should also become a reality, for which the establishment of the EU state is a prerequisite. We have already stated this in the first part of the trilogy 2025: *And this takeover (by the NWO) will take place in Germany and the other EU countries simultaneously.*[47]

[‡‡‡] http://*new.euro-med.dk*

2. Destruction of our living conditions

The global power structure has long ago made the choice to subject our planet (and the entire web of life it supports, including humanity) to an unimaginably massive and destructive climate intervention/weather warfare attack. [48]

Psychopaths

Do not forgive them, because they know what they are doing!

Unfortunately, as long as the world is ruled by psychopaths, we will always have to learn from worst-case scenarios: wars, weather manipulations, mind control. [49]

What we are discussing in this book is so incredibly monstrous that it almost transcends human imagination. The élite of this world want to build the New World Order, which would be dominated by One World Government and absolute Bank domination. They have set themselves the task of enslaving populations, thus gaining absolute power over them. On the face of it that sounds incredible. And incredible things tend to escape detection. To repeat Heraclitus's aphorism (see the epigraph to Agenda 2025, chapter 1): *'Through its very incredibility, truth eludes recognition.'* For example, numerous discussions with friends and colleagues on the question, 'Are there such things as chemtrails?' have shown me that most of them have never heard of chemtrails and they listen in disbelief to arguments that prove their existence. Or they loudly and continually interrupt such arguments. They call for evidence while at the same time they prevent me from presenting that evidence. Witness this commentary on a 2017 article discussing

Chemtrails and HAARP:[§§§,50] *It's hard to believe what's going on. If you air the topic in public you'll be dismissed as a total spin-doctor and conspiracy theorist.* That's exactly what happens to me, demonstrating that people cannot even remotely imagine, and are unwilling to believe, that there could be people and institutions that purposely want to destroy our livelihoods and poison us. Similarly, when asked, 'Do HAARP systems exist and what are they used for?' a common response is, 'How would the élites protect themselves from this?' *These people are protected. All the rest of the population ... are not. The pharmaceutical industry bosses are crouching elsewhere, in their mountains, somewhere, in the fresh air ... They have means to resist, not the stupid people.*[51] There is another aspect. The motivation to do such things, even if those same things can be used in a retaliatory way, is key to the psyche of such people. Behind the projects discussed in this chapter are people who are unscrupulous and lacking in empathy, characteristics typical of psychopaths but also of some top politicians (and top entrepreneurs even more so). Both characteristics seem to be conducive to a high-ranking career in decision-making (and we perhaps need to ask ourselves why this is).

1 to 15% of humanity are probably psychopathic.[****] **S**ystems analysis has provided the following description: An organization with a pyramid structure is vulnerable to the fact that the higher decision-making positions are gradually filled by psychopaths. The older and larger the organization, the more susceptible to this phenomenon the hierarchic structures are. Examples of such pyramid structures are the Vatican, the World Bank, the United Nations, Siemens, UBS (formerly the Union Bank of Switzerland), and Deutsche Bank.[52] And if the leadership of such an organization is at some point mainly occupied by psychopaths, this engenders a great potential for destruction against everyone and everything that hinders that organization's goals, its influence, claim to power, and

---

[§§§] **H**igh **F**requency **A**ctive **A**uroral **R**esearch **P**rogram.

[****] Psychopathy today refers to a serious personality disorder, which goes hand in hand with those affected with ... complete lack of empathy, social responsibility or conscience. (Wikipedia)

maximization of profit. Consider the leaders in the pharmaceutical, medical, and animal-fattening industries. *According to the Robert Koch Institute, between 1000 and 4000 people in Germany already die each year from infection with multiresistant pathogens. In Europe, there are 25,000. In the US every year about 23,000 people are victims of such so-called super germs (superbugs)."*[53] According to a 2016 study[54], collected in 30 countries, about 91,000 people die each year from hospital infections, of which 15,000 were in Germany. Though the numbers from these two sources differ significantly for Germany, these thousands of deaths from multidrug-resistant bacteria are clearly a consequence of the fact that the germs have developed resistance over the years against which the available antibiotics have become ineffective. One cause of this is the irresponsible mass use of antibiotics in animal fattening. This overuse made it possible to keep the animals in a confined space, thus dramatically reducing the costs, and increasing the profits, compared to those experienced by an animal-friendly ethos. However, top industrialists cannot see that they, too, are exposed to the danger of catching resistant germs and dying prematurely. Or they psychologically displace the danger. For, as Karl Marx said:[55] With corresponding profit, capital becomes bold; at 50% it becomes reckless; at 100% it ignores all human laws; and at 300% profit there is no crime that does not risk it, even at the risk of its own destruction![††††]

Another example of psychopathy at the top is the introduction and worldwide spread of synthetic chemical agents in the agriculture and food industries – environmental toxins such as pesticides and insecticides – used for weedkilling or for the longer shelf-life of foods that some medical professionals have identified as causing the rapid increase of cancers, etc.[56] Of course, this increased health

---

[††††] This quote is actually from PJ Dunning (1860), but has been made known via a footnote in *Capital* by Karl Marx: *Capital has the same horror of absence of profit, or of minimal profit, as nature has of a vacuum. With corresponding profit, capital becomes bold. Ten percent guaranteed, and capital applies itself everywhere; 20 percent, capital goes into overdrive; 50 percent, becomes positively reckless; for 100 percent profit, capital would stamp all human laws underfoot; 300 percent, and even at the risk of the gallows there is no crime it would not commit* (SP's translation)

threat also endangers those responsible for the worldwide spread of such poisons: corporate bosses as well as politicians. 'Conspiracy theorits' is the label most often applied to those who point to these incredible things happening around us. Consequently it seems that a substantive discussion of these subjects is no longer possible.[††††]

People who disagree with the claim that global warming is human-made are now being attacked just as much as those who discuss *chemtrails* and *HAARP – ideologically* by politicians and the media, and *objectively* by so-called media experts, including producers of a whole series of YouTube videos. Listen to what host Markus Lanz tells us on a talk show:[57,58,59] *At the North Pole it is warmer these days than in Berlin.* And his talk show guest Dirk Steffens answers: *Yes, and the pair of us will, if all goes well, yet be able to experience sailing a dinghy over the North Pole, because some day it will be ice-free in the summer.* Markus Lanz is obviously spot-on with his statement. But he refarins from saying that the melting of the Arctic is caused by the so-called ELF waves (see HAARP – The Food Slicer in the Sky, chapter 4, 5). This ELF project goes back to a treaty concluded in 1974 between the United States and the USSR aimed at reaching the resources of the Arctic.[60,61]

In this context, the eBook *truth lies*[62] by Thomas Beschorner contains *an online collection of highly explosive and sensitive topics. The articles should emphasize the pros and cons of the individual viewpoints of the population.* In the first article of this extensive work, Beschorner emphasizes that HAARP, as a purely scientific project run by a team of international scientists, is not subject to secrecy. It is also stressed that HAARP in conspiracy theories is referred to as a *secret project associated with global natural disasters such as earthquakes, floods and volcanic eruptions. Sometimes thought manipulation by means of ELF waves is assumed.* In the second article those who make such claims are called spindoctors. However, in the third article, exactly the opposite viewpoint is expressed: *Details and backgrounds of a*

[††††] *The only incontovertible conspiracy theory is that there is never such a thing as conspiracy.* (SB)

madness project that has been developed for years under the strictest secrecy in Alaska by the US military. The High Frequency Active Auroral Research Programme (HAARP) heats the ionosphere with gigantic energy sources (up to 100 billion watts) to affect the Earth's surface and human consciousness using the infamous ELF waves. Here are two opposing views on the project HAARP. Who is lying? The authors of the first two articles, or the author of the third article? Which of the three articles would you *rather believe*, dear reader? I would assume you prefer the first two, because the idea encapsulated in the third article is so inhuman, so monstrous that one simply cannot believe it that anyone would want to engage in research so prejudicial to human existence.

Even so the viewpoints represented in the first and second articles accord well with the objective of discrediting conspiracy theories (conspiracy theory as a term for labelling the enemy). In the following passages we will show that we do well not to reject the third article from the *truth lies*[63] cited above, but to become active ourselves in seeking independent sources.

A number of projects have been launched to
1) drastically reduce the world population and
2) gain absolute control over the survivors.

These projects can be classified as as follows:
    a)   Fomenting wars and civil wars
    b)   Dissolving nation states, partly through the ethnic mixing of populations
    c)   Lowering the average IQ[§§§§]
    d)   Destroying families and communities

[§§§§] If Joachim Sonntag's overall thesis is correct, lowering IQs has been a long-term project, dating from the use of lead in petrol as early as 1922 [cf Landrigan, Philip, 2002, Editorial, in *Bulletin of the World Health Organization*, 80 (10), p768] (https://www.who.int/bulletin/archives/80(10)768.pdf). But it was probably not until the late 60s or early 70s that the élite fully appreciated the population-control benefits in terms of A) reducing world population and B) dumbing down (SP)

e) Destroying human health
f) Gaining absolute control over the people

Such projects would also achieve:
i)   a drastic reduction of the world population
ii)   mentally, physically and psychologically weakened people no longer capable of grasping the political nexus or of having the strength or will to rebel.

What overall strategy are the élite pursuing? An important milestone in implementing these projects was the claim regarding human-made global warming. In the meantime, this claim has been refuted by many serious scientists and is referred to by them as a 'lie to the climate' (see details below). However, that claim continues to be propagated by politicians and the media, serving as the rationale for a series of geoengineering projects that are destroying people's living conditions and health. One such geoengineering projects is the spraying of Chemtrails – highly toxic chemicals, heavy metals, aluminum, strontium and barium compounds in the form of nanoparticles and synthetic fibres in the stratosphere (for facts and sources, see Chemtrails – The Chemical Soup in the Sky, chapter 4, 2). The use of these toxic substances or chemical trails (chemtrails) is either labelled a conspiracy theory by the media or (laughably) claimed to reduce sun exposure, but in reality chemtrails pose an extremely high risk to human health. This risk is due to

1) the spread of highly toxic materials all over the globe, which accumulate in the waters and in agricultural produce
2) these substances being inhaled by humans
3) the additional reduction of vitamin D production in the human body as a result of the obscuring of natural sunlight.

What strikes me is that they take light from us. And reproduction and in general the entire structure of the immune system essentially belong to light. That light is the basis of everything. Sunlight is reduced. We cannot receive the whole spectrum. Clearly, this will affect the reproductive behavior of the next generation.[64] This statement *'they take light from us'* is no exaggeration, s. to the video[65] (from minute 14:26).

Reducing world population

Count all the people in the world
Missing, you'll find, a third.
What's left? Seek in every land:
Half won't understand.
(from *Song of the Linden,
prophecies found in 1850*)[*****]

Almost everyone knows that an expanding world population is one of the gravest problems of our time. In order to limit population growth, there have been a number of measures in the past, such as the introduction of contraceptive pills or China's one-child policy, which (in a global sense) has not yet resolved this problem.[†††††] The élite, on the other hand, are pursuing a completely different, (in their eyes) more effective strategy, appearing on the internet under a variety of names. You can read about this on News-for-Friends.de: Agenda 21, Agenda 2030, Agenda 2050. What these all agree on is a baseline world population amounting to a reduction of up to 95%. The means to enforce this are: *chemtrails (or 'geoengineering'), vaccines, irradiated food, GMO* (Genetically Modified Organisms as outlined in the *Codex Alimentarius), smart meters, 5G use ...*[66] In addition, one must mention here mass migrations from Africa and the Middle East into Europe, which

---

[*****] *Zählst du alle Menschen auf der Welt,
Wirst du finden, daß ein Drittel fehlt,
Was noch übrig, schau in jedes Land,
Hat zur Hälft' verloren den Verstand.*[*****]
(aus „Lied der Linde", 1850; English translation: JS and SP)

[†††††] And indeed, after 35 years of being enforced, China's one-child policy was revoked in 2015, ostensibly through Communist party fears of an unsustainably ageing population. There is now a two-child policy operating in China (SP)

according to the official interpretation is supposed to counteract European population decline. However, this mass migration fails to relieve Africa's overpopulation because population growth on that continent is significantly greater than its population loss due to emigration. In fact, Africa's population is expanding *significantly* faster: by an estimated one million inhabitants within two weeks.

If we were to seriously reduce population growth worldwide the obvious humanitarian way would be to raise education and living standards in high-growth countries to a level comparable to European conditions. In Europe, owing to the high level of education and high standard of living, population numbers are sustainable. On the other hand, according to the super-destructive élite plan, mass migration serves to create a huge potential for conflict in European countries, which may translate into civil wars when indigenous populations become minorities in what they perceive to be their ancestral lands.[67] *Note! Anyone who has been propagating [the idea that] 'multiculturalism failed!' for years and who knows the dangers very well and then later directs this clientele* (i.e. people from other cultures) *to Germany in bulk, doesn't do it 'accidentally',*[68] but on purpose. There is an intention behind it.

For the sake of maintaining power, the world population will be reduced to a minimum. This will be achieved by means of artificially created illnesses, with bioweapons de-clarified as epidemics; but also by means of targeted famines and wars. The reason stems from the realization that once most people can no longer finance their own diet the rich will be forced to provide relief measures or risk a hugely dangerous potential for conflict.[69][‡‡‡‡‡] (see Prologue – The Road to Tyranny, and Inoculated with Glyphosate, chapter 2, 2). This is point 10 in Carl F. Weizsäcker's *Forecasts on Future Development Trends in the World*.[70] As we will discuss in Biological Warfare (chapter 6), this quote already has a frightening reality: for decades we have been working on bioweapons for precisely this purpose.

[‡‡‡‡‡] As stated on the blog falsezitate.blogspot.com on May 1, 2018, this quote and the underlying 12 prophecies might not come from Carl Friedrich von Weizsäcker, but from an unknown author, probably from the year 2007

As far as reducing world population is concerned, there are forecasts for the loss of inhabitants in individual countries. According to one video[71], published on 22.02.2015, which refers to another source[§§§§§], large population losses were forecast for 14 European countries to the tune of 137.7 million (second digit column in Figure 6). In 2017, these population losses were amended to significantly higher values (in total 193.6 million, the 3rd digit column in figure 6.

In this document (Figure 5), one again encounters the year 2025, just as in the two documents discussed in the Prologue – The Road to Tyranny: the weather war document (Figure 1) and the NASA document (Figure 2). So it seems likely that there is a plan, for which I have coined the phrase Agenda 2025, which targets the collapse of the countries of the western world. In every sense this will be the Great Crisis, on the ruins of which it is intended to build the NWO, as David Rockefeller had already formulated in 1994: *We are on the brink of global transformation, all we need is the right all-encompassing crisis, and nations will agree to the new world order.*[72,******]

[§§§§§] www.deagel.com
[******] 1994 on the United Nations Economic Committee - UN Business Council

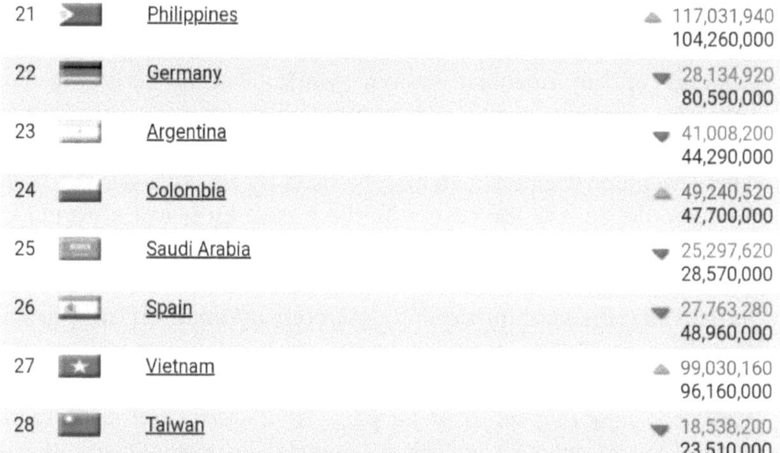

Figure 5: Population projections for 2025 for Philipines, Germany, Argentina, Colombia, Saudi Arabia, Spain, Vietnam and Taiwan. The upper number in each case is the actual population, the lower number in each case is the Forecast for 2025 (extract from *http://www.deagel.com/country/forecast.aspx*).

The company Deagel, which operates this site, trades information of a military nature directly from the CIA, FBI, NSA, US Army, Mossad, NATO, EU. In addition, Deagel.com publishes information on GDP (gross domestic product), military expcnditurc, PPP (purchasing power parity), population figures for each country and forecasts for the year 2025.[73] The population forecasts shown in Figure 6 were published by Deagel in 2014 (2nd digit column in Figure 6) and 2017 (3rd digit column in Figure 6) respectively. As a cause of the high population losses the explanatory text below the table cites the total collapse of the socioeconomic systems in these countries, highlighting (in the depopulation context) the following:

1) Pandemic scenarios (eg Ebola)
2) Collapse of the Western financial system
3) Collapse of Ponzi schemes such as the stockmarket and pension funds

In this justification of the prognoses, wars, civil wars and famines are not explicitly addressed. One can assume, however, that a collapse of the financial system would lead to civil war-like scenarios. Famines can also be brought about by means of weather weapons, as described in the Prologue – The Road to Tyranny. These weather weapons can also be used by the élite against their own people, as was the case with the Forest Fires in California in 2017 and 2018 (see Forest Fires – Human-made? chapter 4, 9).

In the video the narrator says[74]: ... *And this information leads to the fact that by 2025 Deagel forecasts the total collapse of the economic and social system in these countries. This, in turn, would lead to a new migration of peoples, as it were, and millions of people would migrate to other countries or commit suicide or starvation, or else somehow die* ... That would indeed involve a new migration of peoples, but in exactly the opposite direction to the one taking place today. This will go beyond immigraton and lead to emigration pressure on the outside.

Source: Forecast by:	*2) 2017: Population (in millions) **2017**	*1) 2014: Forecast Residents- Loss (in millions) **2025**	*2) 2017: Forecast Residents- Loss (in millions) **2025**
Italy	62,0	-19,0	**-18,2**
France	67,0	-24,6	**-27,9**
Austria	8,8	-1,8	**-2,6**
Switzerland	8,2	-5,2	**-2,9**
Germany	80,6	-1.6	**-52,6**
Belgium	11,5	-2,1	**-3,4**
Netherlands	17,1	-7.7	**-0,3**
Portugal	10,8	-4,0	**-2,7**
Great Britain	65,7	-31,3	**-51,1**
Spain	49,0	-21,3	**-21,2**
Sweden	10,0	-6,2	**-2,8**
Norway	5,3	-3,1	**-1,5**
Ireland	5,0	-2,1	**-3,7**
Greece	10,8	-7,8	**-2,7**
Total	**411,7**	**-137,7**	**-193,6**
USA	327,0	-247,4	**-227,4**
Canada	35,6		**-9,3**
Australia	23,2		**-8,0**

***1)** https://www.youtube.com/watch?v=W8Ifp_O9oRA&feature=youtu.be

***2)** http://www.deagel.com/country/

Figure 6: Forecast population loss for 2025. (1st column: Population 2017, 2nd column: Population 2025, forecast 2014; 3rd column: Population 2025, forecast 2017).

Increasing Emigration Pressure

For Germany, for example, the two forecasts for 2025 made in 2014 and 2017 differ fundamentally: the population loss of 1.6 million forecast in 2014 (2nd digit column in Figure 6) has skyrocketed in the 2017 forecast to 52.6 million (3rd digit column in Figure 6). Taking into account the opening of the German borders in September 2015 – in other words, between these two forecasts – this fundamental difference becomes understandable.[††††††] Because of this million-fold influx of migrants and their obvious need for support by the German government (who meanwhile must also keep supporting the greater part of the German population) the social system will collapse at a certain point in time. The soaring costs of migration and the associated costs of family reunification, amounting to tens of billions of euros per year will no longer be sustainable and collapse will prove inevitable. Precisely when that happens depends on how well lenders are prepared to provide additional funding. It is therefore up to the lenders, the financial élite, to determine the exact time of the collapse. This means that then the state will no longer be in a position to pay pensions and social security. And that is the predicted 'total collapse of the economic and social system' quoted above. As far as the collapse of the economic system is concerned, we have been witnessing for some years how the German economy is being systematically destroyed, in particular the key German industries such as power generation (the

---

[††††††] However, the prognosis for the population figures for Germany was changed several times (on April 23, 2015 changed from 79.6 to 48.1; August 16, 2016 from 48.1 to 40.8; June 22, 2017 from 40.8 to 31.3 and 28 million respectively (https://www.youtube.com/watch?v=t4OwfkSEtlY). The first two changes were made before the German border was opened. However, I assume that the opening of the border did not happen spontaneously, but followed a plan to direct migration flows to Europe, and the forecasts took into account knowledge of this plan. That this plan existed is suggested by the fact that immediately before the outbreak of mass migration to Europe, the United Nations Refugee Agency (UNHCR) drastically cut the already scarce funds for refugee camps near Syria and Lebanon, which caused the number of people who made their way to Europe increase rapidly (*https://www.youtube.com/watch?v=EQ0l0HxNEOY&t=300s*)

nuclear and coal-fired power industries) and, starting in the last few years, the automotive industry as well.

People surviving the collapse will naturally be uprooted. The direction of migration will reverse, no longer *into* Europe[‡‡‡‡‡‡], but *out of* Europe); migration pressure will point to the east. But after the collapse one must assume that the borders will be closed again, secured by mercenaries of the EU army, whose establishment by Macron and Merkel has been demanded or announced for some time. Forerunners of this EU army are the secret armies GLADIO[75] and EUROGENDFOR, which also employ foreign mercenaries who, in following their orders, will even be prepared to shoot at their own people. After the collapse it will no longer be possible to cross the border. The survivors of this Great Crisis will then be the new citizens of the One World State or UN State, without either rights or a worthwhile future. That's the New World Order for you.

A similar prognosis exists for the USA. Figure 7 shows how the forecast for the US has been adapted to the respective circumstances. The largest jump (amendment) in the forecast took place on April 3, 2014, when the population forecast for 2025 was downgraded from 182 million to 88 million, and then, on 24 September 2014, down to 69 million.

[‡‡‡‡‡‡] The German edition reads what would be translated as 'into Germany (or Europe)' [SP]

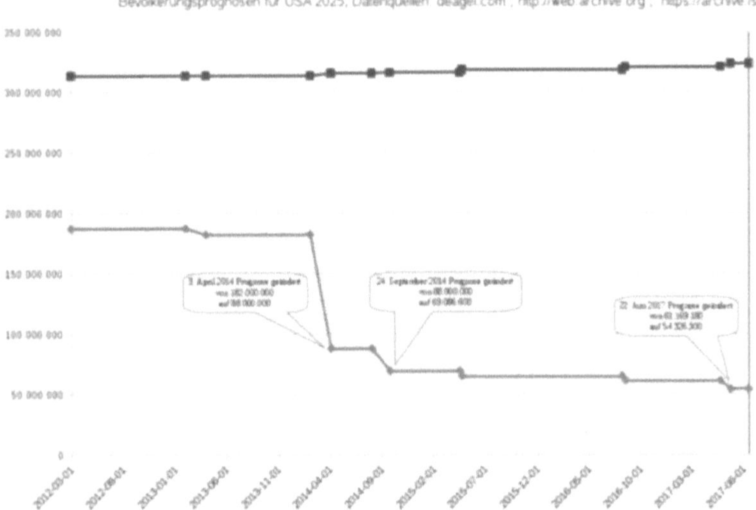

Figure 7: Corrections to the US population forecast for 2025 (lower curve). Top curve: Population "actual" status, based on the respective time on the X axis".[76]

It is noteworthy for the US that in recent years natural disasters seem to increase in frequency and intensity: hurricanes, floods and forest fires. There is a suspicion that these are being helped along by humans, firstly to keep people in fear, secondly to destroy their livelihoods. In California there were two devastating forest fires in October 2017 and November 2018 (see Forest Fires – Human-made? chapter 4, 9). Over the past ten or twenty years hurricanes have also plagued the US. Ceaseless rain and accompanying floods have devastated large tracts of agricultural land there, making sowing impossible. What cannot be sown cannot be harvested.[§§§§§§] The result can be a famine. Michael Snyder describes the US agribusiness situation in June 2019:[77] *America's farmers are facing the gravest crisis in a generation – and the next monstrous storm is already approaching.*[78] *Because of the incredibly wet weather, millions and millions of acres of the best American farmland will have to lay fallow this year, because the moisture does not allow sowing. On further millions of hectares of land, seed is indeed*

[§§§§§§] This has the ring of a modern proverb (SP)

sown, but the yield is likely to lag behind the norm owing to the terrible situation.

Now, of course, one can ask oneself: will the people not fight against this? Won't there be civil war everywhere? Surely this will be the case. But what can defenceless citizens do? Many do not understand what's happening around them nor do they appreciate what causes these anomalies. They have long forgotten how to scrutinize the big connections from a logical point of view. This is the result of an indoctrination that has been going on for decades, a kind of double-brainwashing,[79] a stupefying of the people by the media in support of political actors.

3. Climate Change - a topic for all people

Isn't the only hope for this planet in the collapse of industrial civilization? Isn't it our responsibility to ensure that this breakdown occurs?
(Maurice Strong, first UNEP director 1990 and 1992, organizer of the Rio conference, and chief advisor to Kofi Annan, 1990 in Wood and 1992 at the Rio climate conference[80])

Climate Emergency

Whoever should play with the emergency to restrict freedom will find my friends and me on the barricades of democracy.
(Willy Brandt, 1968[81])

Climate emergency was declared in at least 67 German cities and towns by December 18, 2019 (Wikipedia). On November 28, 2019 the European Parliament in Strasbourg proclaimed a climate emergency for Europe.[82] The Süddeutsche Zeitung (South German Newspaper) commented:[83] *The climate emergency has more of a symbolic character and should build up pressure for concrete legislation. What needs underlining is that Parliament stated that urgent action should be taken because of climate change.* Is this really the case? What is an emergency if not a state in which civil rights are overridden? **Because** a declared emergency prepares the way for emergency regulations, for the undermining of law: *Anyone who calls for a climate emergency today demands nothing more than decisions without democratic legitimacy and aims to override democratic rights,* said MEP Markus Ferber (CSU)[84].

By definition, the declaration of a state of emergency clears the way for emergency ordinances.

On December 11, 2019, the new head of the EU Commission, Ursula von der Leyen, announced the European Green Deal, according to which the EU should be made climate neutral by 2050.[85,86] She wants to make climate neutrality legally binding by 2050, This means that by that year the use of oil, coal and natural gas will have been largely abolished. Enormous financial resources are required for this objective.

Climate Change – The New World Religion

The supposedly manmade climate change is the ultimate pretext to control people, because CO_2 is no more and no less than life. All human action is based on CO_2; even breathing! Who controls the CO_2 emissions of people by law can determine how we have to live and how many people are allowed to live. Just as before 9/11 no one had seen a reason to reduce the Middle East to rubble and ashes, before the climate hysteria nobody would have voluntarily renounced travelling, his pet or even his own children.[87]

All parties in the industrialized world, whether right or left, will adopt the CO_2 warming theory. This is a unique opportunity to tax the air for breathing. Because they supposedly save the world from death by heat, the politicians even receive applause for it. No party will resist this temptation.[88]

Figure 8: Title page of *Der Spiegel* (in German, *The Mirror*) from 1986: starting signal for climate hysteria. 'As long as we don't announce disasters, nobody will listen.' [John Harton, Vice President of the IPCC (Intergovernmental Panel on Climate Change), 1994[89]]

In 1986, *Der Spiegel* (in German, *The* Mirror) shocked its readers with a horrific scenario. The front page of its 33rd edition depicted the bottom third of Cologne Cathedral sunk in a sea that stretched to the horizon (Figure 8). This was the starting gun for a climate hysteria that has since planted insecurity in many people's brains. Fear of the climate, now firmly anchored in the public mind, has developed such momentum that many are convinced that a global climate catastrophe will hit humanity in a few years and that the demise of human civilization can only be prevented by enormous countermeasures. In 2007 Der Spiegel reinforced the drama of climate change with the title page: *SECRET CLIMATE REPORT – We don't have 13 years left to save the earth.*[90] After that, we should expect the worst for 2020 at the latest. This example should already lead to the suspicion that the much-talked-about climate crisis amounts to a major brainwashing, driven by the media and most politicians.[*******]

Human-made climate change is an invention of the élite, which pursues the following objectives:

1) Creating a common project or theme that affects the entire world community with which all humanity – not just individual groups, states, or groups of states – can identify. This commonality serves the élite seeking a One World Government. Dirk Müller points out:[91] *As a global society, we never had a common purpose. To date, there has not been a single issue that affected all the people in the world that they have dealt with and taken care of. Even a world war was only an issue for some of the nation states ... But if I want a World Society, I need a purpose that we all care about as common humanity. And* there's *climate change – apart from 'extraterrestrials' ... few other topics could be used at all. But climate affects everyone. Climate is tangible for everyone, is comprehensible for everyone, affects everyone somehow. And that is precisely the topic that has now been projected as the narrative for the world society, in order to create this world society for the first time, leading to a common understanding of the globe.*

2) Redistribution from the bottom up (CO$_2$ tax[†††††††,92], *constantly new and higher environmental taxes, toll increases, insulation regulations, emissions taxes, CO$_2$ allowance trading, diesel bans and electric cars ...* [93])

3) Legalization of geoengineering (including chemtrails) on the grounds that geoengineering is needed to counteract

---

[*******] Or, might one suggest, driven by leading politicians in the pay of the élite *through* the media (SP)

[†††††††] The report of the Expert Commission for Research and Innovation (EFI) calls on the Federal Government to introduce a CO$_2$ tax

impending increases in the Earth's temperature (circumventing the ENMOD Convention[‡‡‡‡‡‡‡] of 1976)

4) Distraction from other political issues, in particular the creeping destruction of democracy, the new laws on surveillance and censorship of the citizens, and mass migration to Europe. Before the European elections on 26.5.2019, the topic was specifically pushed into the centre of media and public interest, so that actual problems, such as refugees, family reunification, homeland security, social welfare, and poverty in old age have completely taken a back seat

5) Creation of fear and confusion

6) Divide and rule. Human-made climate change is yet another component of this policy. In addition to the deep division in the population (right against left, patriots versus do-gooders, natives against migrants, Muslims against Christians and Jews, conspiracy theorists against mainstream believers, poor versus rich, and now climate change believers against climate change deniers) an evn newer component is Young versus Old, by which an artificial generational conflict is built up and stoked[§§§§§§§]

7) The Dismantling of democracy. Climate activist and founder of Extinction Rebellion, Roger Hallam, said in an interview with *Der Spiegel*:[94] *If a society acts so immorally, democracy becomes irrelevant ... climate protection is greater than democracy.* By *immoral* he meant that, in his opinion, too little is being done by the

---

[‡‡‡‡‡‡‡] The ENMOD convention prohibits the use of environmentally changing techniques

[§§§§§§§] This is particularly evident in the UK at the moment, following the Brexit ballot (the 2016 vote by the UK electorate to quit Europe). In Liverpool a young man approached me in the street and was angling to be abusive to me about my Liverpool FC hoodie, which for some reason he seemed to suspect was the uniform of a Brexiteer, or Leaver. He asked me what I meant by wearing the hoodie, but my answer gave him no reason to assume I was a Leaver – I in fact voted Remain – and he went away clearly disappointed that he was unable to pick an argument, or perhaps even a fight, with a then 64 year-old man who was statistically, though not in reality, a member of the generation said to have betrayed British youth. (SP)

UK government to avert climate catastrophe. Democratic processes ultimately depend on majority decisions, and decision-making can require a lot of time. By contrast, centralist systems are much faster and preferable to a democratic system in respect of meeting the global challenges of today. Therefore, climate change is a prime example of anchoring this undemocratic way of thinking among the population, convincing people that only quick decisions can avert the 'impending climate catastrophe'. In addition, a discussion broadcast on ZDF between the psychologist Richard David Precht and Green Party chief Robert Habeck, suggested that Habeck prefers the Centralist to the Democratic system. Although this statement by Habeck has been postulated as misleading and unintended,[95] it clearly demonstrates a growing tendency to push back democratic principles, justified by the pretext of being able to enforce political decisions more quickly.

8)   The weakening of the European[********] economy (equating with the harmonization of living conditions within the EU) because a governable, united Europe is not possible if one country is rich and another is poor.)

9)   Deindustrialization. Remember the quote from Maurice Strong at the beginning of this chapter? *Isn't the only hope for this planet in the breakdown of industrial civilization? Isn't it our responsibility to ensure that this breakdown occurs?*

[********] Instead of 'European' the German text originally had 'German' here, but British readers need to know that not only does this also apply to Europe as a whole but to the UK too. Even after Brexit the UK is unavoidably and indeed advantageously linked to Europe socially, economically, and politically. (SP)

Majority decision: Climate Killer CO_2?

97% of scientists are certain that climate change is largely manmade. [96]

Or:

0.54% of climate researchers are certain that climate change is largely manmade. [97]

The proponents of the hypothesis that global warming is human-made repeatedly claim that *'97% of scientists are certain that climate change is largely manmade.'*[98] This claim, often used as an argument against climate skeptics is wrong*: Only very few peer-reviewed papers ever go so far as to say that recent warming is chiefly anthropogenic.*[99]

The above '97% claim' derives from a 2013 study, in which a certain John Cook had evaluated almost 12,000 scientific papers. But it is a lie. When this study is scrutinized scrupulously it emerges that: *"A total of 0.54% of the works believes that at least 50% of the people are to blame for climate change."*[100] How does this difference come about? Quite simply, by clever questions and tricks in the statistical evaluation of the answers.[101] The above 97% claim is also refuted in a YouTube video.[102] And yet this claim, still disseminated by the media and the IPCC, is repeatedly used to 'refute climate skeptics'.

This 97% claim is even opposed to a petition (The Global Warming Petition Project, also known as The **Oregon Petition**), signed by 31,000 scientists (as of January 2018), which states that the Global warming human-made hypothesis is wrong.[103] On June 19, 2019, ninety Italian scientists signed a Petition against climate alarm in which the scientific facts that contradict the above hypothesis are more explicitly summarized.[104] As early as 1992, 4000 scientists signed the Heidelberg Manifesto (Heidelberg Appeal), published on the last day of the climate summit in Rio de

Jenairo, in which the signatories demanded that society pay more attention to scientists than to numerous irrational health and environmental activists. And on September 26, 2019, 500 scientists signed the declaration 'Listen to the scientists: 500 researchers are protesting against the inciting of climate alarm',[105] which states that it is *'cruel and unwise, on the basis of immature climate models, to advocate the waste of trillions'*.[106] Fritz Vahrenholt, one of the signatories, stated in an interview: *Climate discussion has become so hysterical that it drives politics ahead. But we have no climate emergency. If Greta Thunberg's demands are implemented, prosperity and development will be massively endangered worldwide.*[107]

Climate change lobbyists[††††††††] react sharply to this Oregon petition with its 31000 signatories. They argue that the Oregon petition is merely propaganda. Or the petition's validity is denied on the grounds that it was signed by predominantly non-specialist scientists. Or: among the signing scientists are also Bachelor, Master or Doc titles in a field related to the natural sciences; but if you compare the number of graduates from higher education institutions since the 1970/71 school year that meet the criteria of the Oregon Petition with the number of signatories, then the ratio is 10.6 million to 31,000.[108] So a majority decision for human-made climate change? What an impoverished scientific credential! 'The earth is a disk' was also a majority decision in the Middle Ages, a view hardly anybody dared to contradict at the time. Or consider the prevailing dogma of the present: The Standard Model of the Elementary Particles, the cosmological theories of parallel worlds and extra dimensions, and bubble multiverses are also majority decisions, followed without contradiction by most specialists. Is that why they must be right? Professor Horst-Joachim Lüdecke[109] from the EIKE Institute wrote about the lobbyists' comments[‡‡‡‡‡‡‡‡]: *The blog ... regards itself as a lobbying association for the manmade climate change hypothesis. A scientific topic has thus become in recent years the weapon of*

[††††††††] represented by the *Huffington Post* in the UK and by www.klimafakten in Germany (SP)
[‡‡‡‡‡‡‡‡] *www.klimafakten.de*

ideological interest groups with a policy that pursues 'climate protection' inculcating objectives entirely different from 'saving the world from heat death'. As a result, all major political parties have now incorporated 'climate' into their programmes ...

Philip Stott, emeritus professor at the University of London, is quoted in the climate report of the UN Climate Change Conference in November 2016 as follows:[110] *The fundamental point has always been the following. Climate change is determined by hundreds of factors or variables, and the very idea that we can predictably manage climate change by understanding and manipulating the only politically-elected factor CO_2 is as absurd as anything... That's scientific nonsense*, he added. Then why has this scientific nonsense become a state doctrine, or more drastically, a state religion? Philip Stott's viewpoint is shared by many serious scientists, who have their say in a Youtube video[111]: tens of thousands of scientists who do not stand with the hypothesis that humans make a significant contribution to climate change. Among these are included more than 70 Nobel Prize winners.[112] In particular, the claim of the representatives of human-made global warming that CO_2 is responsible is refuted by the empirical fact that between 1905 and 1940 a pronounced global warming was measured, whereas between 1940 and 1970, where industrial production and thus human-made CO_2 emissions greatly increased, a slight cooling was effected. What has also been forgotten is that in the middle and second half of the 20th century, a cooling of the Earth, or even a new Ice Age, was announced.[113,114,115] The absurdity of the thesis that human-made CO_2 is responsible for climate warming is also addressed in a 2011 article[§§§§§§§§,116], but no note of this is taken either by politicians or by CO_2 apologists.

The theory that the threat of global warming is fuelled by humanmade CO_2 has a grotesquely satirical side, as an EU member of parliament shows us in a video[117]. MEPs (Members of the European Parliament) and their staff, a total of about 3000 people, move once a month from Brussels to Strasbourg for three nights

---

[§§§§§§§§] on *world.de*

and four days, then back again. Their luggage is transported by truck; the parliamentarians usually take the plane. This monthly move 'gives rise to around 20000 tons of CO_2 emissions per year. That's as much as thirteen thousand flights, London – New York and back, just because we're moving back and forth between two locations.'[118] This example clearly suggests that decision-makers are not concerned with limiting the so-called Climate Killer CO_2, and that the debate about limiting CO_2 emissions is bogus. Also (according to the Court of Auditors), in financial terms, this monthly move amounts to € 114 million a year. *Which company would come up with the absurd idea of relocating 3000 employees somewhere else for three nights and four days each month?*[119]

Equally contradictory to concerns about CO_2 reduction, the 709 deputies of the Bundestag were ordered back from their vacation to attend the swearing-in of Acting Defense Minister Annegret Kramp- Karrenbauer (also known as AKK) at a cost of more than 1 million euros, not including the additional CO_2 emissions.[120]

If Climate Activists were really serious about climate change and the preservation of decent living conditions they would do everything in their power to oppose the deforestation of rainforests in South America or Indonesia. And they would be more resolutely opposed to littering the seas and oceans with plastic waste. They would also advocate a responsible use of available world resources. Although these problems have long been known and feature repeatedly in the media as news or comments, the impression remains that practically little is being done to tackle these problems other than to build up threats such as the CO_2 legend, which then serve as a catalyst for further investment and justification for tax increases or new taxes.

Perennial ice core test series have shown that within the last 100,000 years when the temperature rises or falls, CO^2 changes follow a few hundred years later. *CO_2 does not cause climate change, but follows it. ... So the basic assumption of the theory of manmade climate change is proven wrong.*[121] The explanation for why CO_2 content follows the respective temperature change is related to CO_2 release from the oceans, which rises or falls in line with global temperature. However, the warming or cooling of the oceans themselves is related to solar activity, that is, 'the sun is behind climate change, CO_2 does not matter.'[122]

Originally we were warned of **'global warming'**. However, when it turned out that the average annual temperatures measured had not really increased[123] in the past 20 years, this term was simply replaced by **'climate change'**. *The term 'global warming' (which was still very popular around the turn of the millennium) was almost completely withdrawn from circulation and replaced by the widely applicable universal term 'climate change'. This ... now allows the use of the phrase in a climate-neutral way. Now [climate change] can safely come to an ice age or even to a warm period, which is sure to be the case. It's all about maintaining the drama and not succumbing to contradiction, so as not to endanger the climate replacement trade. This business model thrives solely on a 'sustained' panic in the minds of climate believers, and the blame for whether it is getting warmer or colder can be left completely behind, because it is all about the guaranteed change.*[124],********

It all depends on this one question: if carbon dioxide is not a major cause, then carbon capture, cap-and-trade, carbon trading, and the Kyoto agreement are a waste of time and money. All this diverts resources away from the important things that interest us – how to find a cure for cancer or to feed Somali children.[125]

One article†††††††††[126] gives the following assessment: *The anthropogenic climate change is probably the biggest lie and the greatest scam ever, with the most serious consequences. It is used*

******** By the climate replacement trade, presumably, is meant the battery of technologies designed to change or replace the current global climate or to mitigate its extremes, including those referred to in the next paragraph. The phrase 'guaranteed change' was originally 'securitized change' in the first English draft, which carried the sense of a change that allegedly needed securing while also hinting, rather ominously perhaps, at changes in security. (SP)

††††††††† *https//news-for-friends.de*

exclusively for the redistribution of assets from bottom to top on an unprecedented scale; this means total expropriation in this socio-ecological system in which we unfortunately still have to live at the moment -ultimately the enslavement of all mankind.

In the much cited film by Davis Guggenheim and Al Gore, *An Inconvenient Truth,*[127] which warns of human-made climate change, *on the one hand, facts were kept secret and, on the other hand, adapted to produce the desired effect: creating fear in the population and to obtain legitimacy for the absurd and ruinous 'climate' policy, such as constantly new and higher environmental taxes, toll increases, insulation regulations, emissions taxes, CO_2 allowance trading, diesel bans and electric car woes* ...[128]

What we are experiencing today is the celebration of a climate religion that, unable to do anything with scientific facts, has instead raised human-made climate change to the level of a dogma. The central claim of the representatives of human-made climate change is that CO_2 caused by humans would accelerate global warming, the buzzword being greenhouse effect. Here's an argument that suggests quite the opposite:

The Counter-thesis
to the CO_2 thesis

There is an absolute discussion taboo on the topic of 'climate change', and that's probably the worst thing about it.
(Naomi Seibt, 16-year-old high school graduate[129])

CO_2 is heavier than air; as a result, the concentration of CO_2 near the earth is greater than in upper atmospheric layers. Climate apologists often use this point to refute 'climate deniers' by saying that the swirling of the air masses (via wind, currents) prevents a fall in CO_2 and therefore CO_2, N_2 and O_2 are more or less equally distributed in the atmosphere.[130] However, they suppress another effect, namely the formation of clouds, which takes place at altitudes of about 2 to 13 km. During the formation of clouds, rising water vapour condenses, releasing heat energy absorbed by evaporation on the earth's surface, which is radiated equally in all directions. CO_2, which is more concentrated under the clouds than above them, now causes heat radiation to be greater in the direction of outer space than in the direction of the earth's surface, which means a cooling of the near-earth region compared to the (hypothetical) situation that no CO_2 would be present.[131]

One method of so-called geoengineering, which would limit global warming by solar radiation, is to construct an artificial parasol of the finest metal particles in the upper atmosphere, reflecting direct solar radiation back into space (see Chemtrails – What is their Purpose? chapter 4, 3). This has apparently been happening in Germany since 2003/2004[132] by means of discharging huge amounts of minute metal particles into the upper atmosphere (see Chemtrails – The Chemical Soup in the Sky, chapter 4, 2). The result is a milky-white sky, which actually leads to a decrease in solar radiation incident on the earth. At the same time, however, this milky-white phenomenon reduces the dissipation of the earth's heat into outer space, which in turn contributes to global warming. Without this milky-white sky, the heat radiation from the earth into space would be greater, which would mean additional cooling of the earth's surface. This cooling effect was well observed in earlier years: nocturnal cooling was always particularly pronounced when the sky was cloudless and starlit.[‡‡‡‡‡‡‡‡‡‡] In contrast, dense cloud cover reduced heat dispersal in the direction of outer space, which is why nocturnal cooling was less than it would be in a cloudless sky. While heat radiation from the earth's surface towards outer space takes place continuously, 24 hours a day, the shielding of sunlight through the milky-white sky occurs only during the daytime, namely when the sun is in the sky. On balance this means that this artificial parasol tends to increase, not decrease, the average temperature on the earth's surface.

[‡‡‡‡‡‡‡‡‡‡] In German the adjectives are reversed: *sternenklar* (starlit, or starry) and *wolkenlos* (SP)

Under normal cirumstances the average CO_2 content in air is extremely low: about 0.04%. EIKE (The European Institute for Climate and Energy) makes the following statement:[133] *So 0.038 percent CO_2 is in the air; Nature produces 96 percent of this, the rest, i.e. four percent, is manmade. That's four percent of 0.038 percent, or 0.00152 percent. Germany's share of this is 3.1 percent. ... With this we want to take the leading role in the world, which costs us annually around 50 billion euros in taxes and burdens.*

If so, the question arises: why then is just the opposite claimed, namely that CO_2 causes global warming? The answer is simple:

1)   If one were to say that CO_2 can reduce or reverse global warming, on that basis one could not justify CO_2 certificates and CO_2 tax. It would be harder to argue that coal-fired power generation has to be abolished.

2)   The paradox is that actual global warming is desirable since it sustains the claim that CO_2 is a contributory factor to that global warming. It can be brazenly asserted that we have not yet reduced CO_2 enough, so global temperature continues to rise and CO_2 taxation needs to be more efficient, that is, more expensive. It is assumed that the mass of people do not see through to the true background to the issue and its underlying connections. For if they could the whole climate-taxation project would collapse like a house of cards. That is why media propaganda propagates and fuels the CO_2 global warming thesis, as we can see, for example, in the FridaysForFuture Movement, but more generally in the electoral gains of the UK Greens in the EU election and in the national election.[§§§§§§§§§]

Simultaneous with the fight against CO_2 is the corollary fight against one of the prerequisites for human existence: the plant world. CO_2, a gas without which human civilization could not exist, is also an essential substance for the plant world, as it is used

---

[§§§§§§§§§] In 2017, the German Greens made similar gains in the EU and *Landtag* elections, as JS points out in the German edition of his book. See also The Maoist Blueprint, chapter 3, 8) [SP]

via photosynthesis for energy production. And photosynthesis works only when there is sufficient sunlight. Other measures used to reduce global warming include reducing solar radiation by introducing aerosols into the upper reaches of the atmosphere to absorb some of the sunlight or reflect it back into space. This in turn results in a reduction in photosynthesis.

How is it possible despite the extremely minimal human-made CO_2 contribution that an entire Climate Religion can be built on it? An answer to this is found in the video *The origin of the Climate Lie*[134]**********, in which the narrator states that *media, mostly printed media – of course, TV – were fabricating facts that were not even there! And all these facts arose from devising means of creating fear.* In the short description of the book *The Climate Change Lie* by Hartmut Bachmann we read: *According to a survey, 70% of Germans are frightened by systematic scaremongering about a looming climate catastrophe. However, those who recognize that the underlying evidence for this alleged disaster is* **largely forged** *can conquer their fears. ... the entire structure that is supposed to support climate catastrophe builds on one lie after another told by top international climate authorities down to state governments. After this disclosure the author turns to the question:* **CUI BONO?** *Who benefits from this? In doing so, he cites criminal machinations ... (and) how ruthless exploiters and egotists from business and politics manipulate and frighten people in order to exploit them.*[135]

********** *Klimalüge* in German (SP)

The Climate project –
too big to fail?

Figure 9a shows the increase in the average temperature of the near-the-surface atmosphere and the oceans since the beginning of industrialization (Wikipedia). According to this source it is 'a climate change through anthropogenic [human-made] influences'. Figure 9a represents part of the so-called 'hockey stick climate curve', which is shown fully in Figure 9b: the average temperature in the northern hemisphere since the year 1000, determined from various sources. These graphics are the main cornerstones of the claim that climate change is human-made. And they form the basis for the climate models that climate scientists used to estimate temperature development until the year 2100, assuming we do not reduce CO_2 emissions. Climate reports of the IPCC also derive from these.

The graph, from NASA, was prepared by James Hansen (and co-authors) in 2010, later revised and supplemented by Nathan Lenssen (and co-authors) in 2019. The hockey stick climate curve, was published by Michael Mann (and co-authors) in 1998. It shows a gradual decline in temperature since about the year 1000 but, following the onset of industrialization, a steep increase from about 1890 until 1998.

However, this hockey stick is obviously a curve invented or manipulated by Michael Mann.[††††††††††] For this gentleman has now been convicted of lying by a Canadian court.[136,137] That's a tough judgment. *The highly acclaimed Michael Mann persistently refused*

[††††††††††] To be precise, this curve was invented in 1998 by Michael E Mann and his two co-authors Raymond S Bradley and Malcolm K Hughes. The hockey-stick name for the curve was coined by climatologist Jerry D Mahlman to describe its shape, though Mahlmann is not implicated in any accusations of fraud. On the contrary, in the context of the IPCC case for global warming, he described the emphasis on the hockey-stick graph as 'a colossal mistake' (*https://en.wikipedia.org/wiki/Hockey_stick_controversy*). [SP] *to release his raw data and computer codes to validate his famous artifice.*[138]

A number of publications in the past also questioned the credibility of the data that forms the basis of the graph (Figure 9b). In 2013, *Der Spiegel* online analysed the critics' dilemma regarding the hockey stick climate curve. The author of this article comes to the following conclusion:[139] ***Under pressure from the industrial lobby*** *– Apparently, the 'Hockeyteam', as Mann and colleagues called themselves, was cornered by a powerful lobby made up of industry associations. The lobbyists are not afraid of the deliberate misinterpretation of climate data to trivialize the dangers of global warming* ...So here the tables were turned, it was not Michael Mann and colleagues who falsified, but they were urged ... *to trivialize the dangers of global warming...*, which they did not do.

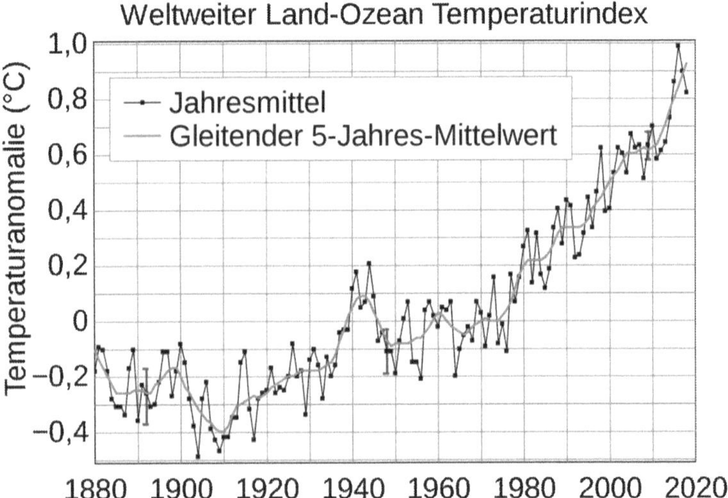

Figure 9a: Global warming or global warming since the beginning of industrialization (copied from Wikipedia)

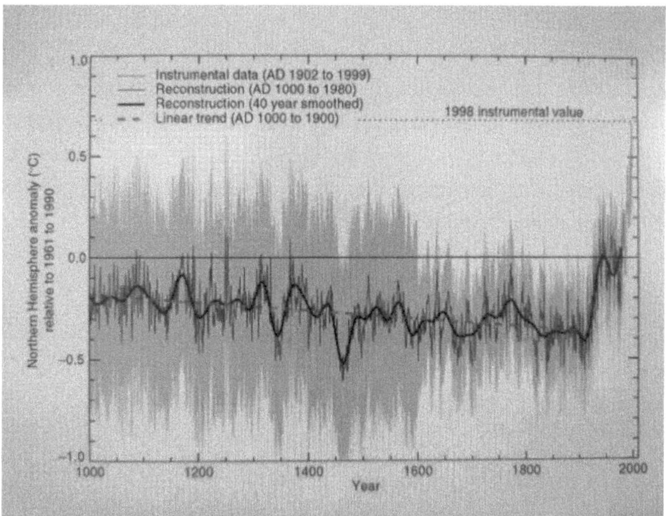

Figure 9b: Global warming or global warming for the past 1000 years (copied from Wikipedia)

Wikipedia concludes: *In the meantime, recent climate constructions of the past 1,000 years have provided a picture comparable to the hockey stick diagram. These actual graphs are largely consistent with the original hockey stick chart and are within the framework of Mann et al. predetermined error limits.* Wikipedia refers to these two sources.[140,141] And another website‡‡‡‡‡‡‡‡‡‡ arrives at a similar result.[142] This verdict is not surprising, because, as we will see in the next section, the 'newer climate construction' is based on manipulated data.

Concerning Figure 9a, the following is to be reported about its alleged author: While no traces can be found on the internet about the author Nathan Lenssen there are entries with surprising results by James Hansen, the 'Father of the Climate Curve', quoted in a 1971 *Washington Post* report. Even before this date he had apparentl warned of a coming Ice Age: *In the next 50 years, the fine dust that people constantly blow into the atmosphere by burning fossil fuels could weaken the sunlight to such an extent*

---

‡‡‡‡‡‡‡‡‡‡ *www.klimafakten.de*

that average temperatures could fall as much as 6 degrees ... 10 Years later, James Hansen is named Director of the NASA Goddard Institute and conjures up a global warming with a curve going upwards from the global cooling and the temperature curve ... going down (Figure 9). Now it was said: 'it does not threaten any ice age, quite the contrary, it is getting warmer, and so warm that soon the polar ice caps will melt.[143]

Manipulating temperature data

... is the biggest science scandal ever.[144]

How can it be that, after very few years, we moved from the Ice Age originally predicted to threatening anouncements of a climate change catastrophe (based around global warming)? Quite simply: through data manipulation: '*... the underlying assets of this alleged catastrophe are (mostly) faked ...*', so goes one statement.[145] We want (and need) to check this claim. Let's take a closer look at some of the data. In an article of the EIKE institute[146] such falsifications were once specifically pursued. For example, the article cites how NASA has manipulated temperature data records measured over a period of more than 100 years at various locations on Earth[147]. In one of the sources cited therein, examples are shown of data manipulations from six different locations in the world where temperatures have been measured: Punta Arenas, Chile; Marquette, State of Michigan, USA; Port Elizabeth, South Africa; Davis, Antarctica; Hachijojima, Tokyo; Valentia Observatory, Ireland.

These new temperature measurement data sets now provide partial warming trends, even in places where there was once a cooling trend. Three examples of data manipulations are shown in Figures 10–12. NASA has changed its original, so-called *V3 unadjusted data,* and published under the new name *V4 unadjustierte*

Daten.[§§§§§§§§§§§] The upper picture shows the original data (*V3 Unadjusted*) over time, the lower picture shows the changed data (*V4 Unadjusted*). In Figure 10, a slight temperature drop has been constructed from a significant downward trend in the mean temperature. In Figure 11, a slight downward trend is made out to be a clear upward trend. In Figure 12,[148,149] the corresponding graphs are plotted for Darwin Airport, located in Northern Territory, Australia, where the V3 Unadjusted data shows a significant downward trend in mean temperature, while the *V4 Unadjusted* data shows a clear upward trend.

Another example of data manipulation by GISS/NASA is the temperature curve since 1900 for the selected measuring station Züurich Fluntern, in Switzerland. The temperature data from GISS/NASA for the time series 1900 to 2018 are significantly higher than in the original measured data.[150] *As a result, Switzerland is given out as too warm in the GISTEMP dataset, which forms the basis of many climate models, with an increasing trend, i. e. New levels of ground temperature reported by NASA for Zürich Fluntern or Switzerland tend to deviate more and more from those identified by MeteoSwiss.*

[§§§§§§§§§§§] Or *V4 unadjustierte Daten* in the German (SP)

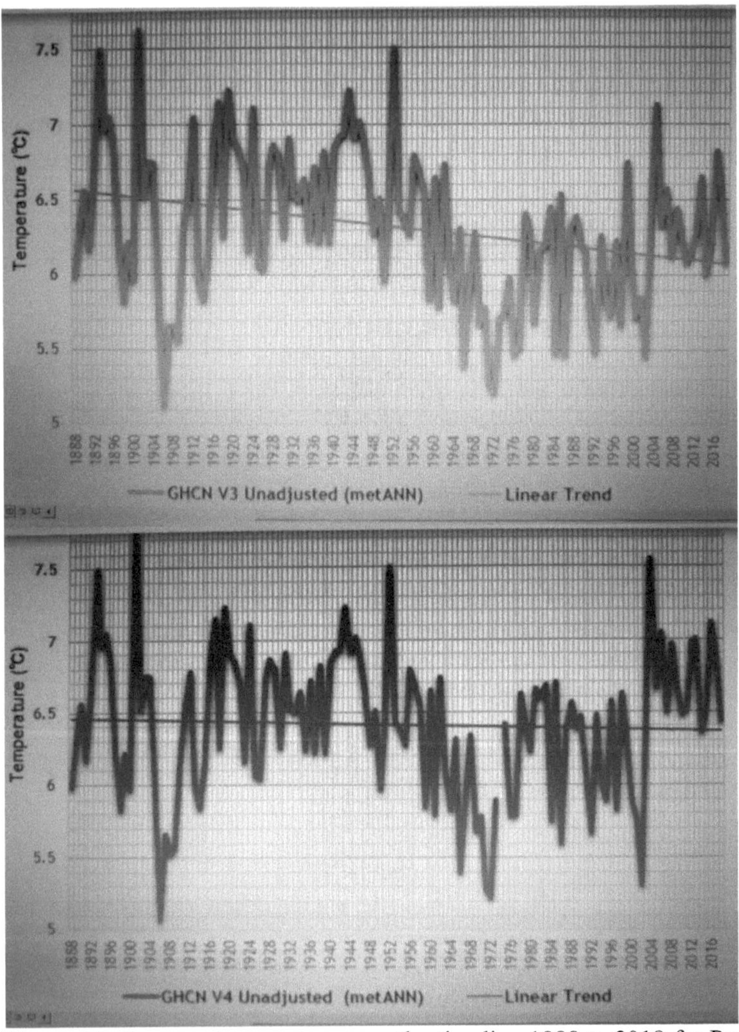

Figure 10. Average temperature over the timeline 1888 to 2018 for Punta Arenas, Chile. Top image: Original data (*V3 Unadjusted*); here there was still a clear downward trend in the mean temperature, which, however, has almost disappeared in the *V4 Unadjusted* data (lower picture).[151]

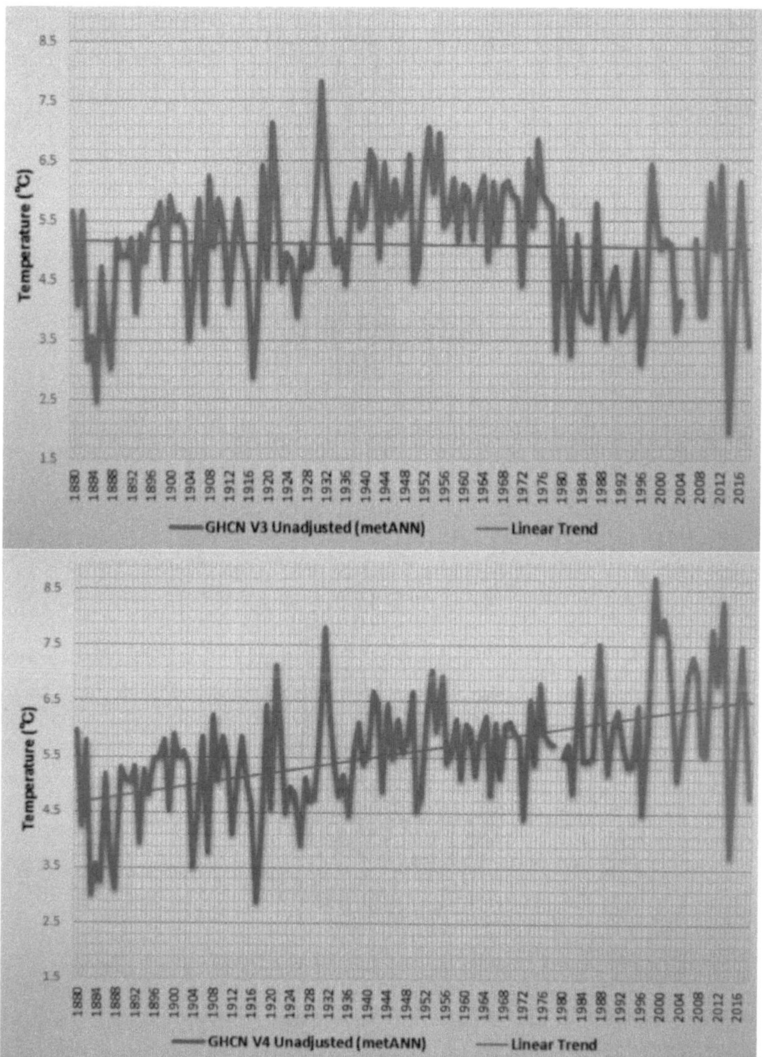

Figure 11. Average temperature over the timeline 1880 to 2018 for Marquette, Michigan, USA. Top image: Original data (*V3 Unadjusted*); lower picture: modified measurement data (V4 Unadjusted). Here a slight decrease in the mean temperature has been turned into an increase in temperature.[152]

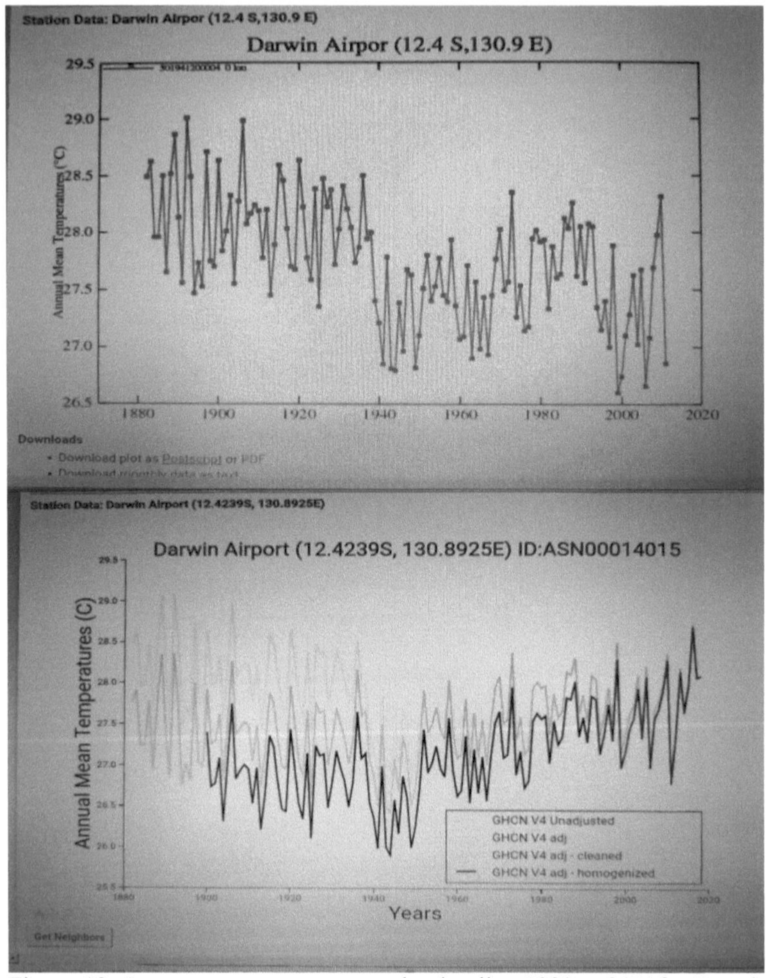

Figure 12. Average temperature over the timeline 1880 to 2011for Darwin Airport, Australia. Top image: Original data (*V3 Unadjusted*)[153] with a clear downward trend; lower picture: modified measurement data (*V4 Unadjusted*)[154] with a clear upward trend.

Another type of manipulation is an increasing weighting of temperature data from warmer areas (cities, settlements) compared with rural areas. Since it is generally 2 to 4 degrees warmer in the cities and settlements, because buildings there heat up more during the day and at night this heat is stored longer, with this type of manipulation, an increase in temperature can easily be pretended.[**********] And that is exactly what happened with the temperature measurement data in Germany. If one overlays the Germany maps with the official temperature measuring stations from the years 1989 and 2018 and looks at the changes in data acquisition, we see that in the last 30 years a lot of measuring stations have disappeared from the cool locations or been moved to warmer zones, in the vicinity of settlements, where it is naturally warmer than it is out in nature.[155] Therefore an increase in the mean temperature in Germany over the time axis has been generated or manipulated. *Nevertheless, it has become warmer in many regions, but only because our streets and cities have grown, and we concrete everything. The asphalt glows in the summer ... The heat comes from the cities, not from the* CO_2.[156]

Over the time axis, manipulations are also found in sea-level measurements. Figure 13[157] shows the changes in sea level from 1880 to 2019 (top curve), as published twice by NASA, once in 1982 and once in 2019. The comparison shows that the curve published in 1982 (lower solid line) only shows a sea-level rise of 8cm, while the upper curve, published in 2019, shows a sea-level rise of 14cm for the similar period, 1880 to 1980. Both curves are normalized to the same initial sea level in 1880.

[**********] Many of us can vouch for this urban/rural heat difference from personal experience. From 1977 to 1985 I lived in High Spen, a remote pit-village (mining village) ten miles out of Newcastle-upon-Tyne and Gateshead, and less than 700 feet (213 metres) up in altitude, yet if there were two inches of snow in the conurbation we often had ten feet (3.5 metres) of it where we were, and the village could be officially cut off for two months a year, yet of course we hardy villagers always found a way out. One day in the early 80s a local radio broadcast warned us that it would be colder in our village that night than it was at the North Pole: it dropped to minus 17F (minus 27C) and we watched and listened as the ice-flowers crackled and formed on our single-glazed windows. I now live in a remote farm near Beverley, East Riding, where six months a year I have to put warm clothes on to go to bed (SP)

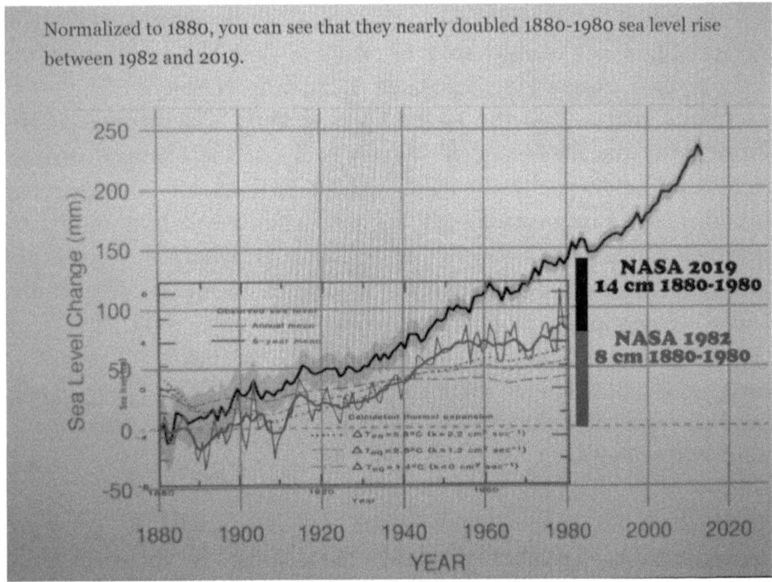

Figure 13. Sea-level changes over time: lower solid curve (red curve) is from 1982, upper curve (black curve) is from 2019; both curves published by NASA[158] Resultant sea-level increases differ significantly for the period 1880 to 1980: 8 cm versus 14 cm.

Chris Frey of the EIKE Institute (European Institute for Climate and Energy[†††††††††††]) commented:[159] *NASA seems to be unaffected by the sun, oceans, water vapour, etc., when it comes to global temperature trends. The number one factor behind NASA's 'warming' does not even seem to be CO_2, but rather their Orwellian falsification of data. If at NASA the data does not match the (invented) models, just change them until they fit. Finally dry up this NASA swamp!*

In my opinion, the *cui bono?*[‡‡‡‡‡‡‡‡‡‡‡] question is the crucial one to ask in order to challenge the claim that there is climate change and that it is human-made.[§§§§§§§§§§§]

[†††††††††††] In German, Europäisches Institut für Klima und Energie
[‡‡‡‡‡‡‡‡‡‡‡] Italian for 'who benefits?' or 'to whom is this useful?' (SP)

In 1976/77, the ENMOD convention was created because of the worldwide rejection of the use of Monsanto's Agent Orange and other geoengineering interventions during the Vietnam War in the 1960s and early 70s. At that time, fear grew that, given their rapid technological development, environmental weapons could be used in conflicts generally. Since then, the use of environmental weapons has been banned.[160] Listed in an interpretation agreement attached to the ENMOD convention (Understandings Regarding The Convention) are the following phenomena capable of being generated by environment-altering techniques: *earthquakes, tsunamis; regional upsets in ecological balance; changes in weather patterns (clouds, precipitation, cyclones of various types and tornadic storms); changes in climate patterns; changes in ocean currents; changes in the state of the ozone layer; and changes in the state of the ionosphere.*

An understanding of this terminology as far back as 1976 should really make us sit up and pay attention.[161] This means that technical possibilities for the artificial generation of earthquakes, tsunamis, disturbances in a region's ecological balance, altering weather (including cloud formation, cyclones, and tornados), and climate change were already recognized as a realistic threat from humans.

How could one circumvent this ban on climate-changing manipulations? Very easily. By creating a hypothetical global threat that needs to be counteracted to avert it. 'Fight manmade climate change' represents the battle slogan against this threat. Which, of course, you are duty-bound to do something about. Climate-change terminology actually 'legitimizes' geoengineering. The very term 'climate change' also fosters fear as a means of

---

§§§§§§§§§§§§ Surely there can be no question that climate change is a reality and that much of it, by your own admission, is human-made – unless you wish to disqualify the military-scientific establishment as humans. From a certain point of view I would understand this perfectly since humanity in general is not directy to blame but only complicit, mainly through ignorance (SP) But global warming has nothing to do with man-made CO_2.

coercing the population into almost universal agreement about this project.

On the basis of the above-described fake measuring data, politics has created a kind of climate religion linked to an indulgence trade in CO_2 allowances, leading to the creation of additional government revenues. I like to compare this indulgence with the 'indulgence trading'[***********] advocated by Johann Tetzel (1465–1519). [††††††††††††] *Incidentally, the Climate Brotherhood does not see itself as a rival to the Holy See, but rather as a unique complement to the maintenance of a modernized* **'Theology of theft'** *that comes with even more terrible stories around the corner than, for example, the Bible.*

Despite these proven manipulations and forgeries the Climate Project – too big to fail? – continues to drive forward. There will always be paid specialists willing to 'prove' that critics are 'wrong.'

The Children's Crusade 2019

I want you to panic
(Greta Thunberg)

Because whoever is in a panic cannot think. And that is precisely the state that our leading social forces, such as the Greens and others, want here.
(Gerhard Wisnewsky[162])

Embroiling our children in the nightmare dissemination of a mounting climate catastrophe – as expressed in the FridayForFuture demos of schoolchildren – displays religious traits

---

[***********] In German, *Ablasshandel* (SP)
[††††††††††††] One does not necessarily need to be a mediaeval historian to have heard about people being encouraged by the Church in centuries past to pay for forgiveness of sins, a pactice that Martin Luther (1483-1546) denounced. (SP)

reminiscent of the Children's Crusade (*peregrinatio puerorum*) in 1212. Then, literally thousands – mostly children and adolescents from France and Germany – were led by visionary boys to an un-armed crusade in the Holy Land. Historically, this was between the Fourth Crusade (1202-4) and the Fifth Crusade (1217–21). The First Crusade (1096–99) was initiated by Pope Urban II in 1095.

In a similar way, schoolchildren are being instrumentalized today, who are taught the upcoming climate catastrophe as a fact at school and usually believe this to be true. And the children are also happy to take part in the "Fridays for Future" children's demonstrations, especially as this is supported by some politicians, who make legal truancy possible. The "Fridays for Future" children's demonstra-tions focus on coal and the shutdown of coal-fired power plants at the earliest possible stage. Just like in the Children's Crusade 1212, visionary children are promoted and marketed as figureheads, like Greta Thunberg from Sweden and *her German counterpart, the six years older geography student Luisa-Marie Neubauer, who co-organizes the "Fridays-for-future" demos ("We are in the greatest crisis of mankind!").* However, she was *caught in the act of travel-ling almost all continents despite her youthful age - her destina-tions included Canada, China/Hong Kong, Namibia, half of Eu-rope, and Morocco,*[163] which, if the representatives of the climate religion are to be believed, should accelerate the "climate catastro-phe" caused by the frequent flights associated with world travel.

Point 6) in the enumeration of goals (see Climate change – the New World Religion, chapter 3, 2) that the élite pursue in inventing human-made climate change is the most significant and at the same time the most dangerous. *Now not only are children sent on the streets (to protest), they are now incited against their parents ... against the older generation: 'You are guilty, you have done nothing (positive), you are a blight.' This is a very, very dangerous development: Now if the young generation is incited against the old and the old world is consequently destroyed on the basis that everything that came from the old was bad, then we are put in a very dangerous situation, as far as the inter-generational contract is concerned, leaving the pension question, etc, etc, etc aside; if now boys are incited against the old. We must again be very, very cautious and very, very mindful of what is happening now in this regard in the next few months, in the next two or three years, and not let that happen; it was bad enough that they split right from leftt, that they split society horizontally. If they succeed in (vertically) dividing and inciting children against their parents, it will be very, very dangerous ...*[164]

The Maoist Blueprint

The masses are brought up as hearing lemmings[165,‡‡‡‡‡‡‡‡‡‡‡‡]

The FridaysForFuture demos are very similar to the beginnings of the Cultural Revolution during communist rule in China (Cultural Revolution, 1966–78). *During Mao's Cultural Revolution, millions of teenagers were incited against the adults. They persecuted teachers, scientists and party officials. They were allowed to stay away from school. In the end, millions were killed.*[166,167,168,169] Cambodia is remembered in a similar way, when the Khmer Rouge (1975–79) ran their terrorist regime: *Money was abolished, books were burned, teachers, traders and nearly all of the country's intellectual élite were murdered …* (Wikipedia)

The analogy between today's FridaysForFuture movement and Mao's Cultural Revolution seems evident; today, with the support of governments and schools, Friday's school lessons are being replaced by student protests, national and European, and even worldwide, led by a highly stylized icon, Greta Thunberg. Again, the dangerous thing about this upsurge of young against old is that this process is creeping: giving youth a unifying idea, in this case the 'climate'; breaking the bonds between children and parents; perhaps eventually developing in a similar direction to that formerly taken by China and Cambodia. That this incitement in

---

‡‡‡‡‡‡‡‡‡‡‡‡ Although the original experiments are the drive of lemmings as a species towards mass suicide have been strongly challenged in recent years, the analogy is still culturally intelligible. (SP)

connection with climate change falls on fertile ground is demonstrated by landslide gains for the Green Party in the UK national and council elections of 2019, as a result of which the Greens[§§§§§§§§§§§] had one MP, one Member of the House of Lords, seven Members of the European Parliament (until January 31, 2020 when Brexit was finalised), and two members of the London Assembly.[************]

In schools and nursery schools[†††††††††††††], little ones are already incited and indoctrinated with the slogan 'Young against old'.[170,‡‡‡‡‡‡‡‡‡‡‡‡‡] In Germany, the most recent example of this propaganda drive is the song transmitted on state television with the title *My grandma is an old environmental pig!* In the final seconds of the song the child singers issue a threat they have memorized in English: *We will not let you get away with this!*[171§§§§§§§§§§§§§]

In the Cultural Revolution in China, Mao-Tse Tung likewise imposed totally irrational measures, *where all the Chinese educated*

[§§§§§§§§§§§] Already in Germany, and increasingly in the UK, the Grüne Partei, or Green Party, is popularly (or upopularly) known as the Greens
[************] (Green Party's UK website, Sep 9, 2019) Naturally, in the German edition of this book the German political situation is described using German figures. Green gains achieved in the German state elections in 2018 amounted to 17.6% in Bavaria, 18.8% in Hesse, and 20.5% in the European Parliamentary election on May 26, 2019. Overall the Federal results for the German Greens gave them and their allies (Alliance 90), 67 seats out of a total of 589, 4 more than they had from the previous election (*https://en.wikipedia.org/wiki/Bundestag*; citing the Office of Federal Returns (Bundeswahleiter).
[†††††††††††††] Likewise, in the original German edition the text, as initially translated by Joachim Sonntag into English, but relating to Germany, would have read: 'little ones are already incited and indoctrinated in this sense, "Young against the old", in schools and kindergartens'
[‡‡‡‡‡‡‡‡‡‡‡‡‡] See *https://www.independent.co.uk/voices/European-elections-2019-brexit-politics-millennials-gen-z-farage-corbyn-a8926801.html*
[§§§§§§§§§§§§§] English readers may, or may not, wish to watch a video of this disgraceful performance (yet entirely innocent on the young children's part) on the following website:
https://www.bing.com/videos/search?q=My+Grandma+is+an+old+environment al+pig&&view=detail&mid=0740C0B885E30E82D5F60740C0B885E30E82D5 F6&rvsmid=3FCD7079B3518B7F6AD83FCD7079B3518B7F6AD8&FORM=V DQVAP) [Notes on this page by SP]

classes were actually cleansed, ie at the very least driven out of office, if not killed. And that's the point here too. You also notice the conflict and anger directed against old white men. There's something else: old white men are the cultural carriers of educational institutions in this country, yes, and they are to be disempowered. And the tone of people like Greta, but also ANTIFAs or even some of the Greens is clearly Maoist, their actions are also Maoist, and the whole concept is Maoist. So, in short, we just have the same modus operandi, the same pattern of action, the same blueprint as the Chinese Cultural Revolution. And that's where it's going to go.[172] Gerhard Wisnewski quotes the demand of Rezo, the German vlogger, from his legendary Youtube video: *This is not about different political opinions; there is only one legitimate attitude!* To which Wisnewski responds: *And if we arrive in a state where there is only one legitimate attitude, then we are in imminent danger.*[173]

It should also be noted that the media conjure up their horror scenes to construct awareness among the general public that climate change is human-made and that human-derived CO_2 emissions contribute significantly to the worldwide catastrophe. Figure 8 illustrates such a horror scenario. This BILD title can certainly be regarded as the beginning of climate hysteria. The media exert a devastating influence on popular fears, which ultimately override the logical mind. Orwell sends greetings. Why are the media at the forefront of this? Quite simple: with catastrophe reports you can make a lot more sales, increase the circulation. For such an increase in sales, no additional investments are needed.[174] But that's just a superficial reason, because more profoundly the media act in the sense and on behalf of the élite.[175]

4. Geoengineering

Human influence on the weather

The only thing that keeps many from believing that the weather is manipulated on purpose is ignorance of whether this is possible at all. Most people think that it is not possible.[176]

Human influence on the weather actually exists in the form of weather manipulation through geoengineering. In one article[177] the author writes: *The US and probably other states are now able to significantly influence the weather with geo-engineering measures (electromagnetic waves/HAARP, chemtrails).* This statement, that it is possible today to influence our weather artificially and allow it to be used as a weapon of war, had already been recognized in the 1970s, leading to the UN Treaty CONVENTION ON THE PROHIBITION OF MILITARY OR ANY OTHER HOSTILE USE OF ENVIRONMENTAL MODIFICATION TECHNIQUES (UN 1976 Weather Weapon Treaty), ENMOD Convention for short.[178]

Artificially generating rain by seeding clouds – spraying silver iodide from aeroplanes – has long been known. Less known is the technical ability to produce dryness and drought by controlling the condensation of atmospheric water vapour, HAARP activities preventing, for example, cloud formation.[179,180] (See HAARP – The Food Slicer in the Sky, chapter 4, 5). Figure 14 shows two radar images of Germany on 2.8.2018, one picture before 1:30pm (right picture), the other one after 1:30pm (left picture).************* The circular area above northwestern Germany shows the result of HAARP activities. So the humid air from the Atlantic is kept away from Germany, and the CO_2 problem can be sold to the Germans

---

************* Numerous similar radar surveys (German *Radaraufnahmen*: literally, radar receptions) can be found on the internet better!^{†††††††††††††} Just imagine: Artificial drought! In the Youtube video[181], this is described as follows: *You pump energy into areas where rain normally occurs, pushing the cloud formation upwards and outwards, where rain does not come off properly and, above all, with simultaneous warming by the energy it is no longer rainy. From the rain radar, only these circular cloud patterns are identifiable ... And that, of course, makes us wonder how such diverse regions of heat and drought in the world can be justified? One might also ask, is it really true that weather patterns in the world are fairly distributed? And if you can trigger drought, then of course you can trigger refugee movements.*

In the summer of 2018 there was such a heatwave in Germany that severe agricultural problems were the result. This heatwave probably had its origins in HAARP activities, as recorded since May 2018 in radar surveys over northwestern Germany. But what was the point of creating a long-lasting heatwave over a rich nation such as Germany? To generate refugee flows from Germany could surely not be the case! It seems that this was was nothing more than a demonstration to tell us: See, the climate warming is real. Do not believe the 'conspiracy theorists' who deny human-made global warming.

Figure 15 shows how extremely high heat prevailed in a narrow area over Mecklenburg-Vorpommern,[182] whereas in the adjacent areas temperatures were significantly lower. This temperature contrast could have been artificially created by HAARP activities in the centre of this heated area: one of the world's largest HAARP facilities is in nearby Rostock.

---

††††††††††††† Naturally, the German edition would literally translate this last phrase as 'sold to us better' (SP)

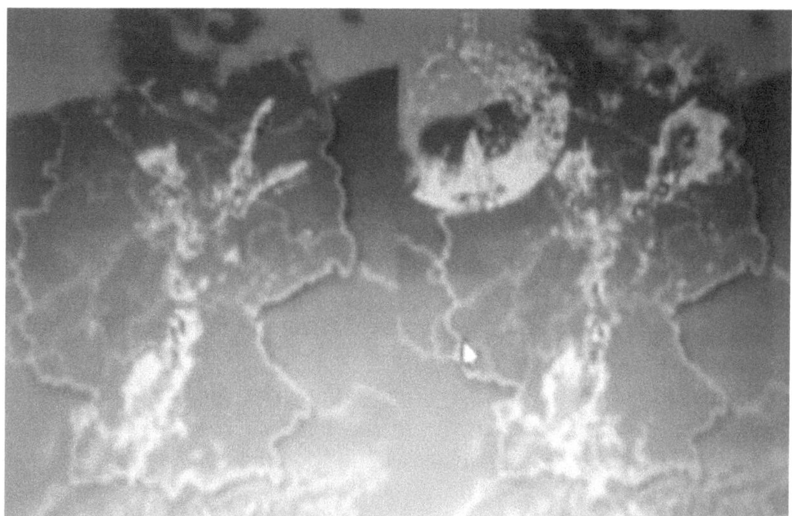

Figure 14: Radar images of Germany on 2.8.2018, one image before 1:30 a.m. (right image), the other image (left) after 1:30 a.m.[183]

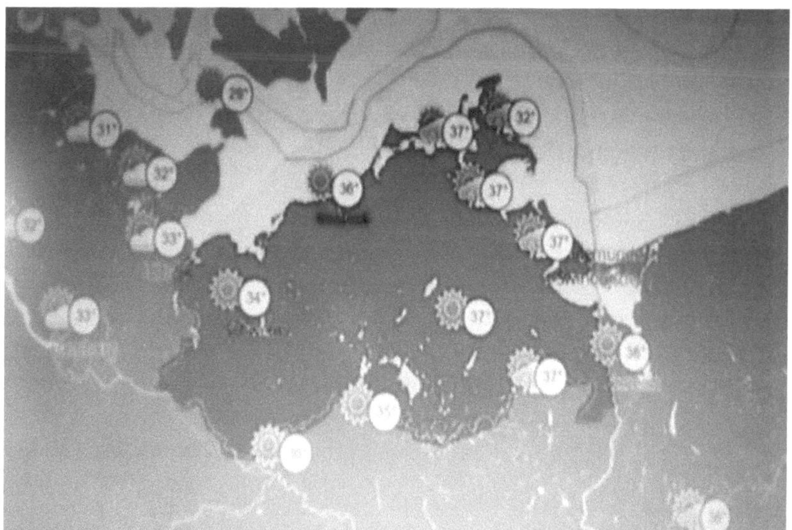

Figure 15: Extreme heat over Mecklenburg-West Pomerania on May 8, 2018.[184]

Another aspect is that this heatwave can easily justify the use of geoengineering via the claim: yes, we need geoengineering to combat devastating climate change.

At a hearing in the Senate Subcommittee on Terrorism, 'Weather War + NOW' on June 15, 1995,[185] Robert Fletcher of MOM (the Militia of Montana) spoke the following: *There are techniques to control the weather. We have a full dossier of evidence ... We have all the patents of this technique. And then we have the testimony and reports of Senator Claiborne Pell that it not only existed but was used in the Vietnam War ...* ‡‡‡‡‡‡‡‡‡‡‡‡‡‡

Chairman: *Are you really saying that the government built a weather weapon so that the – New World Order – quote could starve millions of people worldwide? To subdue the rest ...*

Fletcher: *Yes, sir, right. We have proof documents. Do you really believe 85 hurricanes in the middle of our granary are normal? No, unfortunately not. This equipment exists and it is used internationally. Even if that sounds bizarre, we can prove everything. As bizarre as it is, but there are these weather wars. I quote Senator Claiborne Pell: 'this is the greatest weapon the world has ever seen.*§§§§§§§§§§§§§§

This was the situation in 1995. Development in this area has certainly advanced since then.

The operational concept for **weather manipulation** is as follows:[186] *Part of the weather manipulation system is the selection of techniques that are used to change the weather. With few exceptions, it is necessary to deliver either energy or chemicals to the meteorological process in the right way, in the right place and at the right time.* (Excerpt from: *Weather as force multiplier:*

---

‡‡‡‡‡‡‡‡‡‡‡‡‡‡ Claiborne Pell (1918-2009), a behind-the-lines World War Two hero and statesman, was Rhode Island's most re-elected Senator, serving six terms from 1961 to 1997, and the 19th longest-serving Senator in US history. Famous for his Columbo-like disregard for his appearance (despite his wealth), he wrote three books, of which *Power and Policy: America's Role in World Affairs* (1972) was the most influential and revealing. (SP)

§§§§§§§§§§§§§§ By 'our granary', Fletcher presumably means the arable Great Plains of the US, incorporating Nebraska, North and South Dakota, but also including parts of other states including his native Montana. (SP)

Owning the weather in 2025, Military applications of weather modification)[**************]

Concerning the generation of hurricanes and influencing their direction and strength, see also the Youtube video.[187]

Chemtrails – The Chemical Soup in the Sky

This chapter covers the period until the end of 2019. I have observed no chemtrails in 2020. This may be because President Trump has cut funding for geoengineering projects.

On the topic of Chemtrails we face a huge disinformation and manipulation campaign, unique in its perfection and 'success'. Despite a wealth of unequivocal evidence (see below), the media succeeds in lying to the population and falsely reassuring them.[†††††††††††††††] When it comes to dismissing Chemtrails the media are extraordinarily imaginative. The reason is, admitting that tons of toxic materials are actually being sprayed overhead would be contrary to the officially waged fight against pollution; worse, governments could be sued and held responsible for deliberate pollution. That is why the truth about Chemtrails is something that might never be confirmed.[188] *... It is a state secret; nobody should know because it is illegal... absolutely illegal, it violates criminal law in many ways.... The criteria for all environmental offences are met. It is air pollution: if you* (contaminate) *the air with nanoparticles without permission, that is all, as I said, without administrative approval. And if, in violation of administrative regulations, you release into the air substances that are capable of*

[**************] *http://www.chemtrails-info.de*
[†††††††††††††††] *... mainstream portals and fact-checkers like CORRECTIV, MIMIKAMA, ..., which claim to uncover and refute disinformation, fake news and conspiracy theories.*

harming life, health, body and so on, or things of significant value, then this is air pollution. Of course, we also have soil contamination because the nanoparticles also settle in the soil. We have water pollution because in the long term the water is contaminated, i.e. we have perpetrated all three environmental offences, to a significant extent, practically-speaking a particularly difficult kind of case, because it is happening across the board.

Numerous discussions with friends and colleagues on the question, 'Are there any Chemtrails?' have shown me that most of them have never heard of Chemtrails and listen in disbelief to my arguments proving their existence, or they interrupt me. They call for evidence, but at the same time prevent me from presenting that evidence by interrupting me over and over again. This demonstrates that people simply cannot imagine, and are unwilling to believe, that people and institutions out there could wilfully destroy our livelihoods and poison us. It is precisely because there is such a denial culture on this subject that this section on Chemtrails needs to be a little more verbose.

So-called chemtrails 'are global, civil and military weather change experiments with our atmosphere, that is in plain language, masses of toxic substances that have been intentionally applied in the lower atmosphere since 2003. It is the biggest global experiment with the weather that ever took place. Climate engineering, also known as geoengineering, is the artificial manipulation of global climate, the intentional change in daily weather, the intentional dissolution and modification of whole weather patterns, and the creation of an artificial climate. Every year millions of tons of highly toxic aerosols are purposely sprayed by the military + commercial air traffic into our atmosphere. It is a ... mixture of ... metal oxides, sulphur, including sulphuric acids, highly toxic to humans/animals; nano-particles, artificial fibres/polymers, combined with electromagnetic pulses to which we and our natural world are exposed daily. Not only does it make you sick, in the long run it destroys the entire biosphere of the earth. It contaminates the soil, the waters and our breathing air. Some of these substances are destroying our vital ozone layer.[189]

Is this true? Can it be? Do they really want to destroy us?

As for the above-mentioned denial culture, it should be noted that there are many YouTube videos and articles on Chemtrails disseminated through public service media in which the claim that geoengineering programmes are chemicals sprayed by airplanes, is called conspiracy theory.[190,191,192,193,194,195,196] These are disinformation websites[197] put on the net to spread false reports, labelling Chemtrails a conspiracy theory without true content, all in order to hinder public education. On Wikipedia you can read that chemtrails are normal contrails comprising the products of combustion – CO_2 and water – which arise due to the very low temperatures that prevail at high altitudes. Even the platform Mimikama, which claims independence as an exposer of fakes and false statements, denies the existence of chemtrails. For example, Mimikama shows how aeroplanes have installed tanks[198] that were interpreted by 'chemtrail believers' as transport containers for the toxins to be sprayed, but in reality serve to absorb water. At the end of the article Mimikama concludes: *For over 20 years now the Chemtrails conspiracy theory has been circulating. – And to this day there is no credible proof.*

Even in March 2017, one source *(TAG24.de)* published an article in which the following could be read: *As soon as weird stripes appear in the sky, half the world cries 'Beware, Chemtrails!' Actually, they are normal contrails produced by aircraft. But conspiracy theorists claim that these stripes are poisonous chemicals sprayed on behalf of intelligence agencies to control or eradicate humanity ... Now the plot gets even thicker for the conspirators: Because the scientific World Association of Meteorologists (WMO) has officially entered the Sky Stripes as cloud shapes in the Cloud Atlas ... Because the supposed chemtrails are now officially a cloud type. This cloud is called 'Homomutatus' (Latin: made by man).*†††††††††††††† Figures 16–18 show some Mammatus cloud formations. The Mammatus clouds have primarily nothing to do with chemtrails, but are mentioned in the article

---

†††††††††††††† Perhaps even more interestingly in the context, *Homomutatus* is also translatable as 'changed by man' (SP)

of *TAG24.de* in the same context. Chemtrails and Mamatus clouds have in common that they are human-made. The goal of this article is obviously to trivialize the chemtrails

Figure 16: A New cloud type: Mammatus clouds[199]

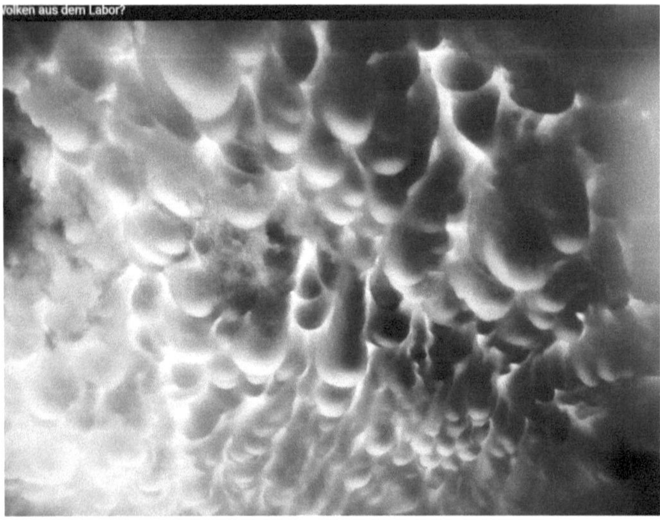

Figure 17: A New cloud type: Further Mammatus examples[200]

Even TV celebrities have joined in the denial campaign against chemtrail advocates,[201,202] as well as the prominent Swiss meteorologist Jörg Kachelmann, who states in a video[203], 'Chemtrails do not exist … the crazies, the conspiracy theorists', but in another video, he put his harsh criticism back into ominous perspective by saying,[204] 'When you're in television, you cannot say "chemtrail'. With that in mind, it's clear that the majority of the population also believes that Chemtrails are an invention of so-called conspiracy theorists. *As soon as 'knowing persons' speak out in public about the true facts of the matter, these people are discredited in the worst possible way or are vehemently threatened and blackmailed.*[205]

This denial campaign originated in the USA.[§§§§§§§§§§§§§§§].[206] *In the spring of 1999, the website www.carnicom.com was created to draw attention to unusual events surrounding aircraft activities over the southwestern desert sky of the United States … Within days, it was obvious that this site immediately attracted the attention of a myriad of high-level government and military authorities, defense contractors, research organizations, chemical and pharmaceutical companies, and health organizations. This interest has been documented over a period of a few months for the same page. Over this period, there was a clear pattern of monitoring of the surrounding research. Over the next few years, an apparent contradiction has emerged. On the one hand, there has been a high level of documentation monitoring, sampling methods, research, analysis and detection efforts, as well as a campaign of continuous devaluation of the importance of the matter. And the refusal to investigate was carried out by exactly the same visitors from this side … Pentagon, several Air Force bases, US Senate, aircraft manufacturers, pharmaceutical companies and drug companies, national security agencies, intelligence and emergency agencies, arms and defense companies, research organizations and the Navy.*[207]

[§§§§§§§§§§§§§§§] Spraying activities in the USA began much earlier than in Germany. In Germany, spraying has only been going on since about 2003

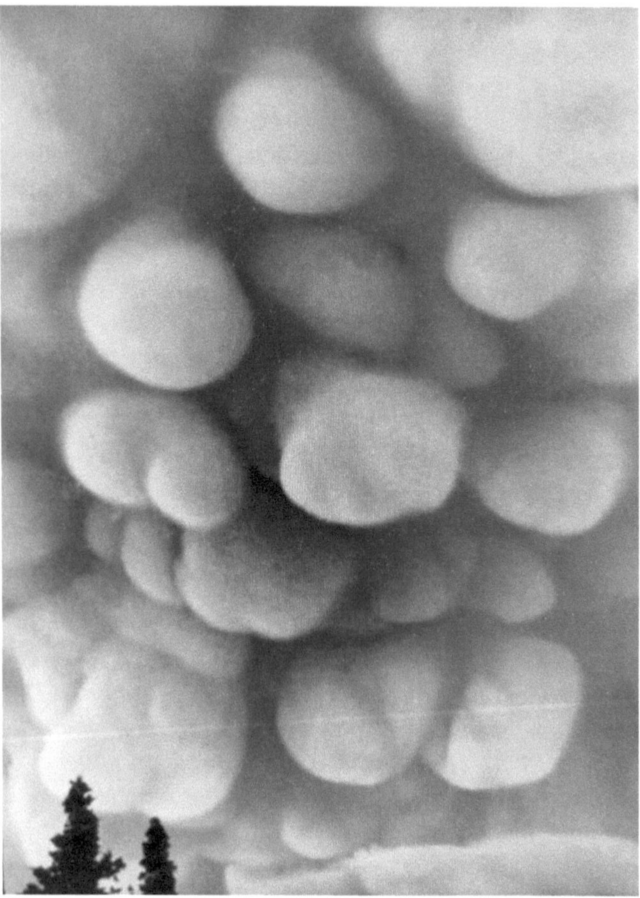

Figure 18: A New cloud type: Yet more Mammatus clouds[208] ***************.

*************** The appearance of these clouds could be artificially created by a special powder sprayed by aeroplanes. Such clouds have the property of binding the water that might have fallen as rainfall. *The powder is extremely absorbent; it can take up 2000 times its weight in water and bind it as a non-toxic gel. When the liquid solidifies, its temperature rises from 10 to 15 degrees. The combination of cloud and gel causes the storm to be deprived of energy.*
(https://www.youtube.com/watch?v=HitwJhUJrT4) Mammatus clouds from the lab? published on 04.01.2018. With this gel you can also dissolve bad weather fronts, which is something positive, as well as prevent precipitation and, in the worst case, trigger drought. On Wikipedia you can find more pictures of this cloud type under the term Mammatus.

So, all just conspiracy theory without truth? In the video[209], pilots, doctors and scientists report on Chemtrails. At a public hearing in Shasta County, California, these specialists challenged the denial campaign by reporting on Chemtrails/geoengineering that chemtrails are real and part of a military project funded through black coffers. And they have pointed out the possible consequences for the environment, health and nature.

Officials have since confirmed that Chemtrails are real, that is, the conspiracy **theory** on Chemtrails, which has long since been formally condemned, is thus absolved by a real **conspiracy practice**: *Telling information from the Federal Ministry of Education and Research shows that the use of weather-changing measures for presumed protection of the climate that has been practiced overhead illegally for years is one area that has left conspiracy theory and now been raised to legitimacy on the level of a scientific-political discussion.*[210] If you enter the page[211] specified in this video on Google, all you will find left is: *The cat is out of the bag – Geo-engineering poisonous ... It is missing: Infografik_climate_engineering*

What does this entry and its deletion tell us? Apparently, the Federal Ministry of Education and Research in Germany[††††††††††††††††] has withdrawn the relevant document again. One reason for this might be the very explosiveness of the statement that Chemtrails exist, for then all the 'experts' who have so far said the phenomenon of Chemtrails does *not* exist, would now appear to be liars or, worse, (bought?) propagandists of those same interest groups who are behind the spraying. In addition, of course, there is (as stated earlier) the risk of environmental pollution lawsuits, which are likely to have a greater chance of succeeding if the existence of Chemtrails is officially acknowledged.

But there have also been contributions from public service television (a mainstream medium which, one presumes, would

---

[††††††††††††††††] (BMBF, for Bundesministerium für Bildung und Forschung) [SP]

surely not want to promote the propagation of Chemtrails), in which the existence of Chemtrails was confirmed. The narrator of One video[212] from the year 2016 starts with the following words: *Would you like to eat plastic right now, maybe for breakfast this morning? Our NDR colleagues from the editorship 'Markt' have tracked down these plastic particles anyway. They are in honey, milk and drinking water, probably in other foods as well. Barely visible to the naked eye, they probably get into the food through the air or water. - We examined rainwater. Rainwater contains large quantities of material. ... The* **chemical soup of the chemtrails** *contains aluminum powder and barium salts, which are supposed to reflect part of the sunlight back into space. In our latitudes today, virtually all people already have a remarkably high level of poisoning by aluminum and barium. How the extremely rare barium gets into our body, you can no longer explain without* **chemtrails** *as a cause.* (Bold print by the author). And the weatherman Gunther Thiersch said in the weather news on 14.01.2009 (where he showed on the weather map for Germany some white stripes, about 500 km long and 10 km wide): *And then there's something here we cannot identify as snow or rain. Here in the west, these snaky lines, probably in the afternoon over the North Sea, have some aeroplanes, military planes, taken out about 5 to 6 km in height, have nothing to do with the weather ...* [213] Another video refers to this material used by military aircraft as follows: *To create the enormously large geister clouds over the Dutch coast, tons of substance have to rain down again and again over the Federal Republic of Germany.* [214] A comment by the meteorologist Karsten Brandt[‡‡‡‡‡‡‡‡‡‡‡‡‡‡‡]: *They set up environmental zones and the like, and apparently this environmental zone in 4 ... 5 km altitude above the North Sea and Germany is not included; hence it does not matter what is being applied there. That's unbelievable ... Every 20 to 30 days, conservatively estimated, there are weather conditions where these particles also appear, from the North Sea ... with a planar particle flow.*[215] This was the situation in 2008. As illustrated in the video: *Today we experience it nationwide several times a week.* Even if

---

‡‡‡‡‡‡‡‡‡‡‡‡‡‡‡ Karsten Brandt is the founder of www.donnerwetter.de (SP)

these clouds do not come from the German military[§§§§§§§§§§§§§§§§§], meteorologists think it is simply absurd that nobody feels responsible for substances that regularly settle over Germany and are actually banned.[216] *Absurd is just a polite description; here the population is deceived.*

A comment from the medical environmentalist Dietrich Klinghardt:[217] *Wow, to save the climate with pollution, this idea you have to come first. For chemtrail activists, however, this is no longer an idea, but already a reality.*

In a collaborative broadcast by the state broadcasters ARD and ZDF, recorded in another video[218], the existence of Chemtrails is clearly confirmed and their purpose explained. In this video the speaker, Joachim Bublath, is almost drowned out by noise, so that one can follow his statements only with difficulty.

On one website[****************] you can read: *While the mainstream media and our people's representatives still deny the topic of chemtrails and geoengineering, the US Space Agency (NASA) has admitted that for 'scientific' aims lithium, barium and other chemicals are sprayed into the atmosphere ... An important part of the investigation work is the following phone call in which Douglas Rowland (NASA staff member) admits that the space agency has been spraying lithium and other chemicals into the atmosphere since 1970. Of course, Rowland also assures us that these activities are safe both for nature and for humans.*[219] However, lithium is by no means harmless but ... *used in psychiatry as a psychotropic drug for manic and bipolar disorders ... causes countless side-effects such as sleep disorders, headaches and suicidal thoughts.*[220][†††††††††††††††††]

[§§§§§§§§§§§§§§§§§] In German, Bundeswehr (SP)

[****************] *Legitim.ch*

[†††††††††††††††††] My father, Wilton Alan Philp (born 1932), formerly a senior officer in the RAF, suffered from manic depression, relabelled bipolarity, for which lithium was prescribed. Occasionally he was affected by a lithium overdose, which displayed symptoms so similar to a minor stroke that it actually camouflaged the minor strokes he eventually began to suffer; so at first his strokes went undiagnosed. Incidentally, in later life he also suffered from sleep apnoea, a tem-

Chemtrails already existed much earlier than in 2003. In 1978, toxic barium had already been sprayed into the atmosphere, not by aircraft, but by a rocket. The German daily broadsheet *Die Welt*[221] reported: *Four more than a thousand kilometres of blue and white barium clouds were sprayed in the high atmosphere on the night of Monday by an American research rocket.*

The NWO is testing the spread of finely divided aerosol particles in the atmosphere. ... They use nano-sized alumina, which behaves like the finest smoke or clouds, and other substances, which are especially visible to satellite weather radar. All politicians, even those involved in the programme, believe they are conducting secret tests to **'darken' the atmosphere in an emergency**, *when the global climate gets out of hand, to limit solar radiation to the earth's surface. But that's just a lie, and maybe that's why* **the whole climate hysteria was created, to carry out covert operations like chemtrails. But in reality the world climate is not important to them.** *The real reason for the chemtrails is that, as I wrote before, they plan to reduce/eradicate the world's population with nano-particles so fine that, once released, they stay in the atmosphere for a long time and throughout the entire atmosphere be distributed globe. For the pre-tests with the chemtrails. The nanoparticles will be like dust and invisible, so you will not know you're even breathing them.*[222],‡‡‡‡‡‡‡‡‡‡‡‡‡‡‡‡‡

Spraying programmes are mainly found in North America, Northern Europe and in the southern hemisphere/Australia ... A four-jet military machine leaves a massive contrail, which will not dissolve as normal. This steadily increasing phenomenon has been observed in over thirty countries since the mid-1990s. The large jet has none of the identification marks demanded by international regulations. Conspiracy theories speak of a non-ratified spray of

---

porary cessation of breathing while asleep, which meant that he had to don an oxygen mask at bedtime. In the night, though, he would wake up happy, thinking he was flying again. (SP)

‡‡‡‡‡‡‡‡‡‡‡‡‡‡‡‡‡ Bold print by the author

chemicals and nanoparticles overhead for the purpose of military weather control and a targeted attack on human health.[223]

Further evidence in support of the thesis that barium and aluminum are sprayed overhead are the concentrations of these elements in the environment as measured by the Bavarian State Office for the Environment. §§§§§§§§§§§§§§§§§§, which tended to increase in the period from 2004 to 2015, while, for example, the measured concentrations of arsenic, another environmental toxin, did not rise.[224] (Arsenic does not seem to be sprayed).

While many scientists point to the fact that sick-making chemicals are sprayed by aeroplanes[225], this subject is not treated by environmental protection organizations. Why are Greenpeace, WWF (World Wildlife Fund), the Red Cross and other organizations with environmental concerns silent about these global environmental crises? One commentator suggests:[226] *Because environmental organizations such as Greenpeace and the WWF, the Federal Environment Agency (UBA), and the Ministry of Aerospace (DLR) itself, are involved in this research. But in public, they deny that this research will be used. What a coincidence that these organizations are on board.*

How can this be? Quite simply, *Any environmental organization that brings uncomfortable truths to the public will be deprived of its 'general utility' as a public lever of Western governments, with devastating governmental disadvantages. They will not risk that for that reason alone. So you can keep these environmental groups in check.*[227]

The environmentalists of the German Federation****************** are no exception.[228] When Greenpeace was contacted regarding the aerosol issue, the spraying of chemical and biological agents, Greenpeace announced in September 2000 that they were *unable to comment* and had *no official position* on the matter.[229]

---

§§§§§§§§§§§§§§§§§§ In German, Bayerisches Landesamt für Umwelt (SP)
****************** JS's original rendering was BUND (SP)

In January 2000, a certified letter containing a physical sample of material from highly unusual fibres[†] was sent to the US Environmental Protection Agency Director, EPA, Carol M. Browner, requesting the material in the interest of the Public, the environment and health. In February 2000, the EPO responded with two letters: *We have no knowledge* of any aircraft programmes that scatter materials into the atmosphere. The EPA does not corroborate the receipt or existence of physical materials in correspondence. Only one and a half years later, in June 2001, the EPA confirmed receipt of these unusual fibres. This confirmation was made on the basis of the Freedom of Information Act, to which a citizen referred. However, the EPA refused to identify this sample by announcing that *it is not the policy of this EPO office to test or analyze any unsolicited ... material samples or objects.*[230]

The Green Party, which many people still believe is committed to protecting the environment, calls for the decommissioning of coal-fired power plants for a cleaner environment. The absurdity of this demand is that today's modern coal-fired power plants are equipped with highly effective filtration systems, thereby minimizing air pollution, and, on the other hand, these same power plants are implicated in practising geo-engineering through the overhead spraying by aeroplanes of tons of their carbon fly ash – ostensibly to reduce solar radiation.[231]

One video[232] also touched on the psychological phenomenon of so many people not being able to see unusual events in the sky, so they are unable to make connections: *The total absence of any awareness and memories about the appearance of a natural sky as it was 10 years ago, makes a critical dispute impossible. They did not see anything unusual in the sky even when it was obvious, but only what they wanted to see or could see, namely nothing. The greatest crime against humanity is the plan to expose our planet to more than 10 million tons of toxic metal compounds until 2025; (it) is not a secret conspiracy; it takes place almost daily in front of*

[†] What these fibres signify is the topic of "High-Tech Bioweapons - Forecourt to Hell, chapter 6, 2

our eyes, above our heads. All we have to do is look, observe and critically question the official media.[233] This forgetting, *the complete absence of ... own memories,* also plays a major role in Orwell's novel *Nineteen Eighty-Four.* The elderly in Orwell's fictional surveillance state, who had lived before the 'revolution', had nevertheless forgotten that time, *because the few scattered survivors from the ancient world proved unable to share the one epoch to compare the other ... They remembered a million useless things ... but all the essential facts were out of their field of vision.*[234]‡‡‡‡‡‡‡‡‡‡‡‡‡‡‡‡‡‡

Pictures 19 to 27 show pictures of Chemtrails that impressively demonstrate the thesis that materials sprayed overhead give the sky an unnatural appearance.

Today, a huge amount of poison was again spread over the Greater Stuttgart area ... Within an hour, a beautiful light- blue sky turned into a grey wall. At least 10 aircraft on the way. The stuff goes straight to the brain. It dumbs. It kills. ... It is unbelievable,

---

‡‡‡‡‡‡‡‡‡‡‡‡‡‡‡‡‡‡ Psychologically, this cultural blindness (a form of cognitive dissonance) is a phenomenon that should be better known. The most famous examples hark back to the landing of the Conquistadors in the New World. When the natives asked how the visitors had arrived, the Conquistadors pointed to their sailing ships in the bay, which were massive compared to the indigenous seacraft; but the natives were unable to see them because such visions were beyond their experience. A more personal example took place in a mining village where I lived for some years. Waiting for a bus one day I fell into conversation with a prospective fellow-passenger and happened to point out to him the beautiful daylight moon. Despite all attempts on my part to reassure him he made the decision to leave the bus-stop and be with his family, because he had never seen a daylight moon before, believed it was unnatural, and thought there was something wrong with the solar system. Fascinated, I have since made a point of collecting similar examples, from which I can only conclude that we do not see what is there but only what seems relevant to us at the time. Surely, therefore, we must pay attention to those who claim to see what we cannot and are able to prophesy concerning the future. A most interesting website, responded to by some quite intelligent bloggers, is: https://www.northcoastjournal.com/humboldt/myth-of-the-invisible-ships/Content?oid=2129921 (SP)

but look at the Deagel list.[§§§§§§§§§§§§§§§§§§] *The population is to be drastically reduced ... When the hell are you finally waking up ???* So reads the post of a Facebook friend on 23.9.2018,[235] and a comment: *They were also busy in Ulm!*[236] And I conclude: On 29.09.2018 and 17.10.2018 the Dortmund sky was again covered in milky-white, already expanding Chemtrails (Figures 23 and 24), whose appearance certainly has nothing to do with natural cloud formations. See also what occurred on 05.08.2019 in the vicinity of Dresden (Figure 27).

During the last weeks of the end of 2019 I have seen no more Chemtrails. The powers-that-be may have taken a break from spraying after more and more photos and information about spraying activities have been distributed on the internet.

The fundamental question that arises automatically is how do the élite protect themselves from their own weapons, especially from the aerosol particles that spread out in the atmosphere, finely distributed? *Surely they have something like underground retreats, which they leave only when everything is over on the surface of the earth.* This was one comment to the above-quoted article[237]. Another comment was: *During the time these tests are being conducted, the so-called élites are not found in the area. The 'élites', who belong to umpteen different branches of the Order of the Golden Fleece, have their own communication systems ... why are no members of the élite dying in so-called accidents, such as September 11th? [2001] Coincidence? ... because they know in advance what will happen on this planet ..."*[238]

Despite the numerous references to Chemtrails, including the three TV videos cited at the beginning, the media continue to deny them. In various video contributions Chemtrails and HAARP are repeatedly dismissed as conspiracy theories located in the realm of fantasy, a dismissal believed by broad sections of the population.

[§§§§§§§§§§§§§§§§§§] In addition to information of a military nature that it receives directly from CIA; FBI; NSA; US Army; Mossad; Nato; EU related, the company Deagel distributes forecasts about the population in individual countries
(see Reducing the world's population, chapter 2, 2)

You invent such deranged terms as 'climate deniers', 'chemtrail believers' and other ridiculous ways to discredit people who want to draw attention to what is being manipulated in this world – and you just continue as before.[239]

Figure 19: Comparison of an ordinary summer sky in 1999 with the year 2019. *The total absence of any awareness and memories about the appearance of a natural sky as it was 10 years ago, makes a critical dispute impossible.They did not see anything unusual in the sky even when it was obvious, but only what they wanted to see or could see, namely nothing.*[240]

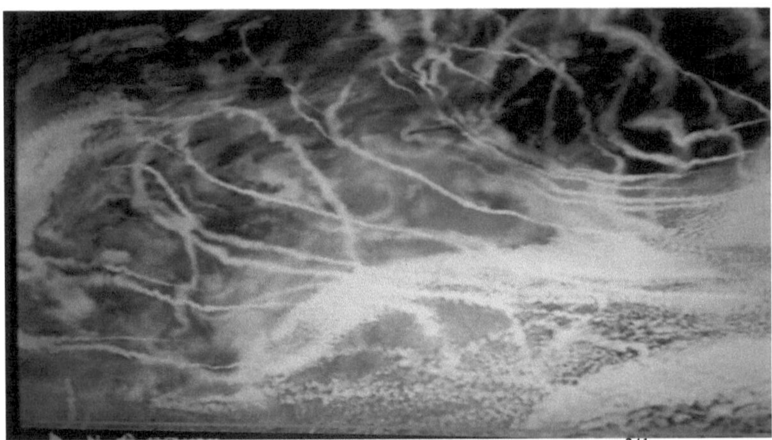

Figure 20: Chemtrails: Result after a spray action on the sky[241]

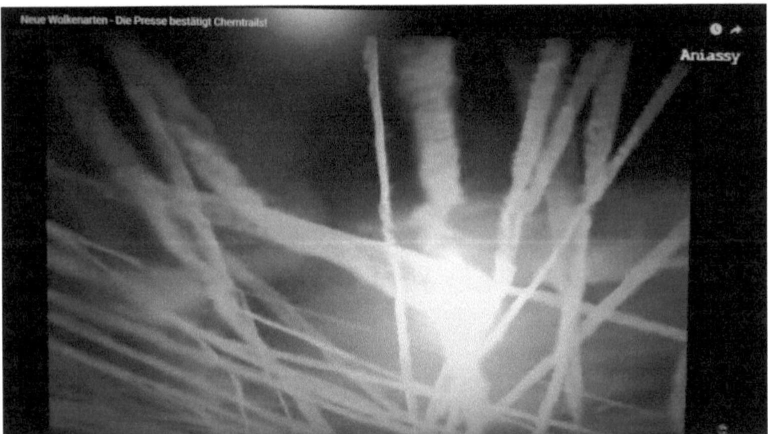

Figure 21: Heaven covered with countless chemtrail traces that widen over time.[242]

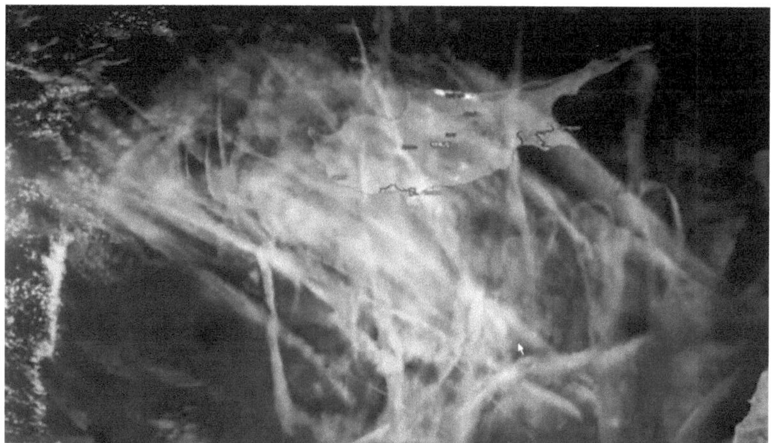

Figure 22: Chemtrails photographed from the aircraft.[243]

Figure 23: New Cloud Species over Phoenix Lake, Dortmund, 17.10.18

Figure 24: New Cloud Species over Dortmund on 17.10.18

Figure 25: Here the Chemtrails are not expelled from the turbines (further proof that they are not merely contrails).[244]

Figure 26: New Cloud Species over Berlin. Dietrich Klinghardt: *My patients from the American secret service have told me that it would not have been possible to listen to Angela Merkel's phone without this one* (he pointed to this photo).[245]

Figure 27: Chemtrails over Dresden on August 5, 2019, 8:40 am.

Now ask yourself: If Chemtrails have been confirmed in *individual* reports on TV and in mainstream media, why are Chemtrails being denied in official reports? Why, despite the overwhelming evidence, is the existence of Chemtrails, the spraying of toxins in the atmosphere, so vehemently contested by mainstream portals and the mainstream media, despite the overwhelming evidence? The answer: Because of the impending legal consequences, as highlighted at the beginning of this section.[246]

An answer is also provided by the 2001 IPCC Report, which gives an opinion on the spraying of materials into the atmosphere to limit global warming. *The report says that it is possible to reduce global warming by spraying different particles. Incidentally, the report mentions sky fading********************* *mentioned above **as a risk for the premature discovery of spray attempts by the public***.[247]†††††††††††††††††††† The underlying reason for this secrecy indubitably has a legal implication. In a case of pollution the polluter would have to be proven guilty beyond any doubt, which becomes more difficult the less spraying is detected.

Having confirmed the existence of Chemtrails in the three TV videos of cited above, we can progress to a substantive discussion of this phenomenon. What exactly are Chemtrails? How do they differ from ordinary contrails? Contrails dissolve after about 1 minute, but Chemtrails stay in the sky, widening gradually and merging into a milky-white blanket that reduces the amount of sunlight. Contrails are continuous, they cannot repeatedly be switched on and off ... However, one video shows this switching in action, in other words, in that particular case contrails definitely cannot be involved.[248] From minute 12:46‡‡‡‡‡‡‡‡‡‡‡‡‡‡‡‡‡‡ you can see how two aircraft fly relatively close to each other, in which one of the trails is switched on and off, and the other remains

---

****************** Sky fading - in other words the formation of a milky-white ceiling in the sky which reduces incident sunlight - arises after prolonged spraying.
†††††††††††††††††† Bold print by the author (JS, SP)
‡‡‡‡‡‡‡‡‡‡‡‡‡‡‡‡‡ AWACS Stop + Go-erwischt in Northern Germany

continuous: in other words, the switching on and off cannot be explained with different air layers, which fly through the aircraft, where the temperatures differ and thus the condensation would switch on and off.

Although we have shown in this section that Chemtrails are real, the cover-up campaign will continue until such time as it becomes possible to legalize geoengineering through the IPCC, on the grounds that without geoengineering the Earth's climate threatens to collapse. Prior to this it will be denied so as not to run the risk of governments being sued for environmental crimes.§§§§§§§§§§§§§§§§§§

Intentional global manipulation of the climate and weather through stratospheric aerosol injections is the largest environmental crime ever to have occurred in human history. It is still unlawful and not legitimized by the respective parliaments. The IPCC is always working to legalize these illegal programmes.[249] In this sense, the media are also paving the way for populations to accept geoengineering activities. On 28.09.2019 an article[250] with the title Geoengineering: It only helps to cleave the climate was published.******************** by zeit.de. The short summary has the rhetorical query: *emit less greenhouse gases? It's good, but it's not enough. In order to stop the earth's overheating, interventions in climate change are necessary – but so far hardly practicable.* The text expands on this: *The dilemma is obvious: In order to keep global warming below two degrees, until the year 2100 humanity is allowed only to blow 700 billion tons of greenhouse gas into the air. Even with rapidly sinking emissions, this limit would have been reached by the 2000s. After that, no more grams of greenhouse gas should be released. Since this is completely unrealistic, the IPCC has long assumed that humanity must intervene. The special report published on Wednesday (25.09.2019) on the condition of water and ice on earth has once*

---

§§§§§§§§§§§§§§§§§§§ There would seem to be a potential for environmental crimes eventually to be included among war crimes, crimes against humanity, and crimes against individual nations; which must make some politicians extremely nervous. (SP)
******************** by zeit.de

again made it clear that things cannot go on as they have been doing so far. In principle, two approaches are conceivable here. The first is to artificially extract carbon from the atmosphere and store it underground for the long term. This is usually referred to as Carbon Capture and Storage, CCS for short. But even if the first projects are successful it is unclear whether CCS can be used on an industrial scale – and what that would cost. Therefore, there is a second approach: researchers also want to artificially cool the earth by allowing the planet to directly reflect incident sunlight. So raise the albedo.[†] *Experts speak of **radiation management**, influencing the radiation balance. There are also different techniques in the discussion, but practically none of them has been tested so far.*

Until such time as these stratospheric aerosol injections (Chemtrails) are legalized, this spraying is kept secret and denied. But how can it be that this overhead spray of toxins can be kept so secret? Since surely at least some of the aircraft pilots involved would eventually get scruples and whistleblow. The answer is that these whistleblowing pilots do actually exist. One video[251] features a former civilian employee of EADS (European Aeronautic Defence and Space Company), who helped to reconstruct an aircraft into a spray plane. He was dismissed after giving details to a Green Party member and providing pictures of these events. This former employee said, *And then the military came and told us to wear full protective suits and respiratory masks; because the tanks must now be filled, and the substances that come in, aluminum, sulphides, barium oxide ... are interspersed with nanoparticle-sized polymer compounds; they are highly poisonous to you; so you have to wear protective suits now. ... So I just wanted to say, we are flying into an ecological catastrophe. And anyone who does not want to understand that, I'd like to be able to show the evidence, and I'll put myself at the disposal of each committee of inquiry ...* There are other pilots who whistleblew.[252] On the other hand, pilots of commercial airliners, fo rexample, often have no idea what they are spraying or that they are spraying toxins. A large proportion of

---

[†] Albedo is the comparative whiteness or reflectivity of the planet (SP)

these toxins are spread by military aircraft, and we may assume that military pilots are required to maintain secrecy and only follow orders. In addition, they usually only know part of their specific job, but not what they spray.

As a possible reason for not having seen any Chemtrails in the sky since 2020, I wrote at the beginning of this section that President Trump had cut back the funds for geoengineering projects. But another reason could play a role, namely that in the past years the evidence for environmental pollution from Chemtrails has become solid, thus increasing the danger of lawsuits against polluters having a greater chance of success. This would have the unintended and unwanted result of inviting considerable publicity.

Chemtrails – What is their purpose?

After having unequivocally demonstrated in the previous section that Chemtrails are real, now let us ask: Why is spraying done? To my knowledge, Chemtrails serve various purposes:

1) spraying **toxins**
2) spraying **bioweapon** components
3) creating a metallized layer above the earth's surface
4) **spraying so-called nano-robots, or nanobots** (Smartdust, intelligent dust) which settle in the human brain
5) **shielding** the earth from **solar radiation**.

In 1), toxins include toxic nanoparticles, barium, strontium, aluminium, titanium, lithium, cadmium, lead, mercury, polymer fibres, dioxins and many other pathogenic substances. This is the result of independent research and analysis in various regions of the world where Chemtrails have been sprayed.[253,254]

2) involves a topic already covered in High-Tech Bioweapons – Hell's annex, chapter 6, 2).[255]

3) includes Radar Range Extent, Airspace Monitoring, Missile Shield, etc. These are prerequisites for HAARP systems to operate globally by reflecting the emitted electromagnetic waves from a metallized sky to strike the earth's surface at remote locations (see Figure 29.[256]

4) serves the objective of global human slavery via nanorobots, after they have been inhaled unnoticed. These nanorobots can be linked to a cloud and controlled remotely. As a result of this intake, both thoughts and actions of people could be influenced.[257] (See 5G and Tranhumanism, chapter 5, 2)

5) seems to me rather to fulfill an alibi function, a legitimization for Chemtrails, so that they are tolerated by the population as necessary to limit global warming by solar rays. As argued in the section "The Counter-thesis to the CO_2 thesis", there is a risk that such a sunshade would tend to heat up the earth rather than cool it.

Effects of Chemtrails on health

There is no one so deaf as one who does not want to hear, or so blind as one who refuses to see.[258]

The health effects of toxins released through Chemtrails are obviously at the forefront of respiratory and flu-like symptoms. Because of the minuteness of the nanoparticles sprayed through chemtrails, these can easily overcome the blood-brain barrier, intercalate themselves in the brain and in the airways of humans and impair their functions. Owing to their high toxicity they can even destroy metabolic processes.

In the US, there was a flu episode in 2000 caused by an 'unknown pathogen', according to the Center for Disease Control.[259] *In 99% of those affected, tests for flu had been negative.*

Already in 2005, the authors of the influential book *Chemtrails – weather manipulation in the sky?*[260] produced a list of immediate health consequences of spraying on the well-known Chemtrail website[‡]: *headaches and chronic fatigue, ... shortness of breath, balance disorders and loss of weight Short term memory, flu outbreaks, conjunctivitis and asthma attacks."*

It is noticeable that many of the health effects of chemtrails (such as fatigue, lethargy, headaches, etc.) are noticeable in victims of microwave radiation from mobile phones. Similar to cases of microwave irradiation, people respond differently to contact with chemtrail fallout. Depending on the 'biological window' of the individual (synonymous with overall health status), there are people whose immune systems can handle chemistry without problems, while others collapse at the first contact.[261]

Particularly insidious are the nanoparticles (aluminium, barium, strontium ...) and nanofibres,[262,263] because of their tiny size. *Via the respiratory tract, toxic substances enter the bloodstream directly and thus ultimately reach the brain.*[264] Substances harmful to humans descend after a period of time dependent on prevailing weather conditions and, absorbed by normal breathing, are stored in the lung tissue where they can cause pathological changes. The residence time of nanoparticles and nanofibres in the atmosphere can be up to one year; but occasionally it can be very short, as Dietrich Klinghardt describes from his own experience in a YouTube video.[265] As a result of contamination by these poisons, disorders such as respiratory distress, asthma, pneumonia and balance disorders, dizziness, and neurophysiological disorders, which are increasingly associated with the rapidly increasing numbers of Alzheimer's disease and premature dementia, are named.[266] Nanoparticles and nanofibres are so dangerous for humans precisely because they cannot be filtered out by the cilia in the respiratory organs due to their tiny size, and they can easily overcome the blood-brain barrier. Their size is in the order of 0.01 to 1 microns, in other words in a range not recorded at all in the

---

[‡] *chemtrail.de*

usual measurements carried out in large cities by the Environment Agency.[§§§§§§§§§§§§§§§§§§§§§§] While breathing air, the human body is able to filter out particles of 5 microns plus in size.[267] However, this cannot be done if the particles are much smaller. With this in mind, environmentalists have taken measurements in areas just below particle size PM = 10 microns and found that in this potentially hazardous area, and especially below 2.5 microns, the particle density increases rapidly. These particles obviously do not come from diesel cars.[268]

In fact, diesel cars are extremely clean when it comes to fine dust. *In fact, air that comes out of the exhaust of diesel vehicles with modern exhaust gas purification is far less polluted than the air that the engine previously sucked in. The diesel (engine) is an 'air cleaning machine' ... Rolf Bulander, head of Bosch Motor Vehicle Technology, explained that exhaust gases contained only one tenth as many fine dust particles as the surrounding air.*[269] But what about this rapid increase in particle density at the low-micron level? Environmentalists are inclined to attribute it to the spraying activity of airplanes, which involves nanoparticles in large quantities. ... *at 2.5μm (or minus that) it becomes criminal ... because these (nano)particles remain in the body and form inflammatory foci. And if these happen to be substances that somehow act chemically catalytically, then I have a chain-reaction in the lungs. That will not go well. And that's why lung diseases are rapidly rising.*[270] This statement is confirmed by independent sources. Respiratory diseases are now number three in the United States.[271] This despite the fact that smoking can no longer be held as the main cause, because the global campaign against smoking, combined with smoking bans in public institutions, should have resulted in a reduction in respiratory illnesses. In 2011, news broke on German NTV about a new, unknown, yet surprisingly common disease called COPD (Chronic Obstructive Pulmonary Disease):[272] According to a new study, *one in four adults suffer at some point in life from the dangerous respiratory ailment COPD. Scientists working with Andrea Gershon at the Institute for Clinical*

[§§§§§§§§§§§§§§§§§§§§§§] In Germany, these measurements are carried out by the UBA (or Umweltbundesamt), the Federal Environment Agency (SP)

Evaluation in Toronto, Canada have said in the British medical journal 'The Lancet' that this Chronic Obstructive Pulmonary Disease increases the risk for heart attack or cancer.

*The mainstream media report that hospital emergency rooms are full of patients with bizarre upper respiratory tract infections. But apparently it does not seem to be a virus. They report it is a 'mysterious' flu and that no flu vaccine is effective. ... 'That's all nonsense, false nonsense,' says Dr Leonard Horowitz. 'It is a fact that we have had this kind of epidemic since the end of 1998/beginning of 1999.' ... The Research Institute of Pathology for the US Forces has registered a patent for a pathogenic mycoplasma that causes the epidemic. You can see the patent report in the book 'Healing Codes for the Biological Apocalypse'.********************* *Mycoplasma is not really a fungus, ... not really a bacterium, ... not really a virus. It has no cell wall. It goes deep into the cell nucleus, which makes it very difficult to get a response from the immune system. It's a manmade biological weapon. The patent report explains how it causes a chronic upper respiratory tract infection virtually identical to what happens all the time (in the case history of the illness).*[273] (See High-tech Bio-weapons – Hell's annex, chapter 6, 2 for details.)

Dietrich Klinghardt – a specialist doctor working at the Sophia Health Institute, Seattle, a leading clinic in the USA for the treatment of people with symptoms of poisoning and intoxication – says: *People with chronic illnesses come to us from all over the world. We have discovered that the fallout from chemtrails is now the most important cause of poisoning in humans, leading to a range of chronic diseases. These include autism in children ... adult disorders, disorders of the entire nervous system, MS [multiple schlerosis], ALS [amyotrophic lateral schlerosis], Parkinson's, neuropathies and all the degenerative diseases of the brain. That the aluminium content in our nervous system has risen exponentially in recent years, cannot be explained away by underarm deodorant or aluminium cooking pots, but can only be*

******************** The author of this book is Leonard G Horowitz, mentioned in the same quotation (SP) *explained by chemtrails.* Klinghardt's last sentence refers to announcements by environmentalists that deodorants and other personal care products, as well as chemicals that harness aluminium, are the pathogenic cause of elevated levels of Aluminium in human bodies. Klinghardt has performed tests on 200 patients with the result that the average aluminium content in their blood is 140 times higher (120 µg/l). than that of lead (0.9 µg/l).. And he notes:[274] *American laboratories testing for aluminium get a letter from the government: 'If you do not stop it, we'll close your lab.' I do not know what's going on in Germany, but ceratinly something similar. The Americans never signed a peace treaty with Deutschland.*[†††††††††††††††††††††] *And every law, and every measure in Germany, can be vetoed by the American government. Most of you do not know that. The Americans are very proud of it – I found out about it from my American friends. Importantly, what is emerging now is that the airspace over Germany is American territory.*

In addition to the increase in *diseases of the nervous system,* another process is taking place in Western countries, the gradual decline in the population's IQ. In a FOCUS article[275] you can read: *Humanity is becoming more and more stupid – that was the result of scientific tests. While [IQ] intelligence quota decreases on average, behavioural problems and autism increase. Researchers assume that so-called environmental hormones are responsible for this.* One certainly cannot rule out the contribution of massive hormone additives in factory farming, but the use of hormones in healthcare also has a negative impact on public health. However, in

---

[†††††††††††††††††††††] This statement referring to Deutschland, which many may find surprising, refers of course to the lack of a Treaty between the USA and Germany in the aftermath of World War Two. There was a US-Germany Peace Treaty of 1921 as a result of the US Senate having earlier refused to ratify the Treaty of Versailles in 1919 (https://en.wikipedia.org/wiki/U.S.–German_Peace_Treaty_(1921). There was, in addition, a trade treaty between the two: The Treaty of Friendship, Commerce and Consular Relations between Germany and the United States of America (1923) – not ratified by the US Senate until 1925. This Treaty of Friendship was updated in 1954. The North Atlantic Treaty of 1949, overseen by NATO, the organization named after it, did not include Germany until 1955. (SP) light of the above, it seems likely that environmental toxins released via Chemtrails are a major cause of the increase in neurological diseases.

Nanoplastic fibres contained in Chemtrails are highly dangerous to the human body. These tiny plastic particles that have since been detected in the human body were also the subject of a contribution from the radio station WDR4, broadcast on 19.6.2018, in which listeners were told how this plastic waste reaches the human body, namely via the food chain. In an informative sense, so far, so good. But Chemtrails as a possible source of applied plastic fibres were not mentioned, but only functional clothing in which plastic fibres are incorporated. These plastic clothing fibres can partly dissolve during the washing process and, after crossing the sewage barrier, leak into the groundwater and from there enter into drinking water. The obvious cause, Chemtrails, as assigned in the above-cited video,[276] was not addressed by WDR4. Instead, the ignorant consumer was presented with another 'enemy' against whom his anger can be directed: clothing and/or washing-machine manufacturers.

Video recordings of spraying campaigns over the Greater Stuttgart area[277] also showed that these campaigns were essentially confined to the urban area, while in the rural metropolitan area around Stuttgart no traces of Chemtrail could be seen. This nourishes the suspicion that these spray actions not only serve weather manipultors but suggests that as many people as possible should want to expose the release of these poison cocktails as having criminal intent. In this context, one should also ask why anyone would use such highly toxic materials such as aluminum, barium and strontium, just to reduce the sun's rays. There are much less toxic metals that could serve the purpose of reflecting sunlight. The answer to this logical question is given in High-Tech Bioweapons – forecourt to Hell, chapter 6, 2).

One video[278] states, *Since the stuff is in the air, we breathe it in. It goes into the respiratory tract, sinuses, and brain. Aluminium (in the brain) is the cause of a variety of diseases, eg. Alzheimer's.*

Over the last five years, the number of patients with Alzheimer's, Parkinson's and other neurodegenerative diseases has increased dramatically, nearly quadrupling. In Hawaii, Alzheimer's is now very common. They spray aluminum nanoparticles, and these nanoparticles trigger cell death in the brain. That's what Alzheimer's is all about. Attention Deficit Disorder (ADD) began in the 1970s when there was no talk of autism, and one in 100,000 had this disease. Today, due to aluminum, one in 48 has an attention deficit/hyperactivity disorder. When heavy metals were released, brains normalized again. There is a risk that the entire ecosystem will collapse because of the many heavy metals, especially because of the aluminum. This is far more than just a little pollution. Monsanto has developed aluminum-resistant plants. I wonder why? ... To this effect there is a US patent with the number US 7,582,809 B2, issued on September 1, 2009.

Spraying (from Al, Ba, Sr) is said to have unimaginably drastic consequences for the health of plants, animals and humans. According to reports, [aluminium has been] sprayed] since 2003 in Germany, but in the US since the 90s. According to experts, they are already faced with the consequences of this environmental poisoning, completely contaminated soil and lakes. Normal seed cannot grow on it. That's what I call really blatant. Would you believe ... that chemical companies have developed aluminium-resistant seeds and earn enormous sums from their sale? Sorry, but it is so.‡‡‡‡‡‡‡‡‡‡‡‡‡‡‡‡‡‡‡‡‡ *If instead of just looking at the telly, iPhone and iPad, we young people would unite somehow and look at all this information properly, then the planes would soon no longer be able to spray what they want.*[279,280]

---

‡‡‡‡‡‡‡‡‡‡‡‡‡‡‡‡‡‡ See, for example, US patent number US 7,582,809 B2, issued on September 1, 2009

HAARP –
The Food Slicer in the Sky

If human megalomania, power madness, perverted thinking and feasibility delusion express themselves somewhere politically, economically, military-technically, it is within the HAARP project.[281]§§§§§§§§§§§§§§§§§§§§§§§§

Officially, HAARP *is a* **US civilian and military research programme** *that uses high frequency electromagnetic waves.*[282] HAARP equipment is used to study the upper atmosphere in terms of radio-wave propagation, communication and navigation. However, operating these systems also offers enormous opportunities for global manipulation, as evidenced by documented patents, such as those found in weather manipulation.[283] The fact that today's weather is heavily influenced by human manipulation that can trigger and intensify cyclones is the subject of a YouTube video.[284]

Figure 28: Chemtrails (left picture), 17 minutes later overlaid with a thin, structured cloud cover (right picture), in which more or less regular rib-like structures have formed, most likely under the influence of artificial HAARP radiation.[285]

---

§§§§§§§§§§§§§§§§§§§§§§§§ Re an analogous context, 'feasibility delusion' has been defined as 'the notion that modern [science] can effect [something] with no problem at all'. The analogy was with modern [medicine] and [sex changes] (https://www.ncbi.nlm.nih.gov/pmc/articles/PMC2697020) [SP]

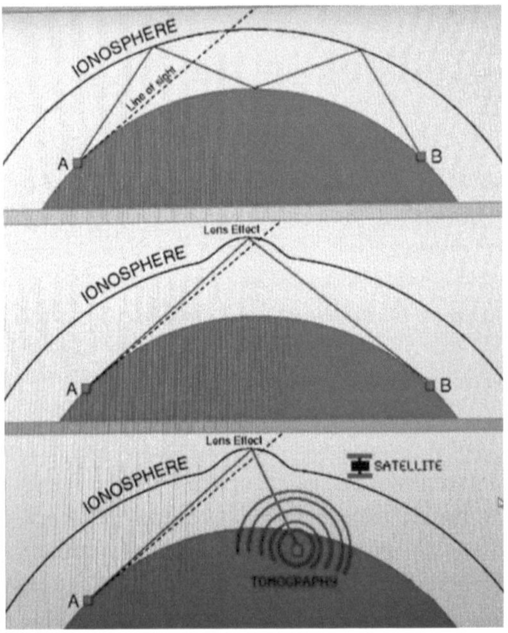

Figure 29: HAARP equipment can operate globally by reflecting emitted radiation on the metallized sky and impinging on distant locations at the Earth's surface.[286]

Figure 30: Surface of the Baltic Sea, showing oscillations resonated by corresponding radar waves generated in the HAARP plant near Rostock. (In the centre of the picture, a bowl filled with water is displayed on a loudspeaker vibrated at a frequency in the range of 2 and 220 Hz). (Picture taken from[287])

The HAARP system is an ionosphere heater ... As with a huge torch, HAARP can heat and then extract parts of the ionosphere before they are lifted up. It cuts a part of the sky, part of the atmosphere. It cuts the part that protects the earth as the ultimate filter and is at the same time the gateway to the universe. The link between WORLD and ALL is dismembered – large holes are burned. Not only can the heated and detached area be raised, it can also be tilted, like a giant oversized shield.[288] If so, one suspects that the ozone hole over the Antarctic could have been created as well. (More in The Ozone Hole – Human-made?, chapter 4,8)

HAARP itself is based on a US Patent of the inventor Bernad J Eastlund (1938–2007) of January 10, 1985, number 4686605, where also the principle of action (energy transfer over long distances by means of microwave radiation using the ionosphere) is described.[289] This patent is based on another US patent[290], issued by Nikola Tesla, number 1119732, for wireless energy transmission. The Eastlund patent was acquired by the US defense company Reytheon, a contractor for the military. *And not only could you send energy to places where there were no electric generators available, you could control the weather as well. You could use it to change the jet streams and bring rain.*[291]

Rostock-Marlow is one of the largest HAARP plants in the world. The Baltic Sea and the sky, when metallized by Chemtrails, serve as mirrors for radar waves to reach virtually any point in the world,[292] including places beyond the visible horizon. This is also the principle in shortwave propagation using the Heaviside layer.********************* In particular, HAARP allows the ionosphere to be deliberately deformed (see the middle and lower image in Figure 29) so that it acts as a focusing mirror, allowing

---

********************* The Heaviside layer – also known as the Kennelly-Heaviside layer after the two independent scientists who predicted its existence in 1902 – is a layer of ionised gas 56-93 miles (90-150km) above the earth, which reflects medium-frequency radio waves (*https://en.wikipedia.org/wiki/Kennelly–Heaviside_layer*). [SP] beams to be focused on a target at the earth's surface. Incident radiation has a very high energy density, a prerequisite for destructive potential. Figure 30 shows the surface of the Baltic Sea, resonated by waves generated in the HAARP plant near Rostock. For comparison, in the middle of the picture, a bowl filled with water is superimposed on a loudspeaker, via whose oscillations oscillation patterns on the water surface with a similar pattern have been produced.

In the above-mentioned article[293], which has been broadcast by ARD and ZDF, the existence of HAARP equipment is confirmed and its purpose explained. As with the topic of Chemtrails, a denial campaign takes place on the subject of HAARP, albeit less focused on whether HAARP exists at all, but rather on the practical appication of its weather-changing programmes. It is often said that HAARP is engaged in purely science-based research. With regard to Rostock the transmitting plant, an online Baltic Sea newspaper[†] described it on 27 March 2018 as:[294] *Marlow radio station ... where the Navy make contact with their ships around the World – by means of twelve antennae distributed in the fenced-off forest area.*

Already in Chemtrails – The Chemical Soup in the Sky (chapter 4, 2) we have found out that Mimikama does everything it can to discredit those in the 'conspiracy theory clique' who are only trying to draw public attention towards locating dangerous developments, as here in connection with HAARP. Countless documents attesting to manipulations by HAARP and Chemtrails are simply ignored by Mimikama. The Mimikama platform takes advantage of the fact that only a small percentage of the population grapples with these phenomena, which seem so incredible that they confound common sense, rendering one unwilling to believe that the government would allow such a thing. On other web-pages HAARP and their activities are played down[‡], and in yet another source [295] the slogan 'conspiracy theory' again crops up: *Whirlwinds in the US have made an old conspiracy theory*

[†] Ostseezeitung.de
[‡] for example, at *https://futurezone.at*

flourish once again: The HAARP transmitter supposedly causes natural catastrophes. This denial campaign serves the purpose of keeping the public in ignorance, so they do not oppose these activities or protest against them – to the detriment of our environment. However, a Report of 14 January 1999 on the Environment, Security and Foreign Policy,[296] authorized by the European Parliament, contains a sub-section with the subtitle *HAARP – A climate-damaging weapons system*, in which one can read: *HAARP, Research Programme for High-Frequency Radiation Research ... is jointly carried out by the US Air Force and the University of Alaska Geophysical Institute, Fairbanks. Similar investigations are also under way in Norway ... in the Antarctic and also in the former Soviet Union. HAARP is a research project in which parts of the ionosphere are heated with strong radio waves using a ground-based system with a network of antennae, all of which have their own transmitter. The generated energy heats up certain parts of the ionosphere, which can also cause holes in the ionosphere and artificial 'mirrors' ... Another serious consequence of HAARP are the holes in the ionosphere, which are caused by the uplift of strong waves. The ionosphere protects us from incoming cosmic rays. There is hope that the holes will close again, but experiences with changes in the ozone layer point in the opposite direction. So, the protective ionosphere has big holes ...* This EU report further notes: *HAARP is associated with 50 years of intense space exploration for clearly military purposes, for example, as part of the 'Star Wars' (project), to control the upper atmosphere and communication. Such research is considered to be seriously damaging to the environment, and it can have a profound impact on people's lives.*

I add two comments to draw further attention to the dangers associated with HAARP: *Global warming, natural catastrophes and extreme weather are not combated by the weather manipulation programme, but rather encouraged and even brought about artificially! ... Total weather control has fatal environmental and health effects. A war against humans and nature !!! The weather became a weapon ...* [297]

Because HAARP uses the ionosphere as a mirror, it can, in principle, reach the whole earth. ... For about the last 10 years, weather catastrophe follows weather catastrophe, starting with the unusually violent El Niño of 1989. Since then, global weather has been chaotic, El Niño comes more often and more violently than normal. It is striking that exactly at this time in Alaska, the large-scale HAARP plant was built and given its first test, and similar facilities were built and tested in the Soviet Union at that time ... These atmospheric manipulations are connected with characteristic physical symptoms – predominant severe restlessness, gastrointestinal disturbances, ocular pains and headaches, and depression, which have been observed to be typical of several such wet-state manipulations.[298]

The technology behind HAARP has a history dating back to the 1940s, beginning in Germany during the Second World War. Postwar, it was adopted by the Russians, then the Americans, and further developed. Large-scale antennae can be used to generate so-called ELF waves. The frequencies radiated by such HAARP equipment are particularly dangerous if they are in resonance with the earth's frequency, which used to be 7.8 Hz, but is now closer to 8hz.[299]-If radiated waves are in the range of the earth's frequency, earthquakes can be purposefully triggered in earthquake zones, simply because relatively small oscillations of the earth's crust there are already sufficient to upset the unstable equilibrium. The closer the frequency of the radiated waves is to the standard resonance frequency, the greater can be the oscillation amplitudes of the earth's crust in such earthquake-prone areas.

Similar cloud patterns as shown in Figures 33–35 were also to be seen in the Fukushima sky shortly before the 2011 Tsunami (Figure 32. More on this topic in Tsunamis – Human-made? chapter 4, 6).[300]

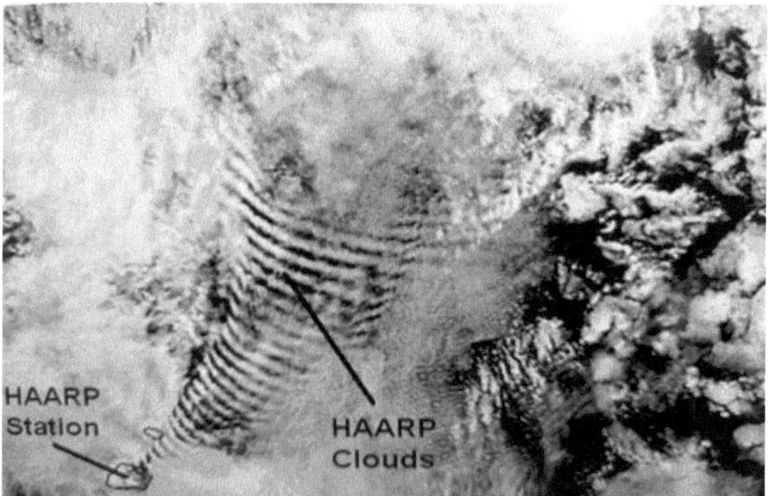

Figure 31: NASA photo: HAARP cloud pattern visibly originating from a HAARP station.

Figure 32 Cloud pattern over Fukushima, Japan shortly before the outbreak of the 2011 Tsunami. (Picture taken from[301]. For details, see Tsunamis – Human-made? chapter 4, 6)

Figure 33: Standing cloud patterns generated by large radar transmitters (HAARP)[302]

Figure 34: Standing cloud pattern: Satellite image of the Iberian Peninsula. The arrow marks waves and ribs that remain firmly in place, as if held tight. Likewise the area immediately outside.[303]

Figure 35: Standing cloud patterns generated by large radar transmitters (HAARP)[304]

Figure 36: Peculiar cloud formation over Dortmund on May 7, 2019, 8 pm

In order for the *metallised sky*[305] generated by Chemtrails to be constantly ready for use as a reflection mirror, it must continuously be re-sprayed, which obviously takes place. Otherwise the metal particles would gradually sink to the earth's surface and the *metallized sky* dissolve, a process which could last up to a year in practice but sometimes happens much faster – depending on the weather, wind, and local conditions. Of course, the larger the metal particles are, the faster they sink to the earth's surface. That is one reason why particle sizes in the nanometer range are chosen. Another aspect is that nanometer sized particles can freely penetrate into human cells.

Figure 37: Peculiar cloud formation over Dresden on August 5, 2019, 8:35 am.

During the Cold War there was not only a nuclear arms race, but a beam-weapon race. Huge antennae systems were built, capable of radiating gigantic amounts of energy.§§§§§§§§§§§§§§§§§§§§§§§§ *The Russians woke up very early to these huge antennae ... they also tried earthquakes in Los Angeles and in the metropolitan area; it works that way on the floes that meet each other, that if you can 'tickle' them for so long with ... very low-frequency vibrations, you can provoke something like that* (earthquake).[306] The Russians started their beam tests with ordinary radar systems, but otherwise planned a huge antenna system in the Chernobyl area, which was to comprise 10 microwave antennae a gigantic 150m high and 600m long, to be built within a radius of 35km.[307] The construction of 16 nuclear power plants was planned to provide the necessary gigantic amounts of energy.[308] *The Russians then had a terrible accident ... when a nuclear waste landfill blew up in response to this huge boost they emitted, and vast areas of Russia have been contaminated.* [309] On a website********************* published on 25.6.2012 an article by Werner Altnickel with the title 'The true cause of the Chernobyl catastrophe' described this tragedy minutely and illuminated its background. This article, supported by evidence, details the Chernobyl accident of April 26, 1986. If true, the media has (once again) lied to us over all these years. For the official cause of the Chernobyl disaster is a meltdown, triggered in connection with a test run by an engineer responsible for ignoring safety regulations. This official version was given out by what was then the KGB (the Soviet Committee for State Security).†††††††††††††††††††††††

---

§§§§§§§§§§§§§§§§§§§§§§§§ This was revealed, and openly encouraged, by President Ronald Reagan (1911-2004) in his Star Wars address of 1983 during his 1981-9 presidency (SP)

********************* *www.chemtrail .de*

††††††††††††††††††††††† KGB, or КГБ (Комитéт Госудáрственной Безопáсности), transliterated phonetically as *Komitet Gosudarstvennoy Bezopasnosti* (SP)

Tsunamis – Human-made?

Destroying the earth, through artificial Earthquakes, Floods, Tornados, Typhoons ... a 'New World Order' Depopulation machine being used to eliminate as many human beings as possible as stated on the Georgia Guidestone. [310] ‡‡‡‡‡‡‡‡‡‡‡‡‡‡‡‡‡‡‡‡‡‡‡

Since we are now capable of doing the following things: setting off volcanoes, exciting tsunamis, opening ozone holes, steering storms, we should ensure that these techniques are not used.[311] We can trigger tsunamis? Is that true? Yes, it's possible; because if it is possible to artificially cause earthquakes (see HAARP – The Food Slicer in the Sky, chapter 4, 5), for example, by bombarding earthquake zones with ELF waves, calibrated to resonate with the earth's frequency of 7.3 to 8 Hz, then this, too, is certainly possible in relation to earthquake zones on the sea floor. *[The growth of] Strawberries can be triggered with ELF waves. ELF waves can vibrate in the ground ... With the right frequency they can have devastating consequences*[312], namely if frequencies are selected in resonance with the earth's frequency. Then the vibration amplitudes in earthquake-prone regions can increase massively until there is a sudden reduction in the internal tensions between adjacent tectonic plates, which would soon manifest as an an earthquake. If such a voltage discharge is caused somewhere on the seabed, a huge wave can be triggered, which would qualify as a tsunami by the time it reached neighbouring shorelines.

If one takes into account the unscrupulousness of the forces behind the monstrosities described in this chapter, then it is only logical to assume that the inhibition threshold should not be too high to test or use these technical possibilities in practical experiments.

---

‡‡‡‡‡‡‡‡‡‡‡‡‡‡‡‡‡‡‡‡‡‡‡ *BE NOT A CANCER ON THE EARTH – LEAVE ROOM FOR NATURE – MAINTAIN HUMANITY UNDER 500,000,000 IN PERPETUAL BALANCE WITH NATURE* (Inscribed on one of the Georgia Guidestones erected north of Elberton, Georgia, USA in 1980)

In the YouTube video[313] cited at the beginning, it is assumed that the tsunami that caused the nuclear disaster in Fukushima was human-made and triggered by HAARP activities. And the picture of the sky above Fukushime immediately before the tsunami looks similar to a cloud cover changed by HAARP activities (see Figure 32). The motive supporting the thesis that the tsunami could have been caused by HAARP activities included:[314] *The Japanese Finance Minister has announced in an interview that Japan has dropped all limits for hedge funds, ie complete financial world, because the Japanese nuclear power plants were blackmailed with a seismic weapon. These statements are older than the last earthquakes in Japan and prove that this is the truth.*[315]§§§§§§§§§§§§§§§§§§§§§§§§§§§§ Brigitta Zuber mentions the same thing in a video[316]: *... then he* (the Japanese Minister of Finance) *said 'be cause Japan received the threat of an earthquake monkey'. I gave the talk on the 1st of December 2009, and I still remember what I said: when you hear about earthquakes and similar things in the near future, remember what has been said here in this lecture and, along with others, hear it - or look at it - with different eyes. Shortly thereafter, Haiti came************************, and then it started; there were more and more horror messages. As for the earthquake in Haiti, it has also been publicly stated that Chavez*††††††††††††††††††††††† *believes it did not arise naturally. And when you see where the earthquake was; it stopped at the borders of Haiti, it stopped. We also have pictures where the sky is electromagnetically charged, all over England, and it stops at the borders of England; it is cut off as if it has been set precisely. Well,*

---

§§§§§§§§§§§§§§§§§§§§§§§§§§§§ Logically, it seems to me that the continuation of earthquakes in Japan would suggest that either there was no blackmail or that the Japanese Finance Minister did not stick to the blackmail agreement. (SP)

********************** The quotation refers to the Haitian earthquake of January 2010, whose epicentre was near the town of Léogâne, 25 km (16 miles) west of the capital, Port-au-Prince. The earthquake measured 7MW and killed somewhere between 200,000 and 300,000 people, affecting 3 million people altogether (cf https://en.wikipedia.org/wiki/2010_Haiti_earthquake). [SP]

††††††††††††††††††††††† The quotation refers to Hugo Chavez (1954-2013), the President of Venezuela (1999-2013). [SP]

we all have that [in our skies], and they do it. That's not just circumstantial evidence, they do it.[‡‡‡‡‡‡‡‡‡‡‡‡‡‡‡‡‡‡‡‡‡‡‡‡‡]

In support of the thesis that the 2011 tsunami in Fukushima was human-made, one video[317] features a man who ... *explains that the University of Alaska owned a server and collected data from HAARP activities, and quite clearly on [the server] it could be seen that before Fukushima, just before it, there was a pulse at certain intervals and on certain frequencies, as had never before been the case, and then nothing after that, so it did not fit the pattern. After Fukushima they just destroyed this server, and now the data is gone. But he recorded it then, yes, look at it.*[318] Data is from a fluxgate magnetometer operated by a station in Gakona, Alaska. Such a machine registers the strength of the magnetic field. Figure 32b shows the registered magnetic field in close proximity to the earthquake that triggered the tsunami: extreme spikes *immediately before and during the quake on March 11, 2011 at 05:46 UTC.*[319] Furthermore, a dramatic heating of the atmosphere over Japan was recorded before the earthquake, interpreted as infrared radiation above the epicentre of the earthquake in the days prior, with a maximum just three hours before the earthquake (see Figure 32c).

Here is an interesting comment:[320] *The question arises: Is the earthquake that caused the devastating consequences in Japan on 11.3.2011, including an atomic catastrophe, of natural origin, or was it caused artificially? In the event that it was caused artificially, the question arises as to who is responsible for this crime, who ordered it and who carried it out. It is very likely that only a few people are required. From this perspective, the question arises as to whether the time was chosen deliberately in relation to other world events (Tunisia, Egypt, Libya, Syria ...).*

[‡‡‡‡‡‡‡‡‡‡‡‡‡‡‡‡‡‡‡‡‡‡‡‡‡] In this context it may be important to note that Shōichi Nakagawa (1953-2009), the Japanese Minister of Finance prior to Hirohisa Fujii (1932-), who is quoted, died in circumstances which have yet to be explained (*https://en.wikipedia.org/wiki/Sh%C5%8Dichi Nakagawa*). In January 2010, Hirohisa Fujii resigned owing to ill-health (*https://en.wikipedia.org/wiki/Hirohisa_Fujii*), with exhaustion described as one of the symptoms, which could be linked with the slurring of speech noticed in his predecessor (SP)

That it is now technically possible to cause human-made earthquakes is also suggested by this source[321]. That the élites lack all scruple with regard to their experiments that put a large number of people in mortal danger, we also know from, for example, revelations by the US whistleblower, Deborah Tavares.[322] Here, too, the question 'Who benefits?' comes to our aid. In this particular case, it is the financial élite who benefit from creating a threat and overturning measures taken against them to control their financial transactions in Japan, as in the above quote from the Japanese Minister of Finance.

And what is the secret behind the devastating tsunami on Dec. 26, 2004 on the Indian Ocean, which killed an estimated 230000 people? This can be read in the India Daily on 29.12.04: *Was this tsunami manmade? Was this an earthquake generation experiment that got out of hand? Did a major foreign power show us what it is capable of? Our navy is urged to clarify what really happened.*[323]

Italian Lieutenant-General Fabio Mini wrote this in an article,[324] *'Owning the Weather. The global environmental war has already started': No one believes any more that an earthquake, a tsunami, or a hurricane are purely natural phenomena. Modern nuclear technology, the production of miniature nuclear warheads or the abundance of atomic mines make it possible to trigger subterranean and submarine explosions, which in turn can lead to earthquakes and tsunami under special conditions! ... And as early as 1977, the international ENMOD convention was outlawed in Geneva for the artificial production of tsunamis, the targeted opening of ozone holes, the control of storms and the electrical change of the ionosphere ... but why should one ostracise something that supposedly does not exist?*

Considering the major powers had no qualms about initiating the Gulf War with its estimated 0.5 to 1 million dead, one must assume that these powers are not afraid to cause a human-made tsunami. Other estimates suggest that around 2.4 million people died in this war.[325]

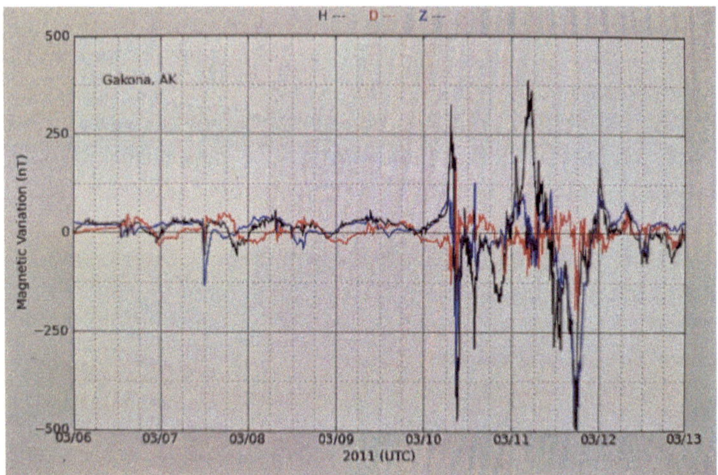

Figure 32b: Measurement of the HAARP Fluxgate pressure gauge in Gakona, Alaska. Extreme spikes *immediately before and during the quake on March 11, 2011.*[326]

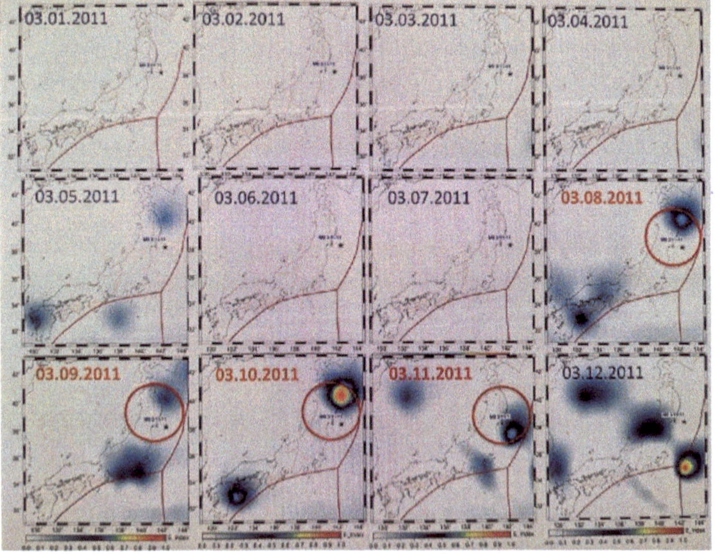

Figure 32c: Measurement of outgoing long-wave radiation… 01/03/2011: *from March 1st to March 12th 2011, in the run-up to the earthquake of March 11th 2011, unusual anomalies over its epicentre (red lines: boundaries between the tectonic plates…)*[327]

Hurricanes – Human-made?

Following on from Human influence on the weather, we pose the question: Are we now technically capable of artificially creating, controlling and amplifying hurricanes? The author of one article[328] writes: *The US and probably other states are now able to significantly influence the weather with geo-engineering measures (electromagnetic waves/HAARP, chemtrails). This also applies to hurricanes, you can even control the direction they take within certain limits and reinforce them if necessary. You can probably even let them emerge ...*

In terms of their destructive power, hurricanes that have hit the United States in the last ten or twenty years far exceed those previously known to us. Has the military contributed to this? For example, the title of an article by Mary W. Maxwell, PhD, LLB (*Manmade Hurricane Harvey: The Military Can Steer a Hurricane*) makes that very claim.[329] Can it be true? This does correspond with what another author, Dane Wigington[§§§§§§§§§§§§§§§§§§§§§§§§§§§§§§] , in a 2010 article, said about Hurricane Katrina. Hurricane Katrina began on August 29, 2005 and lasted 11 days. According to Wigington, in 2005[***********************] NASA carried out an experiment in the Gulf of Mexico called Project GRIP (Genesis and Rapid Intensification Processes), in which NASA used HAARP to transform a tropical storm (then called Earl) into a Category 4 hurricane, a hurricane of devastating proportions which they successfully steered for 11 days in the Gulf of Mexico and from there directly to New Orleans. The city was destroyed. This catastrophe was worsened by the bursting of the levées protecting the city from the sea, so that the city was flooded with water, and

---

§§§§§§§§§§§§§§§§§§§§§§§§§§§§§§ geoengineeringwatch.org
*********************** According to https://ghrc.nsstc.nasa.gov/home/field-campaigns/grip, this experiment was not carried out until 2010, making it impossible for its effects to carry retrospectively back to 2005. Perhaps Wigington is referring to an earlier, spectacularly unsuccessful (indeed disastrous) prototype experiment (SP)

tens of thousands of people had to be evacuated. Witnesses reported that they heard explosions before the levées broke.[330]

There is strong evidence that this catastrophe was an inside job. A
speculator, a certain Judah Hertz (of Hertz Investment Group), had
been buying land in New Orleans in advance of low prices,
especially in the United States Areas where the poorer population
lived and who had been completely evacuated after the disaster. It
begs the suspicion that this speculator may have had some prior
knowledge of the impending catastrophe, as is also known in the
case of 9/11:[†] *As with Silverstein, who hired the
two World Trade Center towers in New York six weeks they were
destroyed, Hertz bought a lot of real estate in the Big Easy, when
prices were low just before Katrina.*[331]

Eva-Maria Griese writes:[332] *Weather extremes as a weapon: The
world climate as a test laboratory – were Harvey and Irma created
artificially? Hurricanes Harvey and Irma are said to be the result
of geoengineering. This accusation is now being raised more and
more frequently. These massive, possibly artificially enhanced
storm systems, designed to dramatically prove the dangers of
global climate change, are evidently directly addressed to POTUS
(President of the United States). The supposedly manmade climate
change is more likely to be a business model in the form of a
climate replacement trade. With pollution rights, dubious
transactions are made that can be bought and sold, even traded on
the stock exchange. The termination of the climate agreement by
Trump now threatens these lucrative businesses, from which
mainly corporations through trade and states have benefited by
CO_2 taxes.*

[†] Silverstein had entered into a 99-year lease on July 24, 2001,
for twin towers WTC1 and WTC2 and for the building known as WTC7, all of
which were subsequently destroyed in the 9/11 disaster, for which he had an
insurance policy of $4.6 billion (Wikipedia)

The Ozone Hole – Human-made?

The ozone hole over the Antarctic, first measured in the 1970s, was officially attributed to the effects of fluorine-chlorinated hydrocarbons.[333] But couldn't it be that environmental pollution in the stratosphere from the Chemtrails[‡‡‡‡‡‡‡‡‡‡‡‡‡‡‡‡‡‡‡‡‡‡‡‡‡] also played a role here? As we can read on the webpage:[§§§§§§§§§§§§§§§§§§§§§§§§§§] *So at least we now know that the chemtrails have a sensitive influence on the formation of ozone and that this could be the reason why why the sun currently has such hard radiation.*[***********************] *And who knows, maybe the technocrats destroyed the ozone layer through their many previous field trials, so they now have to spray like crazy to have the technical plasma layer stop the harsh radiation from the sun.*

In her book *War Weapon Earth*[334], Rosalie Bertell describes this in more detail: *On July 25, 1990, the US military launched a satellite that contained 16 large and 8 small canisters of chemicals – especially barium and lithium (according to the United Nations Registry of Space Objects). Their contents were released into the earth's atmosphere at intervals of 32 kilometres – **only just above the ozone layer**. These activities were repeated on a larger scale and at a different altitude in January 1991...* (bold print by the author)

Over a period of more than 50 years, weather-influencing experiments were carried out in which chemicals were released into the atmosphere and thus triggered reactions ... The chemicals that were thrown into the earth's atmosphere included barium azide, barium chlorate, barium nitrate, barium perchlorate and barium peroxide. All of them are flammable and most have a

---

[‡‡‡‡‡‡‡‡‡‡‡‡‡‡‡‡‡‡‡‡‡‡‡‡‡] Even if the massive spraying (of chemtrails) in the USA only started in the 90s, and in Germany only since 2003, there were prototype experiments like this in 1978 (see Chemtrails – The Chemical Soup in the Sky, chapter 4, 2)

[§§§§§§§§§§§§§§§§§§§§§§§§§§] https://www.sauberer-himmel.de/untersuchungen

[***********************] Hard radiation is radiation typically of high frequency and short wavelength (American Meterological Society) [SP]

destructive effect on the ozone layer. In 1980 alone, about 2000 kilogrammes of chemicals were released into the atmosphere.[††††††††††††††††††††††††††††]

The creators of one video[335] have a slightly different view of the ozone-hole problem: *The Ozone Swindle*[‡‡‡‡‡‡‡‡‡‡‡‡‡‡‡‡‡‡‡‡‡‡‡‡‡‡‡‡] The ozone hole over the Antarctic is not something new, but sometimes heals, sometimes amplifies, depending on the season, as a consequence of ozone redistribution in the stratosphere. At the same time the total amount of ozone would be practically unchanged. This means that the ozone hole is not primarily caused by CFCs, as officially established (in the Montreal Protocol[§§§§§§§§§§§§§§§§§§§§§§§§§§§§]), but is due to a natural redistribution of ozone within the stratosphere. This was discovered by NASA researchers and a Russian group of geophysicists collecting satellite data. If their results are correct, then the global ban on CFCs laid down in 1987 was a mistake. The Montreal Protocol resulted in the worldwide replacement of refrigerators and led to a huge increase in profits for this industry. It should be mentioned here that even before the signing of the Protocol, satellite data corresponding to the later NASA findings was available but not considered. The sun protection industry also benefited and benefits from the Montreal Protocol. *For years, we were led to believe that the sun is one of the main causes of skin cancer, whereas in fact (sun)creams can cause it, as they contain unhealthy substances with many side-effects. Some of these contribute to the development of cancer. Not only that, they can also have a serious impact on DNA. Not too long ago, NASA announced that the ozone layer was slowly starting to recover. Is it possible that NASA did that because many scientists have begun to expose the big lie of the ozone hole? But the worst thing is that the fear of sunbathing has remained in*

[††††††††††††††††††††††††††††] BertellWreckingDeutsch.pdf.
See also *https://www.weather-modification-journal.de/dr-rosalie-bertell-2010-wie-unserer-planet-langsam-zum-wrack-gemacht-wird*
[‡‡‡‡‡‡‡‡‡‡‡‡‡‡‡‡‡‡‡‡‡‡‡‡‡‡‡‡] In German, *Der Ozon-Schwindel* (SP)
[§§§§§§§§§§§§§§§§§§§§§§§§§§§§] The Montreal Protocol of 1987 – ratified in 1989 – was an international treaty designed to protect the ozone layer through the phasing-out of anthropogenetic ozone depletion (SP)

our heads due to the supposed disappearance of the ozone layer. It is to be hoped that someday we will recognize the great benefits of the sun, which are anciently tried and tested. [336] As for the negative health effects of the above-mentioned suncreams (sunscreen, sunblocks, etc), please refer to the (literally) enlightened book *Poison Cocktails in Bodycare: Death lurks in the bathroom* by M Schimmelpfennig[337] ************************** In reducing the positive influence of solar radiation on our health and on our sense of well-being, both physical and psychological, we might mention not only the technological reduction of solar radiation on the earth, caused by the widespread spraying of chemicals overhead, but now include the reduction through sun-screening chemicals. Psychologically, the sun's brightness is among the best remedies for depression; physically, exposure to the sun is the ultimate natural means of producing vital vitamin D. *The sun also works wonders in the prevention of osteoporosis, bone softening, diabetes, high blood pressure, dementia, multiple sclerosis, susceptibility to infections or immune diseases. With the help of the sun, many supposedly terminally ill people can recover."*[338]

Forest Fires – Human-made

California and Athens:

Under the heading 'Experiments on the population – a second 9/11?' (pages 204ff), I have described forest fires taking place in October 2017 and November 2018 in California and on July 26, 2018 in Athens. These three disasters, described in the media as 'forest fires', were most likely initiated from special aircraft. During these forest fires the forest didn't really burn; instead walls and buildings were dusted and cars melted, while other buildings in the immediate vicinity showed no damage. Real destructive aisles had been created, completely untypical for forest fires. Figure 38 features a photo of the destroyed city of Santa Rosa in California.

************************** This is how I would translate M Schimmelpfennig's book title. See the endnote for the German title (SP)

In one video[339] military intelligence is cited as testing laser and particle beam weapons, so-called DEWs, mounted on aircraft.

Figure 39 shows a laser cannon mounted on the bow of a Boeing for targets in the direction of flight as well as in all directions up, down and to the side of the aircraft. Figure 40 shows a laser cannon mounted **below** a Boeing. Laser cannons can also be mounted on drones.

Figure 38: Destruction of Santa Rosa, October 2017: One clearly sees three buildings destroyed down to the foundation walls, while the fourth, adjacent building still appears completely untouched. And the surrounding trees are completely intact.[340]

Figure 39: Laser cannon, mounted on the bow of a Boeing.[341] The laser cannon can be swiveled 360° around the longitudinal axis of the aircraft and at least 180° around the vertical axis, or more precisely, perpendicular to the direction of flight[342] so that it can shoot targets in the direction of flight as well as up, down and to the side of the aircraft.

Figure 40: Laser cannon, mounted below the aircraft,[343] for stationary and mobile targets on the ground. Activation of the laser cannon takes place in the absence of light or sound emission to avoid discovery while in use.

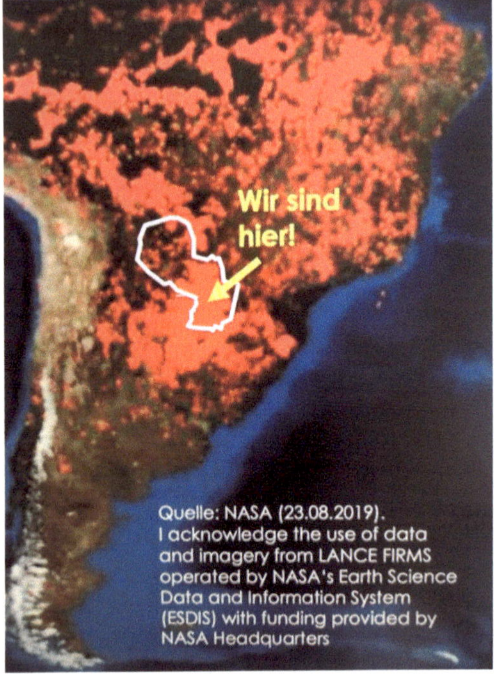

Figure 41: Map of South America,[344] where the satellite-observed fires have been marked in red dots. The area across the border (indicated by the white line) is Paraguay, where in the southern half everything seems to be ablaze

South America:

The situation is different with the forest fires in South America and Central Africa at the end of August 2019, which were certainly not caused by radiation weapons. It is more likely that the slash-and-burn of the past few years will continue, on the one hand to gain more acreage for agricultural fuels[345] and on the other hand to make room for palm-oil plantations.[346] In addition, fires are created by farmers to gain arable land for the next sowing, and to burn waste.

What is evident, however, is that forest fires in South America are used by the media to emphasize human-made climate change and to maintain and intensify fear in people's minds. Such fires were the main news topic, and commentators, consistently assuming a connection with human-made climate change, went so far as to harness impressive satellite images to relay these forest fires into people's living rooms. The burnt areas were highlighted in red. The message: We have to do something about it, and quickly. Because huge amounts of CO_2 generated by these fires will negate our entire effort to save the climate and meet the climate target of limiting the global temperature increase to a maximum of 1.5 degrees. This keeps the popular fear of impending climate crisis simmering, if not fuelled. On one website[†] you can read for August 24th, 2019: *Brazil registers more forest fires than ever before this year.* But it seems this is untrue. In the years 2002 to 2010 the number of fires counted annually in Brazil for 2002 and 2006 were roughly comparable or the figures were larger for 2003, 2004, 2005, 2007 and 2010.[347] This source also claims that the satellite images provided by NASA optics have been processed in such a way that the visible burning areas are disproportionately reinforced in red, giving the impression that huge wildfires struck large parts of Brazil and neighboring countries. For example, on satellite images featured on the internet, all of Southern Paraguay would appear to be aflame (see Figure 41). However, live images from Paraguay,[348] contradict such a horror scenario: here no major fires can be seen in the centre of the area marked red within a radius of about 200 km; there are just small scattered smoke columns where residents are burning waste.

Another, political aspect is interesting. These Brazilian forest fires are used to create a mood against President Jair Bolsonaro, who has been in office since the beginning of 2019. *Like Trump, Jair Bolsonaro opposes the globalist corporate dictatorship. Both reject the neoliberal trade agreement Mercosur.[‡] They have also given the Migration Pact and the Paris Climate Agreement the sack. With this policy, they oppose the establishment and accordingly make themselves powerful enemies.*

[†] *focus.de*

[‡] Mercosur, officially the Southern Common Market, set up by the Treaty of Asunción (1991) and extended by the Protocol of Ouro Preto (1994), is a South American trade bloc. Naturally, the US would not be too keen on such a bloc: hence, no doubt, the continual changes made to the agreement and the suspension at different times of Paraguay and Venezuela (cf https://en.wikipedia.org/wiki/Mercosur#Founding) [SP]

The fact that the Soros NGO network, the mass media and the climate celebrities immediately chose Bolsonaro as a great scapegoat is a coup to politically eliminate him.[349] You have to know that the NGOs are pioneers in war, violence and terror.[350]

Australia:

Forest fires are raging in Australia too, most of them caused by arson; exacerbated by the drought that prevails there every summer. In the news[§§§§§§§§§§§§§§§§§§§§§§§§§§§§§§§§§§], the years of drought in large parts of Australia are held responsible and presented as a result of **climate change**.[351] But is this really the truth? In hot weather, Australia is known for its huge bushfires every year. But in 2019/2020 these bushfires reach a new level. Than climate change? A clear NO. *The official line that is being instilled in people is that the reason (the worst drought) is climate change and global warming. That's what the government pushed through the media, but it's not true, people. In fact, this situation was deliberately created by the government.*[352]

These bushfires are largely human-made, specifically through arson. In 2019/2020, the fact that **they broke out in so many unconnected places at the same time**[353] strongly indicates a planned, intentional, and orchestrated effort. It has become known from various sources that 100 or possibly 200[354] arsonists have been arrested. Well, you could say that this was also the case in previous years. But this year there is an additional motive, to clearly show people that global warming is real and deepen the fear already instilled in people's brains. Furthermore, the question 'who benefits?' comes to our aid once again. Aggressive economic interests lie behind it. Vast tracts of Eastern Australia are suffering from a major drought, with rivers largely drying up because of so many dams being constructed by private investment corporations, albeit largely paid for by taxpayers.[355] This has resulted in the evaporation of numerous rivers that used to provide water to this region. The extent to which water has become scarce in these parts of Australia is made clear by this entry on the Mimikama

---

[§§§§§§§§§§§§§§§§§§§§§§§§§§§§§§§§] In Germany, ZDFheute-Nachrichten, for example (SP)

website:[356] *According to the AFP [Australian Federal Police], two more fires have merged into a huge blaze. The fire brigade in Australia estimates that dry thunderstorms and a strong storm additionally fuel the big fire. The situation in Australia is depressing. At the moment, up to 10,000 [feral] camels are to be shot by snipers, because in dry areas they compete with humans for scarce water.*

The above-mentioned dams are primarily used as a water supply for the fracking industry,[357] which in recent years has experienced a major boom in Australia. Another factor is that a large percentage of these fires occurred in areas where a high-speed rail line is to be built. The people who live there are to be driven out by the fires. The intention is to move these people affected by the fires to other areas, and prevent them from returning to the land to rebuild their homes. One source *************************** reveals: *240,000 people have been asked ... – if you can, you should leave your home – the Australian authorities are calling for evacuation. According to Prime Minister Morrison, there is no prospect of an end to the fire crisis.*[358] But another reason for the deliberate fires could be to make way for the planned high-speed line in Southwestern Australia.[359]

This planned relocation project is dismissed as a conspiracy theory, as can be read at Mimikama, on the above-mentioned fact-check page: *The fires in California from 2018, as well as the current fires in Australia, have nothing to do with respective high-speed [rail] routes. The sharepics published as alleged evidence* (Figure 42) *[show areas] far too small and confined to make a serious claim here.*[360] Figure 43 shows a map where fire areas and areas for the planned high-speed rail line, which have already been laid here, distinctly do match. But according to this same map comparison, Mimikama states *there is almost no overlap between the two areas.*[361] Readers can make up their own minds as to whether the fires were intentionally set or not.

*************************** *Zeit.de*

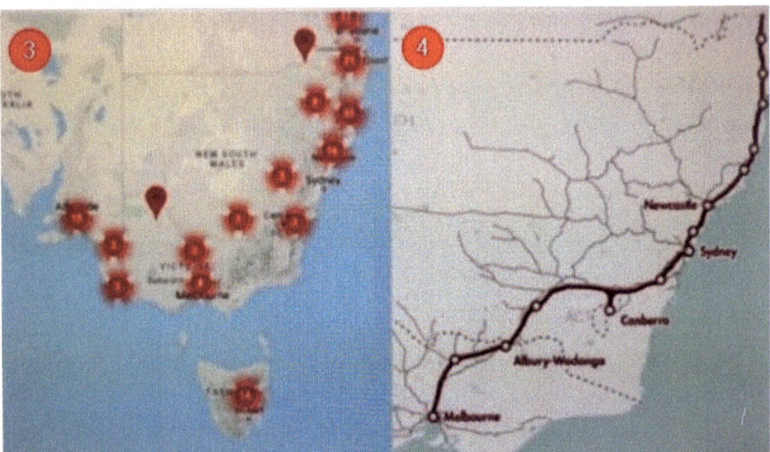

Figure 42: Comparison of the largest bushfires (left picture) with the planned high-speed rail line (right picture).

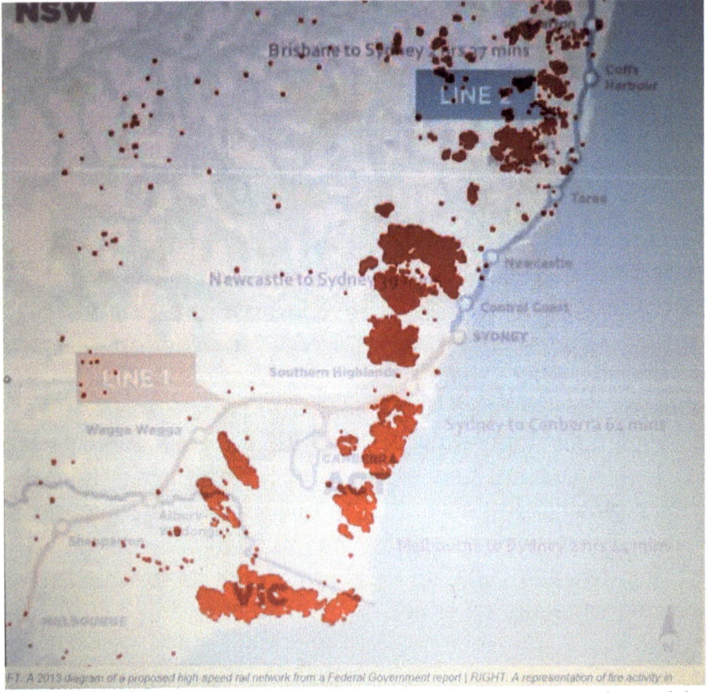

Figure 43: Planned high-speed rail line overlaid by registered bushfire (coloured red)

I am more inclined to the original statement that the fires have something to do with fabricating facts and conditions, not just for the planned high-speed rail line, but for the much larger project behind it, namely Agenda 21 and Agenda 2030: in short, the removal of people from the country to bring them close to cities for tighter control. (See Part 1 of this trilogy, Bring everyone close to the towns[362]). *They [the Australain authorities] use the military to occupy areas and keep people from returning to their homes. So what they're doing here with these fires is throwing [all the people concerned] out of the country ... If you get into trouble the Australian Federal Police will simply remove you for health reasons because you are in a place at risk from* **climate change**. *The military will occupy the area and prevent people from returning to their homes. That's what they're planning, people. They are showing the world how to do it. And that's what you can expect in most countries. Local governments in Australia do not get their orders from the local community, but receive their instructions directly from the United Nations. This is AGENDA 21. This is what is going on here, people, and what is planned.*[363]

---

[363] Bold print by JS. This scenario reminds me very much of what a Planning Inspector told me in Birkenhead, Wirral: *Round here, if they don't get planning permission they simply burn the building down at night; then planning permission proceeds* (SP)

5. Mind Control and Transhumanism

"It seems that you (the cabal) need AI (artificial intelligence) and transhumanism to maintain a life cycle, to work with draconian beings and genetically modify humanity to become work slaves.[364] (Laura Eisenhower, great granddaughter of the 34th US President)

Depressed by communication

Never before has there been such a concerted effort to inform people about environmental health issues, such good systemic cooperation between industry, politics and the media, yet the truth about mobile communications, for example, is ignored ... Those who claim that legitimate means are being used to protect our nature and our health are either not knowledgeable or lying. These are the only two possibilities. If more people do not wake up and help us turn things around, we'll all be sitting in the deadly cage of a digital prison, without cash of course ... [365]

Were these dramatic words – from Anke Kern's speech at the 16th Anti-Acid Conference – exaggerated?[‡] Let's get to the bottom of it. Technical equipment for unlimited communication, created in recent decades, is visible to anyone as part of the radiation masts installed throughout the country.[§] We have been brought the blessing of unlimited communications in the form of cell-phone reception and wifi use, but at the same time – as explained below – the curse of the incipient regression of our mental and psychic abilities as well as the destruction of our physical health. Already, in normal operation, without additional manipulation (or technological

---

[‡] In Germany, this conference is known as AZK (Antizensurkonferenz) [SP]

[§] This is as true of the UK as it is of Germany (SP)

advance), these masts represent a health hazard for us. What we are usually unaware of is the fact that radiation exposure from mobile-phone radiation is extremely high. On average the power flux density at the ear is 2000µW/m², and sometimes much higher. Frequent mobile-phone use therefore represents a potential health hazard. The German Medical Association (Bundesärtzekammer) recommends a maximum permissible power flux density of 1000 µW / m².[366] What is less known is that there are a large number of patents that would make it possible to reduce mobile-phone radiation substantially without affecting the telephony. These patents are locked away in the drawer of mobile operating companies, which raises the question: *maybe ... the same investors sit in the mobile industry as in the pharmaceutical industry?*[367]

It is also noteworthy that upper limit values permitted in Germany are several orders of magnitude higher than the maximum value recommended by the German Medical Association:[368]

German Medical Association: 1,000 µW/m²
UMTS: 10,000,000 µW/m²
D network: 4,500,000 µW/m²
Electric grid: 9,000,000 µW/m²

In a scientific study from 2006 to 2016, the relationship between unusual tree damage and mobile-phone radiation has been investigated in two German cities (Bamberg and Hallstadt).[369] *The notably one-sided damage to treetrunks is striking: not owing to drought, frost, bacterial or viral infestation, fungi, air or soil damage ... etc. On 60 damaged trees a marked difference was found between the measured values for mobile radiation on the transmitter-facing side of the trunk and the transmitter-remote side of the trunk. In the direction of mobile radio transmitters, the measured values ranged between 80 and 13,000 µW/m2, and in the opposite direction between 8 and 720 µW/m2. From the damaged side there was direct visual contact with a mobile radio transmitter in all cases.* This means that radiation loads of 80 and 13,000 µW/m2 have already permanently damaged the treetrunks, values that are still three orders of magnitude lower than the upper limit

138

values permitted in Germany (see above). This is *further evidence that legal limits protect the arbitrariness of industry and not the health of people and nature, so are clearly designed to mislead the population.*[370]

And now it gets really ugly; because the technical mobile radio devices can be used directly as beam weapons by modulating low frequencies: pulses of 8.34 Hz and 2 Hz, for example. These frequencies are in the so-called Schumann range *which is the resonant frequency of the earth, and also of the human brain. One can now modulate this Schumann frequency to transmit certain information; for example, using the brain frequency pattern of a depressive, the brain of the person being irradiated will resonate accordingly and those affected will become depressed.*[371]

For the operation of the human brain, different brainwave bands in the ELF range are characteristic. These extend from 1 to 100 Hz:[372]
Delta waves (1-3 Hz): Deep sleep, coma
Theta waves (4-7 Hz): hypnosis, trance, dream
Alpha waves (8-12 Hz): meditation, relaxation
Beta waves (13-40 Hz): wakefulness up to the highest level of arousal.

Radiation in these frequency ranges can cause psychological changes in humans. The pulsed energy, namely the periodic pulses – particularly in the 1 to 50 HZ range – are dangerous to humans. 1 Hz pulses affect the human heart; 1-3 Hz pulses affect the sleep pattern; 3-5 Hz pulses trigger paranoia and hallucinations; 6-7 Hz pulses cause depression, confusion and suicidal thoughts.[373]

Precise knowledge of these human/pulse correlations allows privileged access to complex neurocognitive processes associated with the human self, consciousness, and memory. When the brain is irradiated with frequencies above a certain level, altered brainwave patterns are forcibly introduced and brain function is interrupted, leading to serious mental disturbances. This manipulation of mentality upsets neurological and physical functions. Health effects can be significant as the human brain and various other organs are always working with electromagnetic waves in the ELF range.

Other types of beam weapon are microwave weapons with which the police should, or should not, be equipped. These microwave weapons work in a similar way to our domestic microwave, heating organic matter from the inside, but with much higher energy. As a targeted person you would feel unbearable heat, apparently coming from nowhere; this odourless, silent and invisible weaponry has a range of 1000 m.[374] Skin molecules could be heated to 55° C. This weapon is even alleged to cause cancer.[375] How? Melatonin in the body is part of the internal cancer police. The effect of technically generated electromagnetic radiation can reduce melatonin production.[376] Melatonin is also the indispensable precursor to serotonin, the happiness hormone. Reducing melatonin via EMF (electromagnetic fields) can therefore be the cause of listlessness, stress and burnout, which we all know is widespread in modern times.[377] Another effect of technically generated EMF pulses is the opening of the blood-brain barrier, limiting the barrier's natural protective function and thus increasing the amount of environmental toxins entering the brain. This leads in the long term to neurological disorders, such as Alzheimer's and dementia.[378]

Microwave weapons can be used against street demonstrators when they assemble in what are perceived to be too large numbers and cannot be combated by conventional violent measures. They can even penetrate masonry.[379]

There exists a US Patent 6506148 B2 'For the manipulation of the nervous system by electromagnetic fields through monitors',[380] which could make it common for an unsuspecting citizen, sitting in front of the TV, to receive from the display a dose of radiation in a certain frequency range that did him or her no good whatsoever.

5G and Transhumanism

The global battle for the human brain has begun ... The further we are from the latest MK Ultra programme[*], *the closer we are to the next one.*[381]

The next generation of mobile communications, the 5G network, is in preparation and has already been installed in some cities. The 5G network involves an even higher radiation exposure for humans than the previous mobile phone generations. As there is resistance and protests in the population against the installation of 5G, the 5G antennas have been partially camouflaged and placed in places where the ordinary citizen does not suspect that they are 5G antennas, hidden in chimneys, street lamps, in inconspicuous street posts. Activists have found that such antennas have been placed near schools, hospitals, sports fields, parking lots in front of large shopping malls, and other central locations populated by many people every day. 5G is the "Internet of Things", based on which really everything can be connected to the network, including self-propelled cars that use a remote-controlled computer to navigate to our specified destination without the need or ability for human/driver intervention. *Devices can react almost instantly to the network. This means that a car brakes fast enough if a vehicle in front starts to skid in a curve - and passes this information on to the traffic behind it.*[382] In an unfavorable case for the driver, however, the car could also be switched off from the outside, perhaps even have an accident if it has become a disturbance in the system.

'Does 5G endanger your health?' Daily we encounter such headings in newspapers and magazines. One such is found on *Spiegel.de.*[383] The headline, in the form of an unnecessary question, sets the tone for the introductory sentences to downplay the dangers of 5G: *Some people, however, are preparing for the transition to 5G – amid often dubious and hysterical reports on the*

---

[*] MK Ultra: the brainwashing programme of the CIA from the 1950s

net. 10 comments in the article mainly cited those who downplayed the dangers of 5G. For example: *Even water is dangerous if it covers the whole head. And too much chocolate. And wifi. And watching TV. There is NO knowledge about radiation-induced cancers, but many stupid people just reject everything that's new. Or anything to do with 'radiation'.* Here not only are the dangers of '5G' downplayed, you have to wonder if Spiegel.de was acting on behalf of stakeholders while they were at it.

Not so in a more informed article †††††††††††††††††††††††††††††††† where W. Kühling is quoted by Martin Luther University Halle-Wittenberg:[384] *He calls 5G an 'experiment on a living object'. The geoscientist believes it has been proven that brainwaves are influenced by high-frequency radiation from mobile communications, genetic information is destabilized and sperm are damaged. ... The International Cancer Research Agency (IARC) of the World Health Organization (WHO) classified electromagnetic phone radiation in 2011 as 'possibly carcinogenic'. And there are a number of researchers who advise increasing the risk level to 'probably carcinogenic', as in the case of glyphosate.*

The main danger with 5G is that it interferes in a special way with the biosphere of our body. Although the previous system 4G does that too, for the individual it does not do so as conclusively. In 4G, humans were still able to escape this radiation influence, for example by switching off the WLAN (Wireless Local Area Network) or by rearranging the living environment; with 5G this is hardly possible any more. The dangerous thing about these electromagnetic waves is that they can intervene directly in human cell communication, even at the DNA level. This fact is officially downplayed, though it is true that our brain and nervous system also use *tiny electrical impulses*, the official version obstinately states that there is no proof of danger: *'Previous studies have been superficial but relatively consistent effects on brain activity from mobile radio-related high-frequency electromagnetic fields have*

---

†††††††††††††††††††††††††††† in *Young World* (*Junge Welt* in German)

been found', says expert Driessen. However, sufficient evidence for health-relevant effects has not been established.[385]

However, a 2002 patent[386] suggests that the 5G system can be used from outside the human body to create certain states of consciousness. Along this track, human thinking and feeling can be manipulated at the DNA level and, for example, depression may be triggered. An even more serious consequence of 5G is that specifically selected people can be targeted for heart disorders by altering their heart rhythm. 5G is a major technological step towards the **Transhuman Agenda**, which should be completed by 2045,[387] assuming the élite's plans are allowed by us to be brought to fruition. The aim is the complete domination of people via mind control, removing the capacity of people to pretend or disguise their identities. How such mind control works is explained very impressively in the video[388] referring to this patent, whose underlying invention relates to *means and methods for transmitting information over long distances using electromagnetic radiation without the need for electronic aids in the receiver ... According to the invention, bundled modulated electromagnetic radiation is transmitted into the organism of the receiver in such a way that reactions are triggered corresponding to an intentional transmission of thought.*

Page 3 of this patent states:
... In contrast to conventional directional radio communication, however, the electromagnetic beam (thought beam) is coupled directly with the recipient's organism, e.g. in the head, the cerebral cortex, the inner ear, the auditory or optic nerves. Depending on particular signals introduced into the electromagnetic beam (e.g., by amplitude modulation), this coupling at the receiver causes an intentional change in thought ... e.g. in a simple model of a thought-transmitting device, the operator of the device (observer) speaks the thought to be sent to a microphone, the electrical signal of the microphone is converted by means of electronics into a series of impulses (...), which result in modulations on the microwave beam sent to the receiver, sent at such a low intensity

that the receiver has no conscious perception of the transmission, but only acts subliminally ...

The patent description continues: *... in a more complicated model of a thought transmitting device, the operator (observer) downloads the thought to be sent to a computer (...) which uses tables or neural networks to translate the thought into a sequence of signals modulated on the microwave beam that is transmitted to the receiver.* Here the Microwave beam is (ominously) epitomised as: *what we have now and what we expect in the future.* [389] On page 10 of this patent, points 24 to 27, one can read about the potentialities of this radio relay method: that

24: *... the bundled modulated electromagnetic radiation acts on the recipient's organism in such a way as to produce a more than 95% probability of a deliberate change to the recipient's thoughts or actions.*

25: *... a feeling-influence based on the effect of modulated microwave energy is involved.*

26: *... thought transmission to a targeted person takes place through objects made of concrete, stone, plastic or wood.*

27: *... thought transmission to a targeted person more than 10 km away* is achievable.

With this directional wireless technology, one can totally take control over the thoughts, feelings and will of the target, even from a distance and through masonry.

And the systematic timing of this microwave technology with very high power flux densities ... now surrounds the whole earth, because we already have thousands of satellites orbiting the Earth. With 5G now, even tens of thousands are (automatically) added ... Not to mention all the radio masts, of course. Combined, they have such strong levels of radiation that they impose a systematic frequency on all living organisms billions of times higher than the natural radiation of the earth. [390] *Strong radiation levels,* as mentioned in this quote, are not the most serious problem of 5G, but the **biorelevance**: the timing of the radiation in the same range as that of cell-level communication – in other words, 5G can be used to radio-penetrate massively into the biological functions of living things, including humans, and to disrupt internal biocommunication. This interference is further intensified by wave polarization in 5G communication.[391] Microwaves, even at very low intensities, can be used to control the ion channels of human cells, which directly affect our immune system. *Voltage-sensitive ion channels act as sluices: depending on the membrane voltage, they control the flow of ions between the inside and outside of the cell: when the sluice is open, ions flow from the location of the higher to the location of the lower concentration on their own, i.e. without any further energy input. An irregular opening or closing of these channels, forced by external radiation effects, disrupts the natural electrochemical balance between the interior of the cell and its environment and can thus set in motion a harmful and possibly damaging cellular chain reaction. The outcome overall being oxidative cell stress.*[392]

Even more dangerous for the human organism are: *Polarized (!) electromagnetic waves* (such as 5G) ... *able to activate the voltage-sensitive ion channels (channel proteins) in the cell membrane irregularly, irrespective of biological necessity, even at low intensities. Unpolarized waves – such as sunlight and many other natural electromagnetic waves – cannot do this even at significantly higher intensities and comparable exposure times, but will only cause heating, which is not biologically dangerous except at much higher intensities or exposure times.*[393]

On the dangers of 5G, one video[394] claims, *The real reason for 5G [being implemented] is 1000 times worse than radiation.* Specifically, 5G is about planting nanobots in the brain of humans to take control of neural activity and remotely control them via a 5G cloud. *Nanochips and smartdust are the new technological tools to push the* **agenda of human microchips.** *Because of their unbelievably small size, both ... can penetrate the human body, settling there and building a synthetic interior network that can be remotely controlled from the outside.* We're talking about intelligent dust particles (smartdust) which, embedded in the brain, form a completely new interface between brain and machine. (See Chemtrails – The Chemical Soup in the Sky, chapter 4, 2). This involves nanobots being sprayed into the air, all unnoticed by (and indeed invisible to) humans, where they can be linked to a cloud and remotely controlled. The size of these microchips is in the range of a quarter of a human hair (as of 2016), i.e. they are practically imperceptible.[395]

This project, intended to influence the way people think and act, amounts to ... *the ultimate enslavement from which there will be no escape, at least not independently.*[396]

This ultimate enslavement is part of the élite's Eugenic, or **Transhumanist Agenda**.[397]‡‡‡‡‡‡‡‡‡‡‡‡‡‡‡‡‡‡‡‡‡‡‡‡‡‡‡‡‡‡‡ The successful experiment with the remote-controlled beetle, ranked as one of the top ten technological innovations of the year 2009 (and repeated in 2015§§§§§§§§§§§§§§§§§§§§§§§§§§§§§§§§§§§), has shown that this futuristic vision is not something weird or fantastical.[398] *At minute 1:18 in the video (faded in), we demonstrate how a beetle is remotely controlled with a smartphone, and the goal of the research is to do the same with humans!*[399]

From this, one author draws the following conclusion: *(What is happening right now is a nightmare.) Ironically, most [mobile phone users] ... are staring unsuspectingly at their smartphones while radiation is gnawing away at their DNA. Anyone wondering why the government, practically behind closed doors and so negligently, is waving through the rollout of 5G cloud (technology),must know that the health risk of 5G technology*

---

‡‡‡‡‡‡‡‡‡‡‡‡‡‡‡‡‡‡‡‡‡‡‡‡‡‡‡ Where and if the Transhumanist Agenda falls short of being achieved – that is, not entirely succeeding in eliminating all members of the human race bar the élite – the Agenda might merely be described as cybernetic, at best compromising humanity and at worst replacing it with a conscienceless and brainwashed human/machine hybrid slavishly dedicated to that same élite. Sadly, some of us already have this mental attitude as a default (SP)

§§§§§§§§§§§§§§§§§§§§§§§§§§§§§§§§§§§ The 2009 experiment was a military-sponsored experiment by Assistant Professor Hirotaka Sato and his team at NTU (Nanyang Technological University), Singapore

(*https://www.ncbi.nlm.nih.gov/pmc/articles/PMC2821177/*;
https://www.telegraph.co.uk/news/science/science-news/11485231/Flying-beetle-remotely-controlled-by-scientists.html) [SP]

stands in the way of a more important plan. Swiss television has published the transhumanist agenda in a political broadcast of March 8, 'Who is afraid of 5G?' Somewhat sneering but amazingly honest, it is about connecting all people to a global 5G cloud via microchip implants, similar to what is already the case with smartphones today. Implanted microchips are the further development of smartphones that most people already wear permanently on their bodies. Moving them into the body is only a small step away and unfortunately, for many, almost a matter of course. Pioneers of the truth movement, such as Alex Jones or David Icke, have been warning of this development for decades. What was then considered shocking and unimaginable is now perceived as normal by large sections of the population because the agenda has been pushed forward in small steps.[400]

On 12.04.2019 one source (t-online.de) reported:[401] *The Belgian government has halted the 5G project in Brussels. Belgium fears that radiation protection values are not adhered to ...* ***************************** The question immediately arises: why Brussels? Could it be because the EU Parliament and the European Commission are in Brussels? I believe that the latter is an extension of the NWO, who are pushing for globalization with all their might, as lobbyists for the global élite. Is this just about ***their*** protection from the effects of radiation? *The European Commission had asked each member state to equip a city with 5G. In Belgium, the election had fallen on Brussels. Here, three vendors had teamed up and made an agreement with the city to relax the city's stringent radiation regulations, Fierce Wireless said. The city has the strictest radiation regulations in the world.*[402]

From a test area in England where 5G has been put into operation on a trial basis, it has been reported that there are no more insects and birds in the local parks.[403] And in an experiment with 5G in The Hague, hundreds of birds are supposed to have fallen dead

---

****************************** In April 2020, according to the *Financial Times*, Switzerland also called out a halt to the rollout of 5G, expressing health concerns while omitting any mention of a link to the continuing spread of Coronavirus (https://www.ft.com/content/848c5b44-4d7a-11ea-95a0-43d18ec715f5) [SP] from the trees. There *large flocks of migratory birds had gathered and sat in the trees around to make their way south together. Suddenly, hundreds of them were found lying dead on the ground. The animals all died of heart failure, although they were physically healthy. There was no sign of disease, no virus, no bacterial infection, healthy blood, no evidence of poisoning, etc. The only reasonable explanation left was the effect of microwaves. Because these have an effect on a bird's heart!*[404]

Nevertheless, these bird deaths were attributed in the above-cited article (tagesschau.de)[405] to a different cause: *poisoning from yew-tree cuttings*[†]. Another source claimed ... *that (the birds) have died from poisonous constituents of the egg-berry.*[‡] What's the truth?

Gender mainstreaming and Transhumanism

Within 30 years, we will have technology for superhuman intelligence, and soon after, the human era will end.
(Vernor Vinge)[§]

We elders are the last generation who will not have to see this through to the end. The nightmare is dawning on our children and their descendants.

What is gender mainstreaming? *Many people believe that 'gender mainstreaming' is just a new term for women's empowerment and*

[†] In German, the cutting of yew trees is known as *Eibenschnitt* (SP)

[‡] Presumably, *Prunus padus Albertii* , also known as Bird Cherry, is being referred to (SP)

[§] Vernor Vinge (1993), retired Professor of mathematics and computer science at San Diego University, is now a multiple Hugo Award winning sci-fi author writing on transhumanist themes. The quote repeats one of the epigraphs found in the fly-pages (SP) *equality. A fundamental error – intentionally so by the creators of this term! Many people think that the issue of gender, whether boy or girl, man or woman, would have determined (the individual's) nature clearly, as well as clarifying who is the mother or father. That was certainly true for the last 5,000 years, but not any more. There are people who want to actively change this – and they do it very successfully.*[406] The proponents of this ideology claim that the biological sex, male or female, is merely a sociological construction.[407]

The basis for this project is a documentary titled 'Cuddling, Touching, Playing Doctor'[408] at the symposium *Early Childhood Sexual Education in the KiTa.*[*] On this basis, state governments have already decided on the so-called Gender Plan, which adds to existing sex education and is supplemented by the introduction of gender ideology, beginning as early as the first grade and even at preschool age. *In its 'Standards for Sex Education in Europe', WHO actually suggests that toddlers aged 0-4 years should be informed about masturbation and given opportunities to explore their gender identity. At the age of 4 to 6 years, children should be taught about same-sex relationships and respect for different standards of sexuality.*[409] Behind these aspirations for the early sexualizing of our children is the UN with its specialized agencies UNICEF (United Nations International Children's Emergency Fund[†]), IPPF (International Planned Parenthood Federation), and UNFPA (United Nations Population Fund).[410] Kindergarten children in several German federal states are already acquainted with books and playing materials on various family models and gender diversity (LGBT-TI[‡])[411]. Children over the age of three are taught that it does not matter which gender they choose, or how a family is made up.

---

[*] In German, *Kuscheln, Fühlen, Doktorspiele ... Frühkindliche Sexualerziehung in der KiTa. KiTa stands for Kindertagesheim* (in English, children's day care centre) [JS, SP]

[†] Now UNICEF prefers to describe itself as the United Nations Children's Fund, but for some reason has not altered its acronym accordingly (SP)

[‡] Lesbian, gay, bisexual, transgender, transsexual and inter-bad people

The Gender Mainstreaming project is therefore not just about equality between men and women or different partnerships; it is in fact an attack on the dual sex of humans, on the marriage of men and women and on the conventional family.[412] However, ... *the result is not the free person, but the mentally crippled person who has poor self-confidence, is unable to bond, cannot found a family, cannot practice solidarity and is reduced to the lowest instincts - the perfect subject (for manipulation).*[413]

There is even more behind the Gender Mainstreaming project. Its ultimate objective being the **physical** dissolution of the differences between man and woman. In the long term, however, gender mainstreaming has four goals: to
1) increasingly shift the educational influence of family and parents on to the state
2) destroy the family
3) dissolve gender, thus creating one of the main prerequisites for replacing the natural reproductive process with test-tube reproduction
4) eliminate what is, from an elitist perspective, the uncontrollable natural process of 'love between two people of different sexes' because it harbours a private sphere of life beyond the élite's direct influence.[414]

The Nightmare

Man is denied his humanity.
The master man plays God.

Gender mainstreaming as taught and practiced in our schools today, as propagated and promoted by the Ministry of Education, relevant government agencies and the public media, is only a harmless preliminary stage of what the future may hold. Gender mainstreaming was originally created as a strategy to promote gender equality, according to the official view. However, there is much more to it than that. Gender mainstreaming opens the way to a variant which, if one looks at the ultimate goal, must certainly be counted as part of transhumanism. The ultimate objective of gender dissolution, in the minds of the élite, is the biological[415] termination of the sex difference between a man and a woman and the replacement of the birth cycle with *in vitro* birth. Re-designing posthumous people for future quasi-generations, via the test-tube, will become the task of so-called scientists who will willingly implement the wishes of the élite. This is part of the Transhumanist Agenda (see 5G and Transhumanism, chapter 5, 2). Of course, this is only for the common people, not for the élite.[§]

It doesn't take much imagination to foresee how things will develop once the NWO is established and the élite begin to implement their transhumanist plans, for which they originally created the project.

This is what the future of humanity will look like if the élite are not successful in preventing the super-élite (or Deep State élite) from taking power. Through the technical possibilities associated with test-tube births, the sex characteristics of artificially created people (clones, etc) will gradually yet systematically be re-developed through genetic manipulation and hormonal manipulation. Once this is technically realized, one of the sexes will effectively be abolished. One of two courses of action will take place: only clones with male sexual characteristics will be allowed to exist, or alternatively only those with female sexual characteristics will be permitted. At the same time, sexual intercourse between male and female human beings will be prohibited, along also natural birth will be prohibited and drastic measures will be taken to prevent this. A decision will be made as to which cloned humans, male or female, will be allowed to live. The choice made will simply depend on which of the two sexes are the more effective work slaves. These slaves of the future will have a lot in common with the livestock of today; they will be the livestock of the future. The selection could be made along similar lines to the selection of

---

[§] Interestingly, this would amount to a cunning reversal of the scenario in Orwell's *Nineteen Eighty-Four*, in which only the proles (proletarians) were allowed to procreate normally (SP)

chicks in Chicken breeding: the male chicks are shredded shortly after birth, quite legally, because they have a lower utility value than the female chicks.

There will also be a chemical intervention in the hormonal balance of individuals with the aim of further dissolving the male-female relationships developed over thousands of years, altering puberty and menopause. While in vitro, the first-generation offspring of work slaves will be biologically programmed, as will the reproduction of egg and sperm cells as the starting material.

But how can one control the mass of slaves, keep them in check, prevent possible revolts? This is done, for example, via 5G, by sending out special low-frequency slots over it, which influence their brains (see section: "Depressed by communication").

Death of slaves will also be regulated on the basis of their utility. As long as the slave remains useful (that is, corruptible), he can continue to live; if not, he will be switched off, that is killed. This sorting out or dying is then carried out at the "push of a button", for example via 5G, through identity-related signature slots, which can trigger the self-destruction of the individual (see section: "High-Tech Bioweapons - Forecourt to Hell").

The overview of whether a slave is still useful and allowed to live on will be provided by a system of digital certification created for all slaves, unambiguously assignable by means of chipping, just as occurs in livestock farming today. For many years, preparations have been underway to introduce microchips into humans as well. The country of Sweden is a pioneer: In Sweden, many people have already voluntarily had an RFID implanted under their skin. This is accompanied by public advertising to have such an RFID chip implanted under the skin: *After all, more than 4,000 Swedes have already had a chip the size of a grain of rice (2 x 12 mm) implanted under their skin by the market leader Biohax. This is not a major intervention and, as we hear, not a very painful one either. But once you have this chip under your skin, it can make your life much more relaxed.*[416] However, technical development has not stood still; the chips are becoming smaller and smaller (a quarter of the human hair - status 2016[417]) and can also be administered with a normal syringe, for example at the same time as the vaccination serum. As a result of the "coronic" panic, fueled by the media, a large number of people are longing for vaccination against the flu virus Covid 19. The global-ist Bill Gates openly says what is planned: *At some point in the not-so-distant future we will all have digital certification to show who has recovered from what, who has recently been tested, or when our vaccination dates were.* (There has already been a proposl by Bill Gates to this effect in connection with the Covid 19 virus. [**]) This amounts to totalitarian control over people. *"This is the ultimate enslavement from which there will be no escape, at least not by your own power."*[418]

The young generation expects a worse fate than the war generation of 1939-45, if we don't fight back. Fate has a name: Transhumanism & 5G.

Dear reader, if you think this apocalyptic scenario is exaggerated or, in other words, just another conspiracy theory, then give me another reason why Gender mainstreaming has been introduced. Is this just to promote decadent thinking and behaviour, or to weaken or destroy family cohesion? This is also true. But in my opinion the crucial thing, is the ultimate aim of making people dependent and controllable for all time, manipulating them in such a way as to eliminate all risk of political power ever being lost again. It is with this in view that bioenginering has become a practical, ongoing reality. What is technically, or in this case more precisely, biotechnologically possible, is done.

[****] It is both fascinating and disturbing how, in the media, corona virus became Covid 19. This appears to be part of a deliberate strategy to keep most people in the dark about the disease. It becomes increasingly difficult for the ordinary person to join up the dots. If you want to research patents, Covid-19 is the essential styling; otherwise the planned vaccination programme appears to address Covid 19, not Coronavirus, which surely gives the vaccinators the opportunity to substitute one vaccine for another. In short, when we're being vaccinated we don't know what the hell we're being vaccinated with! (SP)

6. Biological Warfare

„Der Covid-19-Hype ist wie ein Vorhang, damit wir nicht sehen, was hinter dem Vorhang geschieht. Hinter dem Vorhang ringen zwei Mächte: Der Tiefe Staat weltweit (Deep State) und die Lichtkräfte. Für den Deep State /Illuminati[††] ... ist es die letzte Chance, die Neue Weltordnung einzuführen; daher Corona, und gleichzeitig der Versuch, durch Massenimpfungen die gesamte Menschheit zu implantieren, Bargeld abzuschaffen, Trump zu beseitigen usw. "[419]

Bioweapons Development

The Biological Weapons Convention,[420] signed in 1972 by almost all countries in the world, came into force on March 26, 1975. Article I states: *Each State Party to this Convention undertakes to ... never, under any circumstances, develop, produce, store or otherwise acquire or maintain any such biological weapons. Whether viruses, bacteria or allied insects 'they all fall under the* **Biological Weapons Convention***, which was signed in 1972 by almost all the countries of the world, including the Americans'.*[421]

But bioweapons are still being developed, tested and used.

Infectious diseases that have sprung up worldwide over the past decades – such as Ebola, AIDS, SARS, Lyme disease, EHEC, and Morgellons disease – are most likely developed as biological weapons in secret military laboratories. That's what this chapter is about.

On the basis of a treaty between the US and Georgia, a bioweapons laboratory, the Lugar Centre, also known as the Laboratory of Death, was built in Tbilisi, Georgia's capital, and inaugurated in 2011. Through the publication of documents (via a 'defector') it

---

†† For more details see chapter "Epilogue - Elite and Deep State.".

has been made known what kind of experiments take place in the Lugar Centre. Bacteria and viruses suitable for bioweapons development include: (bubonic) plague, hare plague (tularaemia), anthrax, Brucella, hepatitis C, hantavirus (from rodents), EHEC (Entoerohaemorrhagic Escherichia coli), and CCHF (Crimean-Congo fever) [See Figure 45].[422]

In recent years, epidemics of exotic diseases are increasing among Georgian people, diseases where the pathogen is completely unknown, and it is thought that these epidemics are related to these laboratories. [423] Figure 44 shows in which parts of Georgia so far CCHF (Crimean- Congo fever) has occurred in recent years.

The Lugar Centre is not only experimenting with deadly bacteria and viruses, but also with their potential carriers, the so-called 'allied insects' whose development is expressly prohibited by the Biological Weapons Convention. But the Lugar Centre continues to work on them: ticks, sandflies, tree bugs (aphids, beetles, moth caterpillars, weevils, woodlice, etc) and Asian tiger mosquitoes (Figure 46). Aside from the tree bugs, these are all bloodsucking insects that can infect humans and mammals with bacteria and viruses. Since November 2016, the Pentagon has operated a programme called Insect Allies (Figure 47). *And apparently, these bloodsuckers in Georgia have already been released for testing purposes. Since October 2017 the inhabitants of Tbilisi have been reporting sandflies coming out of the sewers into their baths and biting them while they are naked in the bathroom. Normally, these sandflies are found in the Philippines, not in Georgia ... Although the sandfly can fly only a few 100 m, it has also been found in the Russian Republic of Dagestan, 100 km away, in the same month in which it was sighted in Tbilisi for the first time. The emergence of the sandfly in Dagestan could be related to this US patent (Patent No .: US 8,967,029 B1, Mar.3, 2015: TOXIC MOSQUITO AERIAL RELEASE SYSTEM), which until recently was still publicly available on the Lugar Centre website:*[424] This video also reports another patent for the spread of contaminated insects over enemy territory through drones.

Figure 44: Georgia: In the areas highlighted in colour the Crimean-Congo fever appeared epidemic; the source is believed to be the Lugar Centre biological weapons laboratory, inaugurated in 2011.[425]

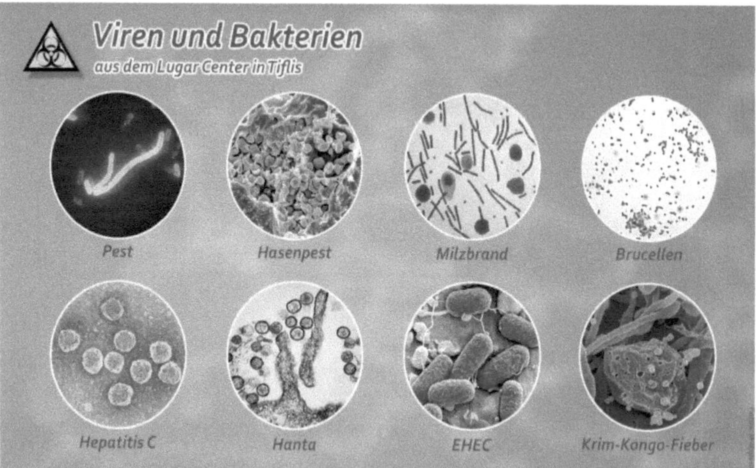

Figure 45: Bacteria and viruses being researched at the Lugar Centre include: plague, rabbit fever, anthrax, brucella, hepatitis C, Hanta, EHEC and Crimean-Congo fever.[426]

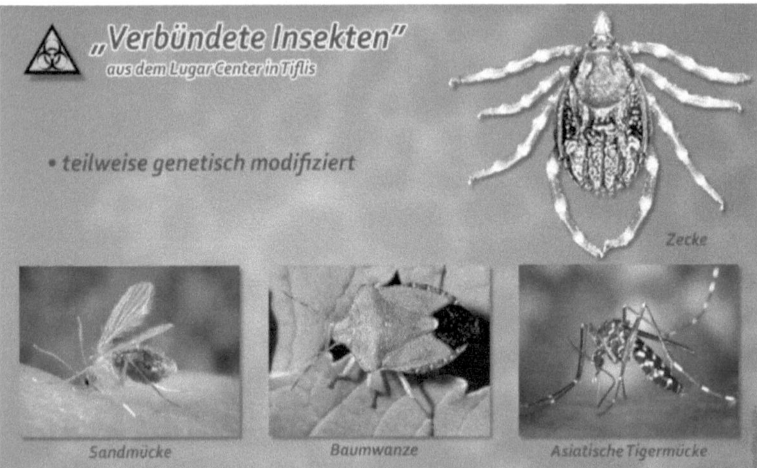

Figure 46: 'Insect Allies' that are being experimented with at the Lugar Centre in Tbilisi: ticks (top right), sandflies, tree bugs and Asian tiger mosquitoes (bottom from left to right).[427]

Figure 47: Since November 2016, the Pentagon has operated a programme called Insect Allies.[428]

Figure 48: In the Ukraine, Pentagon biotech laboratories have been created throughout the country. In recent years (highlighted in red), near the eastern Pentagon laboratories there has been a hepatitis epidemic with hundreds of patients.[429]

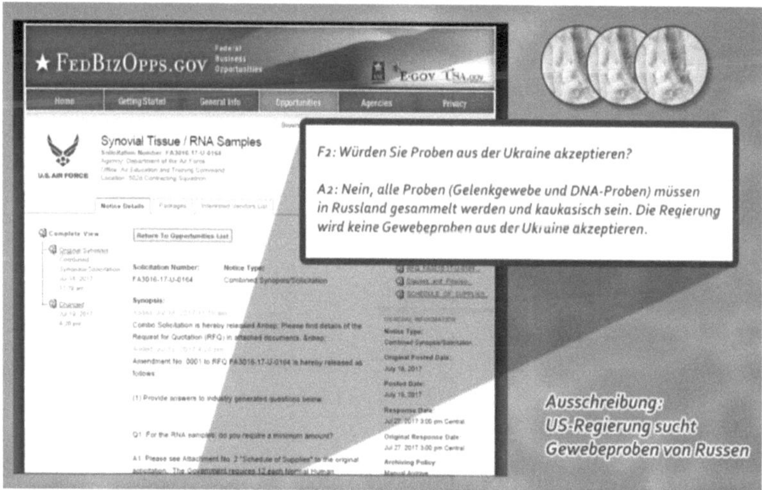

Figure 49: US Government Call: Search for tissue and DNA samples of Russo-Caucasian people. [430]

Biotech laboratories have also been set up by the Pentagon in Ukraine (see Figure 48). *In July 2017, the US government issued a request for tissue and DNA samples from Russian people of*

Caucasian descent. The fact that this only referred to tissue samples from Russian people was clarified in the tender (see Figure 49) ... *Incidentally, the American gene database NCBI, based on Pentagon research into Pesterregern, also came from the Russian Caucasus region.*[431] As stated in the above-mentioned documents, in the Lugar Centre, experiments are carried out on anthrax and porcelains, etc – as well as on plague pathogens ... *so there is a reasonable suspicion that in the Lugar Centre in Tbilisi research on Pesterregern, aimed at destroying specific ethnicities, is also being done ... on a scale that would even surpass the ethnic cleansing of Adolf Hitler and Josef Stalin.*[432]

The fact that the US is interested in ethnicity-specific biological weapons is also evident from another source: *Published in September 2000 ... 'Project for a New American Century', a document in which Dick Cheney called race-specific biological weapons a politically useful tool.*[433]

These things are essentially revealed through research by the team at MarkMobil. However, there is also criticism along the lines that in the above presentation a too one-sided view was chosen, because other countries – the former USSR in particular – were among the first to intensively research biological weapons and are thereby *by far the most guilty*[434] (having broken the contract according to the Biological Weapons Convention). In a longer article the author writes: *For this subject, the research on viruses, bacteria and toxins, one should generally deal with the history of it, in order to get a diverse picture. There are many on earth who have researched such things. State institutions, civil and military, but also private research centres. And it's not just the Americans who work along these lines. There are important reasons for doing this research, especially for the sake of preventing and warding off diseases that really threaten mankind.* However, we are permitted to ask: Does the fact that other countries intensively research, or have researched, biological weapons make it acceptable for us to do so?

In doctors' surgeries one often encounters posters advertising vaccinations against tick-borne infectious diseases. In the past the tiny ticks were merely annoying, they did not transmit any dangerous diseases. In the last ten years this has changed, and we have to ask why it is that the tick has become such a pathogen? Could it be as a result of experiments in military laboratories such as the Lugar Centre in Tbilisi? In Europe, tick-borne diseases such as Lyme disease and TBE (Tick-Borne Encephalitis) are on the rise.

High-Tech Bioweapons – Forecourt to Hell

Society is dominated by an élite ... that does not hesitate to enforce its political goals through the use of the latest modern methods of managing the people's behavior and keeping society under close surveillance and control.
(Z Brzezinski[435])

Dear Reader, in the quote from Chemtrails – The Chemical Soup in the Sky (Chapter 4, 2), our TV pundits told us that our food contains microscopic plastic particles, aluminium powder and barium salts and that these materials, probably from the Chemtrails chemical soup, are responsible for the fact that, in our latitudes, *virtually all people today already have a remarkably high level of aluminium and barium poisoning.*[436]

That such a message should be relayed by a TV commentator is amazing, because in recent years, the existence of Chemtrails has been vehemently denied. Equally amazing, in this broadcast it is admitted that people are being poisoned by Chemtrails. Why are we being told the truth now? Maybe this commentator's honesty was not premeditated? Or is there so much evidence in the meantime (the internet also contributes to its dissemination) that someone clicked on the 'fast forward' button? Television theming ensures that the outraged anger of those who have protested for years against Chemtrails, together with the emergence of more and more evidence of their existence, and more and more people becoming aware of it, has to be channelled. In this new atmosphere of openness it can even be pointed out that spraying activities were necessary to avert the climate catastrophe, without there necessarily being an awareness of the side-effects.[437]

However, those responsible were well aware. Not only were the side-effects approved, they were part of a programme to install a bioweapon in humans, which now revolves around those in the body who have *"remarkably high levels of aluminum and barium poisoning."*[438] That's an assertion which we want to prove below:

Anyone who has been able to endure reading previous remarks about Chemtrails will now be led on a horror trip, where the most perfidious struggle of humans against humans is thematized. It is the so-called Morgellons disease. In 2012 an article was published on Spiegel online under the title[439] *Morgellons Disease – Bad Skin Disease is probably based on imagination*. And another article used the term parasitosis[‡‡] for Morgellons Disease, a clear expression of this illness's 'delusory' nature. A similar (shallow) conclusion is arrived at in yet another online article[§§] , where we learn that there has even been a study with the following result: ... *most likely it is Morgellons Disease, simply a new variant of the so-called parasitosis in which affected persons are convinced that they are infected by pathogens, parasites or other small creatures.*[440]

Today, however, we know that Morgellons Disease is by no means imaginary. In addition I recommend watching a Youtube video[441] with Domian as well as an interview[442] with the operator of a website at the cutting edge of this research.[***] . This page displays an array of microscopic images and analyses of Morgellons. The statement that these fibres are 'living optical fibres' is supported by the microscopic studies of independent authors.[443,444]

[‡‡] In German, Dermatozoanwahn (also see later reference to parasitosis) [SP]
[§§] in welt.de, under the heading *New form of delusion*
[***] https://www.morgellons-research.org

There is no one who does not have the stuff in the bloodstream. What is known about Morgellon Syndrome is that only a few have developed a defence mechanism and can excrete these fibres through the skin: That's where they extrude.[445][†††] We all carry these Morgellons fibres inside ourselves, as a kind of organic/inorganic hybrid, and those who suffer from Morgellon Syndrome grow these fibres from the skin, mouth, nose, eyeballs, ears, genitalia, in fact anywhere on the body, and they are also found in sperm.[446] Dr. Manfred Doepp, one of the few doctors in Germany to have dealt with this disease thoroughly, gives the following description: *They extrude from the skin like that, and it itches awfully. And we have had patients with complete Morgellon Syndrome; they almost went insane with itching,*[447]

Morgellons are artificially created parasites that can permeate the entire body and lodge in many, if not all, organs. If you have a strong immune system you may not have to worry about it for the time being, because your system obviously has the ability to control the growth of fibres in your body. Since the human body is used to dealing with parasites and in its healthy state the host body establishes a dynamic equilibrium with invasive parasites, it can be assumed that even in the special case of artificial parasites a *status quo* prevails – but only provided the body *is* healthy.

[†††] If this is the case it may be somewhat reassuring for Morgellons sufferers to know that they may be in a better position than those who cannot extrude these fibres and must therefore retain them in their bodies, doing whatever damage they do internally. This somehow reminds me of my rare reaction to air pollution in the days when lead in the atmosphere was at its height. I used to naturally form what for all the world seemed like a plastic coating over my lips, perfectly moulded to them, which I could peel off when I got inside. This coating smelled disgusting and I was glad to dispose of it. It was far too thick to be a layer of skin and when I peeled it off my exposed lips did not feel sore in the least, as they would have done if I had removed a layer of lip, but retained their moistness and good condition. Of course, I never publicized this defence mechanism until now. Could the regular nosebleeds of myself and others – a known reaction to high G – in forming a crystalline blood-barrier in the nose, also protect a person from radiation to some degree? (SP)

Morgellons can be counted among the group of biological weapons.[448] These optical fibres can grow like living beings. A number of videos provide a 'live' feature of very small to very large Morgellon fibres, demonstrating viability outside their host and, relatively free movement and resistance to rips in their fabric.[449,450,451,452,453] Because of this ability to survive even outside the host, one must also fear a non-disappearing infection potential from person to person. This becomes clear in an interview titled 'Morgellons: The Pandora's Box is Open'.[454] There, the interviewee (who presents his own case[455] as a person affected) answers the question: *'So these fibres eat themselves back into the skin?'*

Yes,exactly. I first noticed that when I went into the sauna to sweat out the fibres. But no sooner had I sweated out a few fibres, showered or wiped, these fibres caught on my feet and I got there immediately new pustules. When I once put on an older, contaminated T-shirt that I had not worn in three or four years, I was already covered in new pustules and blisters after two hours, even though I had washed the shirt before. By this I actually noticed that these fibres are infectious, even after years. Such long survival times are actually known only from fungal spores or worm eggs.

Morgellons are also thematized in the book *Betrayed, Sold, Lost* by Gabriele Schuster-Haslinger.[456‡‡‡] In this book, Morgellon Syndrome – a condition which in the UK, as in Germany, seems to interest neither politicians nor representatives of medical institutions – is associated with biological insecticides[457] used for pest control. The fibres penetrate the human body as a side-effect when it comes into contact with these insecticides, the cotton fibres originally used having been replaced as a carrier material for the insecticides by polymer fibres in a (successful?) attempt by the insecticide manufacturers to ensure a longer shelf-life for the microorganisms on these fibres. However, under the guise of this seemingly logical explanation of 'longer shelf-life', lurks a perfidious motive attached to the creation of these Morgellons.

---

‡‡‡ In German, *Verraten verkauft verloren*, which I would translate less literally as *Sold Down the River* (SP)

Because these polymer fibres, these optical Nanofasern, serve the purpose of manipulating the people.[458,459] This is only apparent when one looks at the details and appreciates that barium, strontium, titanium and alumina are applied **simultaneously** with these nanofibres, which are sprayed into the atmosphere via Chemtrails. So far, people have wondered: why are highly toxic materials being sprayed overhead? Simply to reduce earthbound solar radiation? Other metals, far less toxic to humans, animals and plants could be used. But these toxic materials - especially the compounds barium strontium titanate and aluminium oxide – when incorporated into the fibres, fulfill a specific function, a capacity for technically realizing a given optical working principle.

Morgellons, artificial creatures consisting of a DNA mix of individual multi-cell fungi, grow like mushrooms, forming fine capillaries. And these capillaries like to take in nanoparticles belonging to two specific classes. It's exactly these classes that are being employed in spraying activities. The result is that we get small, as they say in English, self-assembling nanohybrids.[§§§] These are, in principle, living optical fibres that, along with different nanoparticles, fill the inside (of the body) and act as small quantum lasers, which I can activate and control electromagnetically from outside. The reason this thing is so scary is because laser technology, if you look at it in (medical) biology, you find that they do similar things with synthetic carbon fibres, and not with self-replicating fibres, but with this thing it's essentially the same. With these lasers I can create single photons that can set up full two-way communication with DNA at the cellular level. I can create a light stream whereby I can inject foreign impulses into the body as if they were the body's own. Conversely, I can pick up light pulses and convert them into electromagnetic signals, which then go out as a radio signal from the body. This plays a role in person monitoring because every human being infected with Morgellons and all of nature (as far as I could ascertain from the researchers who have detected fibres) is infected.[460]

[§§§] In German these go by the deceptively cute name of *Nano-mischlings* (SP)

I have always wondered why Chemtrails contain just these materials: aluminium, strontium, barium, titanium, plastic fibres and certain organic materials. You cannot just spray this poison, so toxic to humans, into the atmosphere?! Don't the persons responsible see that this must have devastating consequences for the health of humans and animals? And why use nanoparticles whose production is so expensive? Now we know why: a combination of strontium, barium, titanium, plastic fibres and organic material is precisely what is needed for the realization of these artificial creatures. Aluminium is a material known to be responsible for a variety of degenerative diseases in the human brain (see "Effects of Chemtrails on health, chapter 4, 4). And nanoparticles, because they greatly increase the reactivity of the materials, owing to their tiny size, are also able to cross the human blood-brain barrier. It is the aim of those responsible to control defenceless people who are ill-educated about these materials and human-made creatures.

This is bad enough, but the worst is yet to come. Through the overhead spraying of these materials for many years, we have all come into contact with them; consequently, they are contained in our blood, taken in through the air we breathe. In other words, *we are all, as it were, infected, we all have a network of optical nanofibres within us, accessible via radio waves, which in principle can take over our light body.*[****] *So everything that is known from Indian culture about chakras, the assignment of certain qualities of light, frequencies that affect emotional qualities, expressiveness, intuition, all these centres of*

[****] The light body equates with, or interweaves with, what is also known as the subtle body – *one in a series of psycho-spiritual constituents of living beings, according to various esoteric, occut, and mystical teachings. According to such beliefs, each subtle body corresponds to a subtle plane of existence, in a hierarchy or great chain of being that culminates in the physical form* (*https://en.wikipedia.org/wiki/Subtle_body*). Without the light body, many of us, disconnected from the Holy Spirit, would be unable to continue functioning as spiritual human beings, but would be devoid of love for humanity, compassion, and benevolence. This would be the ultimate triumph of secularism, whose darker name is Satanism (SP)

consciousness in the body are thus controllable from the outside. Worst of all, if I do not provide the light response to the electromagnetic signal, they'll bleed in the light anywa. ... It's just a way to keep people down, and, incidentally, reduce their self-organizing ability by breaking down, as it were, the barn door of autoimmunity to degenerative diseases.[461]

For external manipulation to work, and to control the biochemical processes at the light level in our body, an interface is needed to allow external radio signals to communicate with the human biophoton exchange process within and between human cells.[462] And this interface is realized through microscopic quantum lasers formed by living optical fibres that can be electromagnetically activated and controlled externally. Through exposing these optical nanofibres to external light, signals can be sent to trigger various activities in the human body and to initiate programmes at the DNA level. Excessive red or infrared light at this level can give a signal similar to a *disease signal in biology*[463], triggering a process of self-destruction. Excessive blue light on this level can send out a signal, *where panic-stricken Morgellons begin to multiply* (flood the body, as it were). *I've seen pictures where you put 4 Morgellons in the Petri dish and after 24 hours it's overflowing. And that's an (internal) firing squad for the body when the body starts glowing internally; then the Morgellons start eating you from the inside. The usual symptoms are nosebleeds, ear bleeding, bleeding from the ... (?), stroke or heart attack. And the procedure takes about 10 months in the current application, so the process is slow, unnoticeable. But it is also rumoured that in military application it can progress within minutes. And there was just such a series of incidents, when so many species fell from the sky, such as birds, which simultaneously fell in their hundreds, bats likewise; there was a mass extinction of the whale population; in all carcasses the symptoms are the same. This, so to speak, applies the term signal in its most concentrated sense.*[464] *If I summarize this technique, I get the picture of a total biological control control system at the light level.*[465] *The Morgellons' fibres have the same properties as Chemtrail fibres.*[466]

It should be recorded at this point, however, that the above-mentioned mass extinction of animals, for which the probable explanation is biological shock, cannot be clearly assigned to the action of a biological weapon. Nevertheless, this mass extinction has certainly not been triggered by natural causes.[467]

If the content of the quotations above is a proper reflection of reality, such an internal 'firing squad', if sent into the body, can cause self-destruction and shut down the capacity of certain people to work against the system. The same author who has uncovered these connections has put a number of other videos on the net, in which, so to speak, he also names horse and rider – which companies and institutions are conducting this inhumane research and who finances them – as well as listing the sources that anyone can verify. Even the physics behind the phenomena described is plausibly and comprehensibly explained.[468] Could it be that this application is already taking place today? Also, how can one explain the statistically unlikely demise of several nuisance critics? For example, Andreas Clauss, Udo Ulfkotte and Friederike Beck, who had revealed in numerous videos and books the aims and objectives of the élites and warned of their machinations; or of testimony witnesses during the NSU Trial (National Socialist Underground Trial: 2013-18) in Munich, where a total of 5 witnesses suddenly died before they were able to give evidence.[469] Even before the opening of court proceedings, the constitution protection authority[††††] were suspected of involvement in the NSU murders, a suspicion fed by the destruction of NSU files by the constitution protection authority and by the fact that the NSU files are under lock and key until until the year 2134, so that no access to these files can be gained until then. What did the 5 witnesses know? Could they have supplied incriminating material?

In search of independent sources claiming that Morgellon fibres act like 'small quantum lasers' controllable from the outside,[470] I came across publications that reveal parallels between Morgellons and *'autism-related rope worms.*[471] *Despite the different appearance,*

Morgellon fruiting bodies and the so-called 'rope worms' found in the intestines of autistic people have a number of things in common. This indicates a biological relationship or a common biotechnological source.[‡‡‡‡]

While autism was very rare in the 70s of the last century, today this health disorder is found much more often, especially among young people. It is therefore conceivable that there are other artificially created parasites that have found their way into the human body via chemtrails or vaccinations (see also section "Effects of chemtrails on our health", chapter 4,4).

So if it is possible to "switch off" or make the people ill from the outside via these artificial living beings living in the human body, the thought suggests itself that this is actually happening. "Who benefits?" It benefits the elite to be able to manipulate us, to keep us down, through the mechanism described above. It benefits the powerful who want to dominate us. If the barium strontium titanate and the aluminum oxides didn't serve a purpose, they wouldn't be sprayed.

According to the author Harald Kautz Vella, 2014 there are about 300,000 Morgellon patients worldwide with severe symptoms.[472] In Germany, too, there is now a relatively large number of affected people who suffer from Morgellons that have gone out of control in their bodies.[473] The human body tries to get rid of these Morgellons. And this happens, as described above, by growing out of the body.

Now for the good news:[474]

In a healthy person with a stable internal environment, without any heavy metal poisoning, the Morgellon fibres have little chance of spreading and forming what is known as the Morgellon Mushroom,

---

[‡‡‡‡] There is a suspicion that autism is also caused by certain vaccinations linked to intestinal complications (kla.tv/14793, minute 9:50. - kla.tv/14793 can no longer be accessed on YouTube; however, you can find it embedded as a video at *https://systematikgesund.de/gesundheit/impfen/kindersterblichkeit*)

because in this case the normal immune system is preventative. However, under certain conditions – for example, under the influence of great stress where the body over-acidifies – the higher the propensity for Morgellons disease to form and permeate the body. The spread of Morgellons fungus in the body is supported by pre-existing diseases or weakening of the immune system – for example, as a result of heavy metal poisoning which promotes hyperacidity.

Now for the bad news:

The weakening of our immune system happens, for example, through glyphosate, which inhibits heavy metal detoxification in the body. In a genetically modified plant there is likely to be something that promotes the development of Morgellons.[475] It is worth noting how, despite fierce resistance from the population, both the glyphosate and genetically modified substances have not received a political ban; instead they are increasingly finding their way into our everyday lives. Also noteworthy is 'the United States and the Codex Commission's steadfast refusal *to label genetically modified organisms (GMOs) as such.*[§§§§] Officially, the Codex Commission's[*****] mission is to protect consumer health and to guarantee and promote fair food trade. In truth, however, it does exactly the opposite[†††††]: *Controlled by big industry, the secret purpose of the new Codex is to increase the profits of global corporate conglomerates while gaining world domination over food ...* [476] From the new Codex guidelines it's obvious that the Codex Commission is also part of the 'Population Control' project.

[§§§§] *https://www.zentrum-der-gesundheit.de/codex-alimentarius-ia.html?fbclid=IwAR17zPrh9oKnPMo5k2sQKdoti8jglrDXC5c-rFD8yNcKweR_mTeTDifCTtA#toc-gesundheitliche-selbstbestimmung-ist-bedroht*

[*****] Codex Alimentarius

[†††††] Over the years, who has failed to notice that government departments, and even commissions set up by those departments, are inclined to do the opposite of what the voting public expects them to do – perhaps in order to delay reaching a state of ultimate resolution in which they fear that all politicians would become redundant. To quote JS from earlier: 'Orwell sends greetings'. This is, of course, a witty piece of irony from JS. Foreshadowing Sonntag, that great political observer George Orwell despised this brand of governmental chicanery, which in his famous political sci-fi novel *Nineteen Eighty-Four* he dubbed 'double-think' (SP)

These guidelines include:[477] *All micro-nutrients (such as vitamins and minerals) are considered toxic and must be removed from all foods, as the Code prohibits the use of nutrients to 'prevent, treat or cure disease' ... All Foods (including organic foods) should be irradiated to remove any 'toxic' nutrients ... Any nutrients (such as vitamins A, B, C and D, as well as zinc and magnesium) that have any health benefits are considered inadmissible in therapeutically effective quantities. They are to be partially reduced in such a way that their effect on health becomes negligible.* These micro-nutrients remain available in the pharmacy, although in special cases only by prescription,[‡‡‡‡‡] but again one must say that they are often significantly underdosed, so that their therapeutic effect is low to non-existent: this has long been the case, for example, with some vitamin C supplements.

The heavy metal mercury, which has long been used as a preservative in vaccines but has been removed owing to its toxicity, will continue to be introduced into our bodies during vaccination by disinfecting the inoculation kits before use with mercury-based solutions. The mercury, no longer in the vaccine, is in the syringe.[478]

In the UK, people who have amalgam fillings in their teeth, or who inhaled mercury vapours while having these amalgam fillings removed, are in grave danger when aluminum is added to the mix. And the mercury amalgam, which is the principal one used in dental fillings, and the only one for which health insurance covers the cost[§§§§§], releases mercury into the human body around the clock. The toxic effect of aluminum is further enhanced by the presence of mercury.

[‡‡‡‡‡] For example: Vitamin D preparation Dekristol 20000 I.E..

[§§§§§] My understanding from Sonntag is that the fillings situation may be even worse in German dentistry than it is in the UK, if in some parts of Germany 'the amalgam ... is the *only* one still used ... for which health insurance funds cover the cost'. Several medical observers link mercury vapour and aluminium ingestion (from saucepans, etc) with the onset of Alzheimer's disease (SP: literal translation from the German edition where quoting)

Halogen lamps release mercury when they break. High sugar consumption, antibiotic abuse in medicine and in the animal-fattening industry, not to mention the intensive addition of hormones to growth accelerant used in animal fattening have a negative influence on the internal environment of the human body. In our everyday life, all these these factors, in addition to **a) glyphosate, b) genetically modified substances, and c) heavy metals**, promote the onset of Morgellons disease. By having a healthy lifestyle you can avoid such a disease. However, a large part of the population is already pre-damaged by the above-mentioned influences, which are difficult to escape in a normal everyday life.

A basic milieu in the body is of paramount importance as a prevention of Morgellons disease. In the case of previous damage, however, it is difficult to uphold the standard internal environment. So writes the well-known critic Dr. Leonard Horowitz:[479] *Aluminium, barium, and strontium in highly dangerous chemical compounds affect large parts of humanity every day ... Suddenly you develop a secondary bacterial infection. Now, antibiotics can have a negative effect on you, causing your body chemistry to turn sour so that you get rashes and other things; your liver fills with poisons that show up on your skin; hypoallergenic reactions occur in connection with the other chemicals.* So if you get a bacterial disease besides this intoxication by Chemtrails, because, for example, the immune system is already weakened, the body tends towards an acidic environment, brewing optimal conditions for the formation of Morgellons disease. That's a vicious circle if ever there was one.

Are Ebola, AIDS, SARS and EHEC bioweapons?

If Morgellons represent a biological weapon developed in secret military laboratories, the question automatically arises: Could it be that the newer diseases such as Ebola, AIDS, SARS and EHEC are also diseases that were developed in such places? The author G. Schuster-Haslinger writes:[480] *Interesting in this context is the fact that the US Department of Health owns the patent for the Ebola virus.*[481] However, according to Mimikama, the Ebola patent has not yet been granted and probably will not be granted.

As far as the infectious disease EHEC is concerned, the pathogens of which are also being researched at the Tbilisi Lugar Center, as can be seen from the documents cited above, it is worth recalling the EHEC outbreak in Germany in May 2011. The question arises: Could this EHEC outbreak have been a false-flag operation carried out by intelligence agencies as a punishment for Germany? Previously, on February 18, 2011, Germany had voted against Israel at the United Nations and shortly thereafter abstained from voting on the Libya resolution to establish a no-fly zone. Thus, the FRG had clearly positioned itself against the interests of the USA, which could be seen as a violation of the Secret State Treaty of May 21, 1949 and the **Chancellor's Act.**[482] So at least the interpretation in a video with the title **"Eye Opener! The Subjugation of the Chancellors of the FRG"**[483] Whether this corresponds to the truth, one will probably never find out. The EHEC epidemic was one of the largest ever experienced in the FGR. 53 people died.[484] And there *are* some indications that this was staged: the pathogen appeared as if from nowhere and vanished just as quickly, without the trigger for it being discovered. The ebbing of the disease, at the end of June 2011, coincided with Merkel's unannounced trip to the United States on June 21. In a review of the situation more than two years later, Spiegel online asked the following: [485] *Did the federal government deceive the public over the 2011 Ehec scandal? After more than 3800 people became ill with the intestinal germ Ehec, the authorities presented the alleged carrier.*

In fact, according to Foodwatch, only a tenth of the cases were attributed to him. One year after Foodwatch presented its first report, the Institute (Robert Koch Institute) acknowledged that to date only 350 of the 3842 Ehec disorders could be explained ... However, since the total number was significantly higher, it follows that the majority of sufferers were not associated with one of the outbreak clusters known to Task Force Ehec and/or that the number of sufferers per cluster could be significantly higher than that known either by RKI (Robert Koch Institute) or the Task Force. [486]

The suspicion that **AIDS is a bioweapon developed in secret military laboratories** is well-founded. Those who collaborated with Wolfgang Eggert in the writing of his book *Planned epidemics AIDS, SARS and military genetic research* give tangible evidence.[487] A review****** read: *The book reveals that, as has long been suspected, organic weapons are out of control. Why else is the pharmaceutical industry not interested in drugs that physically suppress the virus instead? After all, it's like a money-printing machine when no vaccine or medicine comes on the market. As a person affected, I know what I'm talking about.*

Such a conclusion, citing a *money-printing machine* for the pharmaceutical industry, written down by a person affected, might seem obvious. But is it true? Is the pharmaceutical industry, or its directors, really so unscrupulous? Or are these artificially created diseases (assuming they are by-products of scientific research, which has not yet been proven) genuinely incurable? Here's a statement from a highly respected scientist, Clifford Cranicom, who reports a meeting between an investigative journalist and a well-placed military source:[488]

1. *The operation is a joint project between the Pentagon and the pharmaceutical industry.*
2. *The Pentagon wants to test biological diseases for war purposes on unsuspecting populations. SARS was*

****** at Amazon.de

found to be a mistake in that the expected mortality rate should have been 80%.

3. *The pharmaceutical industry earns trillions from medications designed to treat both deadly and non-fatal diseases that infect people.*

4. *Bacteria and viruses are freeze-dried and then attached to fine threads for release.*

5. *Metals released together with the pathogens are warmed by the sun, creating a perfect environment for bacteria and viruses to multiply in the air.*

6. *Most countries sprayed are unaware of the activities and have not agreed to them. He explains that airliners are one of the distribution systems.*

7. *Most of the 'actors' are old friends and business partners of President Bush Senior.*

8. *The ultimate aim is to control all populations through targeted and accurate spraying of drugs, diseases, etc.*

9. *People who have tried to reveal the truth have been incarcerated and killed.*

Items 5 and 6 refer, of course, to Chemtrails.

That the reference to artificially created diseases applies especially to the AIDS epidemic (and probably also to Ebola) is suggested by the authorial collective around Wolfgang Eggert. In an interview, Eggert analyses why official explanations/assumptions about the origin of AIDS discussed in the media are so unlikely.[489]

At the same time Markus Egert (not to be confused with Eggert) describes one of the official versions/conjectures about the development of AIDS as a common disease in his book *A Germ Rarely Comes Alone.*[††††††][490]: *Variants of the SI virus (Simian Immunodeficiency Virus) occurring in monkeys were found to have been probably transferred to humans several times in the early 20th century. Around 1920, Kinshasa may have been the type of HIV that is now widespread around the world, which then spread*

[††††††] In German, *Ein Keim kommt selten allein* (SP)

over decades in the Congo Basin before reaching the Caribbean in the 1960s and North America in the 1970s. A similar orthodox statement was made on Spiegel online:[491] ... *AIDS conspiracy theories are ongoing. There is no evidence for these, of course. Major Ebola outbreaks began in 1976 in the Democratic Republic of the Congo (formerly Zaire), the Republic of Congo, in today's South Sudan, Uganda and Gabon. As transmitters, researchers suspect apes and especially fruit bats. Humans are likely to become infected with the virus if they consume the meat of wild animals.* This statement precisely echoes the official version. Wolfgang Eggert begs to differ. Asked in an interview, *And how did the virus get into the public domain?* he answered as follows: *There are several complementary explanatory approaches circulating among AIDS pundits on this point. Again and again the hepatitis B vaccination plays a role, [a programme of] which was carried out in November 1978 exclusively on young sexually active homosexuals. That was in New York. Shortly thereafter, these vaccinations also took place in San Francisco and Los Angeles. And then AIDS appeared in exactly these cities, in the vicinity of exactly these test groups. It is really scary when you look at how quickly this experimental zone was infected with HIV. Interestingly, this hepatitis study was headed by the New York City Blood Center, which also supplied serums and blood to Central Africa at the time. So to the second epicentre of the development of AIDS. I am not the only one inclined to think that some of the supposed immunization products were contaminated with the super virus designed in 1969. Be it inadvertently or intentionally ...* [492]

Another article makes a clear statement about this qualification *whether by mistake or wilfully,* suggesting that AIDS was the first large-scale biological warfare experiment. ... *Dr Robert Strecker found that the AIDS virus was produced in the 1970s by the WHO [World Health Organization] in collaboration with the Cancer Institute at Fort Detrick in Maryland (USA). As official documents show, the political decision was taken on June 9, 1969.*[493]

Covid 19 - a bioweapon?

If the complete eradication of the virus is not successful, the only option left is to make the lockdown, i.e. the extensive stoppage of public life, permanent until a vaccine is available.[494]

No wonder that WHO scientists have identified the SARS/Corona virus so quickly. ... This unsupervised research is producing dangerous artificial viruses, many of which have the potential to be a bioweapon.
(Dr Alan Cantwell, virologist[495])

There is also a patent for Coronavirus, which has been spreading worldwide since the end of 2019. This patent was granted on 20 November 2018 under the number EP3172319A1 at the European Patent Office. [496] *'Corona' is a large family of viruses. There are several patents on Corona viruses, which anyone can look up on 'Google Patents'.*[497] This novel strain of Coronavirus, 2019-nCoV (or Covid 19) *first spreads undetected and with the symptoms of a mild flu and later leads toserious and fatal diseases such as pneumonia.(CAPS).*[498] Coronanavirus was first identified at the winter solstice of 2019 in the Chinese city of Wuhan.[††††††] The Chinese authorities soon quarantined Wuhan and other major Chinese cities with a total population of about 60 million. On January 30, 2020, the WHO (World Health Organization) declared an international health emergency.[499]

The fact that this virus was most likely developed in a bioweapons laboratory is not only evident from the patent granted for it – viruses of natural origin cannot be patented – it also follows from a genetic analysis: *Genetic material* (from Coronavirus) *was found in two different bat viruses in combination with the good old SARS virus. This pathogen appears to be artificial and therefore a bioweapon, unless bats at night secretly kiss fish infected with SARS. As pathogens, viruses are highly selective; without an intermediate*

[††††††] The capital of Hubei Province in the centre of the People's Republic of China (SP)

host, bat viruses cannot simply recombine with any fish virus. However, 2019-nCoV seems to do exactly that, which is extraordinary and, in my opinion, reinforces the suspicion that it was bred in a laboratory.[500] That the 2019-nCoV virus is not of natural origin, however, is classified as a false assertion in an article on zeit.de.[501]

Many Chinese believe that coronavirus was an attack aimed at weakening the country's economy, which is why the authorities had to take such a radical approach to contain the spread of the virus. Because, if the WHO were to classify the new virus as a global threat, it would be a pretext for China's enemies to quarantine the entire country with its 1.4 billion citizens, which would mean the end of China. [502]

As so often, the primary question of who's behind this requires the secondary question, 'Who benefits?' To which the video just quoted gives the following answer: *And viruses designed as bioweapons do not have to break out immediately. In a healthy person they could switch to hibernatory [or sleep] mode, in the form of a normal wave of flu and await activation ... in response to which they would then lethally switch on.*[503] This means that the outbreak of the disease could then occur at the same time as the next seasonal wave of influenza, which would then have pandemic potential.

What a corona pandemic would mean for us was simulated on October (18) 2019.[§§§§§§] The result of this simulation was: 65 million deaths within the next 18 months as well as a global economic crisis of unimagined extent. *The pandemic exercise, entitled 'Event 201', put participants in the middle of an uncontrolled coronavirus outbreak that spread like wildfire from South America and wreaked havoc around the world. 'In the simulation, CAPS (coronavirus) led to a death toll of 65 million people within 18 months,' said John Hopkins University.* On the same day, 18 October 2019, the Military Games (a sports event comparable to the Olympic Games) began in Wuhan, in which 9000 or so soldiers from 110

[§§§§§§] This simulation was carried out by its initiators, or actors, just weeks before the outbreak of the Corona epidemic. Now that's what I call inside information countries around the world took part. That was only a few weeks before the spread of Coronavirus began. This may mean that a large proportion of the soldiers involved in these military games became infected with the coronavirus, which then spread to the population after returning to their home countries.

The fact that the whole thing is an NWO (New World Order) project is suggested by the list of participants and initiators of this pandemic exercise Event 201, including globalization fanatics Bill Gates and Tom Inglesby of the John Hopkins Center for Health Security. As a result of the simulation, the call for increased efforts towards globalization is raised: **Event 201 calls for globalism as a solution to pandemics.**[504] *The intention that they (the globalists) are pursuing with this is that governments will and should cede their societal obligation regarding health care, their power and their responsibility to an international body, namely the World Health Organization.*[505]

Another aspect seems to play a role: namely the outbeak represents a huge business model for the pharmaceutical industry, which would make billions of dollars in profits if a Coronavirus vaccine were now to come on to the market. *The World Bank has for the first time (mid-2017) set up a pandemic fund to provide emergency financing for a pandemic outbreak worth 500 million dollars ... Equity fund for a pandemic. The reason why they are doing this is the idea that you can make a lot of money with a pandemic in the near future.* And lo and behold, after less than 2 years a pandemic breaks out, and the virus is exactly the same as the one that the pandemic rehearsal Event 201 revolved around. [506]

The same globalists who own the virus patent and who first predicted and initiated the rise and spread of the virus now announced that they would develop vaccines for the deadly coronavirus. According to business insiders, 'a coalition supported by Bill Gates is funding biotech companies' that are trying to develop a coronavirus vaccine. So what do you think? Is this all just a big coincidence? [507] And who knows if such a vaccine will again have side-

effects such as those deriving from the Spanish Flu vaccinations of 1919/20 (see section "Vaccinated with glyphosate").
More contagious than any virus is the fear of being infected. [508] And fear would lead many people getting vaccinated against coronavirus.

In the case of Italy, where an above-average number of fatalities of the corona "pandemic" have been recorded, a comparison with the "Spanish flu" from 1918 to 1920, which caused about 20 million deaths, is striking. However, the "Spanish flu" was apparently triggered by mass vaccinations (for details see section "Vaccinated with glyphosate"). It has since become clear that mass vaccinations had indeed been carried out in parts of Italy. *According to bergamonews.it, 185,000 flu vaccinations were ordered in Bergamo in October 2019. ... Furthermore, according to bsnews.it, in January 2020, ie shortly before the alleged Corona massacre, 34,000 people were vaccinated due to a meningitis emergency in Brescia and, nota bene, Bergamo.* [509]

Whether the number of deaths caused by Coronavirus will actually increase as drastically as the simulation shown (pandemic exercise Event 201), will depend decisively on how badly humans have already been damaged by poisons from the air we breathe and the food we eat (see High-Tech Bioweapons – Hell's annex, chapter 6, 2, subsection *Now for the bad news*) and how much fear is spread by the media, which is known to increase stress levels. Finally, long-lasting isolation and anxiety lead to spiralling depression and weakening of health.

The repeated grossly negligent, disastrous handling of medical statistics, in particular by the head of the Robert Koch Institute (RKI), Profes-sor Wieler, has - essentially left uncorrected by the second decisive medical advisor of the Federal Government, Professor Drosten - caused a tsunami of fear and panic in the minds and souls of the population, which can hardly be stopped even with the most well-founded and persistent medical education. [510]

But the crisis is largely a foregone conclusion. The white figures indicate (and this is not my opinion now, but what doctors are saying - I'm only quoting them because they don't get a word in edgewise) that this corona pandemic will proceed more or less like a severe flu epidemic, but in Germany it will be considerably lighter than a flu epidemic. So there is no reason at all for this lockdown. ...There is no overloading of the health care system. ... My demand is that all lockdown measures be lifted now and that no new measures such as compulsory masks and compulsory vaccinations and whatever else may come.[511] The Corona state of emergency is a staging.

The WHO kills?

A non-validated and non-diagnostic
approved test provides the pretext for the application of an
life-threatening medication - and all this with a
Infectious disease for which there is as yet no evidence that it ex-
ceeds the risk of annual flu.[512]

As is well known, the normal global episodes of illness have been referred to as 'pandemics' since the swine flu of 2009 in an inflationary manner and focusing on individual pathogens. In this context, vigilance and historically justified mistrust have long been called for. For if our normal, changing and globally circulating viral winter guests, such as the H1N1 viruses in 2009 (swine flu), already meet the criteria of a pandemic, then the term has become meaningless ... From a medical point of view, and considering the available data, special precautions are now superfluous - even if the government says otherwise.[513] The lung specialist and epidemiologist Dr. Wolfgang Wodarg found out in his research: *The area-wide testing, the fixation on respiratory stations, the emptying of clinics for the announced flood of Covid-19 victims and triage exercises caused panic and thus made it possible for a highly intimidated population to obey. But why? What makes the government so sure that it considers it necessary to annul the Basic Law in essential parts, to drive the middle class into bankruptcy and to let workers and employees fall into unemployment? What else is threatening us?*[514]

The WHO kills? ... A blatant question, which unfortunately must be answered YES, if Dr. Wolfgang Wodarg, internist, pulmonologist and specialist for hygiene and environmental medicine, is right with his report about the background of the numerous Corvid 19 deaths in Italy, Spain and New York. The result of his research is that the WHO recommends a drug (the anti-malaria drug hydroxychloroquine (HCQ)) for the treatment of people suffering from Covid-19, which can kill them if they lack a certain enzyme ('G6PD deficiency'[*******]). But this is exactly what happened to many of the Covid-19 victims in Italy, Spain and New York. It *must be noted that a high prevalence of G6PD deficiency has also been described for some regions of Italy, and that in Italy up to 71 percent of those who tested positive with PCR, as well as the staff, had a prophylactic high level of HCQ. The same applies to Spain.*[515]

How many times this lethal combination has resulted in victims is unknown. There has been no discussion of the issue among those responsible in the WHO and in governments. There is also a frightening lack of knowledge and responsibility among doctors who are responsible for the treatment of Covid-19 patients or for the staff treating them.
Once again, this connection applies not only to Africa, but also to large parts of Asia, South and Central America, Arabia and the Mediterranean region.[516] *And in the course of global migration in recent years, a large proportion of the population in Europe, the USA and Australia also originates from countries where G6PD shortages are widespread.* ***These cases have nothing to do with Covid-19 disease. A PCR test result leading to the prophylactic***

[*******] *"It's something called glucose-6 dehydrogenase deficiency, or 'G6PD deficiency', one of the most common genetic peculiarities, which can lead to threatening haemolysis (dissolution of red blood cells) in most men when certain drugs or chemicals are taken". ... such as the hydroxychloroquine (HCQ) recommended by the WHO for the treatment of Covid-19.*

prescription of HCQ is sufficient to cause severe disease in up to a third of the people from high-risk populations treated in this way.[517] Dr. Wodarg goes even further by saying:[518] *"...and I think this is grossly negligent homicide, what is happening here. And if the WHO programs it that way, ignores it, even recommends it as an exceptional medication, which is now being taken out of necessity; for me it is nothing more than killing a lot of people in a targeted manner, so that we get scared, so that fear is created in Africa, in Brazil, so that we take this disease seriously and say, yes, it is so bad, and we urgently need vaccination. That is perfidious, it is diabolical, it is something for the public prosecutor. It's not for the epidemiologist anymore. It's so obvious.*

The Corona Panic is a staging

The Corona Panic is a staging, it's a scam. It's high time we understood that we're in the middle of a worldwide and mafia-like crime.
(Press conference of " Wir Ärzte für Aufklärung "[†††††††] on 7.5.2020)

This year, the German Television Award honours Corona reporting with a special prize. The prizewinners in the first are: ...: Editors-in-chief of ARD and WDR, responsible for ARD extra: Die Corona-Lage."[519],[‡‡‡‡‡‡‡]

As with climate hysteria, fear and insecurity are generated in the population and are firmly planted in their brains. This "corona fear" is now firmly anchored in many people's minds and has developed such a momentum that many are convinced that they will die in agony if they are infected with the "dangerous" virus. In the news

---

[†††††††] „ We Doctors for Enlightenment "

[‡‡‡‡‡‡‡] *Texto original: „Der deutsche Fernsehpreis würdigt die Corona-Berichterstattung in diesem Jahr mit einem Sonderpreis. Die Preisträger im Ersten sind: ...: Chefredakteure von ARD und WDR, zuständig für ARD extra: Die Corona-Lage. "*

of the public media pictures of people falling down in the streets, stacked coffins, crowded hospitals in Wuhan, Italy, Spain, New York, ... Shuddering stories are spread about how the virus is raging all over the world, and figures are faked to show how many people have died from the Corona virus. *Agonizing death from the corona virus.* ***COVID-19 in the final phase is like drowning, only slower.*** This is the lurid headline in "THE FREE WORLD": *"Those who die from the consequences of COVIC-19 experience their end in full consciousness. Reports from Italy correspond exactly with those from China. The affected person(s) have the feeling of slowly and lonely drowning."*[520] People are awakened to the primal fears of suffocation as a result of a corona infection. The pattern is exactly the same as we have already experienced with the climate hysteria. Placing people in fear and panic leads to people without will, with whom anything can be done, even depriving them of their fundamental rights, as we have seen in the context of the corona crisis.

After the three-month withdrawal of civil liberties, a habituation effect and conditioning of the population began to emerge from June 2020, where they learned to come to terms with the restrictions. An obvious symbol of this new "normality" is the wearing of mouth/nose protection masks in public places, not only in the prescribed supermarkets, petrol stations, DIY stores, public transport and on the premises of public authorities. No, also on the street, also in private cars, even when people are travelling alone. People who refuse to accept this "normality" and do not wear a mask in the supermarket, for example, will be attacked, in the worst case they will be thrown out and/or the public order office will be called in, where they will face heavy fines. And as announced by various politicians and their experts, there will be a "2nd wave", which should ensure a further continuation of the disenfranchisement of the population. The Covid-19 law (Covid-19-Regulatory Extension Act[§§§§§§§]), which was passed by the Bundestag on 16 June 2020, serves exactly this purpose. Together with the Infection Protection Act, this ensures a possible continuation of

---

[§§§§§§§] Covid-19-Rechtsverordnungsweitergeltungsgesetz

the co-rona measures until 31 March 2022 (!). It can be assumed that this 2nd wave is certain to come, namely the next seasonal wave of influenza, which can then easily be relabelled as the 2nd wave.

An essential component of the new "normality" is the requirement that people in public spaces should keep a distance of 1.5 ... 2 m between themselves. This requirement ensures that people can be clearly identified by the new vision recognition systems, a basic prerequisite for seamless control and tracking of people's movements. This new "normality" also includes the restriction of the freedom to travel, not only in the direction of other countries, no, also within the country. This is already indicated by the mass "positive tests" carried out by the employees of the Tönnies slaughterhouse, and subsequently also by the poultry breeder "Wiesenhof".******** The consequence, restrictions also on the freedom of travel between neighbouring districts. These restrictions on travel are a major goal of the elite, because they can keep people under control more effectively. This can be classified as part of the demand "Bring everyone close to the cities" (as a section in Part 1 of this book series reads: "2025 - The penultimate act"). These travel restrictions also prevent effective public resistance by the population. Demonstrations can no longer take place on a large scale. Experience has taught us that demonstrations directed against the restriction of freedom are stopped by the police on a

---

******** *"Almost all animals for slaughter have been vaccinated against corona for years...an exemplary vaccine for cattle is: "Rotavec® Corona". Similar vaccines are also available for pigs and poultry. Conversely, this means that in almost all slaughterhouses, corona fragments in the aerosols ghost through the farm. These are then regularly inhaled by employees and can lead to so-called "cross-reactions". Why is this not discussed in a broader context?*
If experts are already pointing out that such cross-reactions can occur in slaughterhouses, why don't we take a closer look at this? If there is no discourse, the suspicion will rise that the whole thing is no longer about medicine and health, but only about a less well-intentioned political agenda.
Surely such a question must be allowed? Another interesting aspect would be the scientifically ascertainable degree of contagion among production employees - as opposed to those in administration. If there were a significant difference there, this would speak for the cross-reaction mentioned in the manual, i.e. meat-processing, area of the company." (net find)

massive scale and with brute force. On the other hand, demonstrations are tolerated which are beneficial to the system or at least cannot be dangerous to it (examples are "Frydays for Future" and "BlackLivesMatter"). In these demonstrations the restrictions on civil liberties are practically not enforced.

Nevertheless, there is hope, with real experts in the health field raising their voices and exposing the Corona Panic for what it is, a staging, a worldwide crime, behind which the WHO is behind, a tentacle of the Deep State, the coming New World Order NWO. These experts are either hushed up by the public media, or their competence is denied:

We 'Doctors of Reconnaissance' criticize the measures taken in the wake of Covid 19 as excessive. The measures we are all experiencing have nothing to do with adequate suppression of a virus. So, who is actually being suppressed here? We do not have the plague. And this year's corona virus, SARS-Cov2, is behaving in the same way as seasonal flu viruses, which we actually have every year. That's basically good news. The bad news is that we're all experiencing a panik. [521]
It is currently being argued that the measures should be maintained more or less until the entire population can be saved by vaccination. A year and a half of a 'new normality' without holidays, festivals, cultural and sporting events is demanded and compulsory vaccinations, compulsory tests, tracking and immunity apps are promised. [522]
However: *The majority of experts can already no longer deny that the danger of infection in Germany and its neighbouring countries is over, without embarrassing themselves for the rest of their careers. And yet, there are people in governments, government offices and the scientific community who want to lock us up with fear and carry on with their activities.* [523]

We are accustomed to seeing authorities fail collectively on a regular basis, ... But there seems to be a quality to it ... where the neuralgic points are obviously occupied by people who have a job to do. Because that is what is behind it, ... That means that the ques-

tion is now open, of course, whether this is a criminal action running in the background, which is simply not discussed with anyone.[524] This is the assessment of Andreas Popp from www.wissensmanufaktur.net in response to the almost 200-page analysis [††††††††],[525] of the shutdown by a speaker in the KM4 (Critical Infrastructure Protection) department of the Ministry of the Interior. The reaction of the Ministry of the Interior and the mainstream media (Tagesschau) was timely: they placed this analysis and its content in the realm of conspiracy theories.

A systematic fraud:

"After the government has demonized CO2 in the interplay with the lie press due to a science fraud, the attack on the air we breathe (O2) follows. According to the new narrative, the air is contaminated with an invisible pathogen and free breathing is correspondingly highly dangerous to deadly." [‡‡‡‡‡‡‡‡]

"The most important point here is to understand that 'Corona' in that sense does not exist. It is a mild cold that occurs every year and causes the death of those with a compromised immune system. The deaths in Wuhan, which Merkel visited in September 2019 (strange), go back to 5G. The emission of the electromagnetic disease signature[§§§§§§§§] *by pulsed microwaves was (intentionally?) too strong; the pulmonary alveoli burst and the sick people spat*

[††††††††] *A speaker in Unit KM4, that is 'Protection of Critical Infrastructures of the Federal Ministry of the Interior for Building and Homeland Affairs' has, after unsuccessful attempts to talk to superiors about his alarming and extensive analysis and the effects of the shutdown, sent this to the crisis management team and its specialist working groups at federal level in all resors as well as with the states of all federal states, i.e. a huge distribution list. His request to submit the alert to the minister had been rejected without examination of the content. An informant from the circle of those contacted provided the explosive analysis.*

[‡‡‡‡‡‡‡‡] *There is neither a correlation between atmospheric CO2 levels and climate change nor a scientific experiment that proves such a connection. Similar to the Corona scam, the theory is based solely and exclusively on models that can be calibrated at will by the "scientists" to say what the client wants them to say.* (Correlation in the sense that the CO2 content has a major impact on climate change)

[§§§§§§§§] For details see section "'5G' and Transhumanism".

blood. To hide this, they were cremated directly. The Covid-19 hype is like a curtain, so we can't see what's happening behind the curtain. Behind the curtain two powers are struggling: The Deep State worldwide and the forces of light. For the DS/Illuminati (in witch's language "Moreya" - The Conquering Wind) it is the last chance to introduce the New World Order; hence Corona, and at the same time the attempt to implant all of humanity through mass vaccinations, abolish cash, eliminate Trump, etc." [526]

Both the climate swindle and the corona swindle are an attack on human freedom and prosperity. While humanity bleeds, the power elite rubs its hands. The Corona fraud is an example of how the state does not protect us from criminal activities. In practice, the state serves as a vehicle for criminals to realise their claim to world domination. So anyone who wants to solve the problem with new laws and regulations is merely feeding the beast.
*Just as plants cannot thrive without CO2, so humans suffer without oxygen. According to the Warburg Effect, lack of oxygen leads to hyperacidity, which turns the organism into an optimal environment for parasites and infections. So if you wear a respiratory mask and cannot get UV light because you are afraid to go outside because of corona hysteria, you increase your risk of illness.*********,[527]

********* *UV light converts oxygen (O2) into ozone (O3). Ultraviolet radiation is used to treat water, air and surfaces. Due to the speed of the reaction - microbes are inactivated within fractions of a second if a sufficient dose is applied - UV lamps can be used not only to disinfect surfaces but also to disinfect water, air or even air flows guided in air-conditioning ducts. (see Wikipedia)*

Corona - The coup from above

__The NWO program:__
Refugee crisis,
CO2 crisis,
Corona crisis,
Economic crisis
... Crash
TAKEOVER THE POWER

We are on the verge of a global transformation, all we need is the right all-encompassing crisis and the nations will agree to the new world order.[††††††††††] (David Rockefeller)

What damage does this lockdown cause? And it's not just damage that is short-term or that has been left fallow for a short time. It is the destruction of the entire economy. If you look at the whole thing in connection with the last few years, where the economy has already been destroyed without this Chinese sniffle argumentation, it could obviously be ... almost a __finale of a concerted action that was planned for many years.__[528] And exactly this assessment hits the mark; in my earlier book "Germany in Free Fall" I had already described how the policy of the German government was directed against the German economy and obviously had the goal of destabilizing the country.

Actually, the "European Green Deal", announced by the head of the EU Commission on December 11, 2019, was intended to trigger the crash predicted by many economic experts (see section "Climate emergency"). With the corona hype, things are now moving even faster, and the blame for the economic crash can now be placed on the corona "pandemic". *... because this slight cold, inflated to a (pseudo) pandemic, is supposed to create global chaos*

[††††††††††] 1994 before the United Nations Economic Committee (UN Business Council). (*https://wahrheitinside.wordpress.com/2017/04/19/zitate-zur-neuen-weltordnung/*)

188

at the last moment, if the Satanist élite has its way! FEAR[‡‡‡‡‡‡‡‡‡‡]
(engl.: fear = something based on 'erroneous data that appears to be real', is exactly what has been successfully used during centuries of mass hypnosis and is supposed to work this time as well, and as we can see from the whole panic, it does![529] *... These measures are self-destructive. And, if society accepts and implements them, it is akin to collective suicide.* (Professor Sucharit Bhakdi [530])

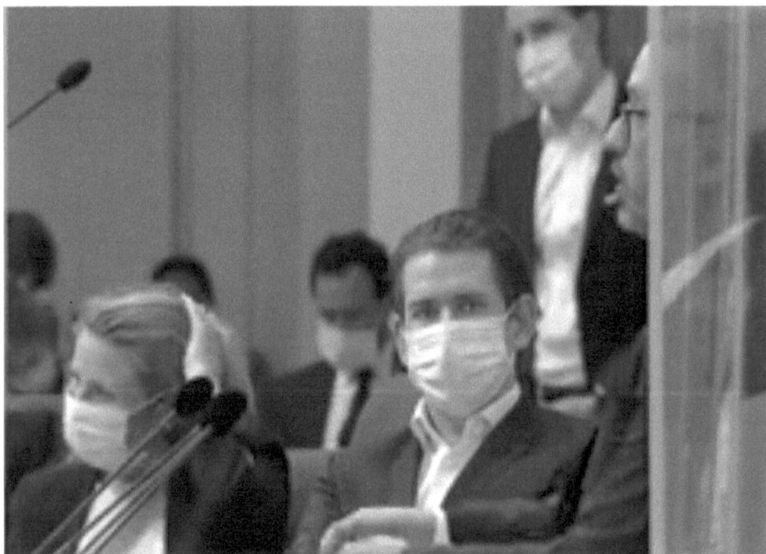

Figure 50: A picture for the history books - I: The Austrian Parliament takes stock after 5 weeks of exceptional circumstances. [531]

[‡‡‡‡‡‡‡‡‡‡] *Chaos* would appear to be the prerequisite for people's acceptance of the New World Order (as Rockefeller virtually proposes); indeed itwill be longed for as a release from the great crisis. The Satanic élite are closely linked to the Deep State (more on this in the chapter "Epilogue – Élite and Deep State")

Figure 51: A picture for the history books - II: Demonstrators demonstrate against the creeping annulment of Basic Law. [532]

Figure 52: A picture for the history books - III: Chemnitz on 18.04.20, arrests of demonstrators opposed to the creeping annulment of Basic Law. [533]

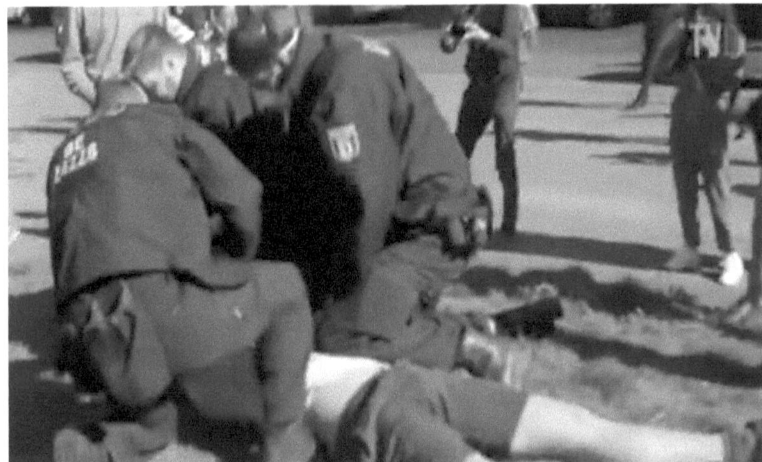

Figure 53 A picture for the history books - IV: Berlin on 18.04.20, arrests of demonstrators opposing the creeping annulment of Basic Law. [534]

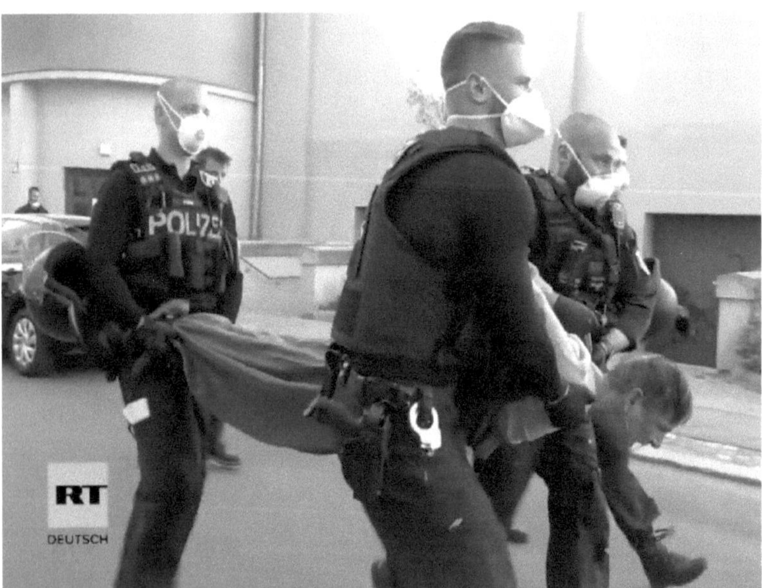

Figure 54: A picture for the history books – V

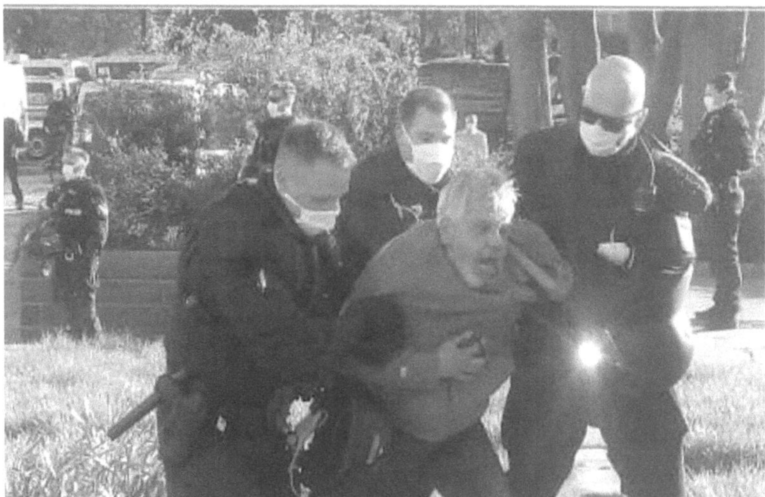

Figure 55: A picture for the history books - VI: Senior citizens who take to the streets to stand up for their rights are taken away like serious criminals.

Figure 56: A picture for the history books – VII.

Figure 57: A picture for the history books – VIII.

Measures so far taken by politicians to contain the virus have had a negative impact not only on public health, but also on the national economy, especially on small and medium-sized enterprises, which are no longer able to cover their running costs. It will lead to thousands of small to medium-sized enterprises being abandoned. The financial aid promised by politicians to these companies will not stop this process of destruction; on the contrary, the loans promised will still have to be repaid at some point, and one-off aid payments will be recovered by the State via the tax office.[§§§§§§§§§]

Measures taken by the politicians have also served the following agenda:[535]
- *Corona hysteria is perfect for restricting or abolishing civil rights.*
- *Corona makes it possible for people to voluntarily place themselves under quarantine, which is nothing more than another form of detention.*
- *Corona makes it possible for us to get used to increased police and military presence on our streets.*

[§§§§§§§§§] How many times have we seen this – that the public pays for everything, the rich for nothing? (SP)

- Corona makes it possible that people are no longer allowed or willing to gather! Restriction of the freedom of assembly (France's yellow vests are fading!)
- Corona makes it possible that people can be vaccinated against their will and at the same time be microchipped. The constitutional 'physical integrity of a human life' has then become passé.
- Corona makes it possible to abolish cash, under the pretext of avoiding contagion.
- Corona makes total surveillance possible in order to maintain public order.
- Corona is the perfect alibi for the breakdown of the financial system. It keeps the real reasons and the real culprits in the background.
- Corona may distract from the fact that the people in Wuhan have fallen ill and died from 5G radiation, but not from the virus. Because in Wuhan, 5G has been completely rolled out and in operation since autumn 2019! Was Corona invented to deflect from the exposure to 5G?[**********]
- The Corona virus creates fear. This fear is more contagious than the virus. And it seems deliberate! Because once a person is afraid, they let it all happen to them. (net find)
And you can always extend the curfew.

On 8 April 2020, the lawyer Beate Bahner filed an emergency petition with the Federal Constitutional Court against this **coup from above.** In this emergency petition, she complained that the Corona Ordinances issued by the federal and state governments were "blatantly unconstitutional". *The reason for an emergency petition is, according to the lawyer, confirmed by the fact that the Federal Republic of Germany is on the way to becoming a* **'dictatorial police state'** *by 'restricting almost all basic rights'. Bahner also fears for her freedom through arrest and police custody, as she would receive a visit from the Heidelberg police.* [536]
This urgent application was rejected on 10 April 2020. *Unfortunately, I did not succeed in saving the constitutional state and the free democratic basic order in Germany, especially our*

[**********] Of course, another possibility is that 5G radiation lowers resistance to Coronavirus (SP) *constitutionally anchored basic rights and the unbreakable human rights from the worst global attack and the lightning-fast establishment of the most inhuman tyranny the world has ever seen. Today, the rule of law is dead. ...*[537]

But what she certainly hadn't expected was that she was then taken to a psychiatric ward by police force and treated like a dangerous felon when she was arrested. [538]

Forecast - What's next?

Dress rehearsal for the emergency? - Step by step we slide where we don't want to go. (Henryk M. Broder)[539]

This constitution is in grave danger. - Keyword Corona. And I would like to take this opportunity to show that what is happening in this country is extremely dangerous for this country, and that the numbers 33, 89 and 20, i.e. 2020, can be mentioned in one sentence. For what is happening here before our eyes at the moment is a scandal and a **medium catastrophe if we do not oppose to those who are doing that. ... Anyone who openly displays the Basic Law in Merkel Germany will be picked up by the police.**[540]

"We are on the verge of a global transformation, ...", triggered and initiated by the WHO, the long arm of private donors, mainly financed by the Bill Gates Foundation. That there is a strategic plan behind it, worked out in think tanks, can be seen, for example, in the fact that the politicians in connection with the reunification had taken a series of measures which made the transition from the FRG to the NWO very simple. Since 1990, the FRG is not a state, but a limited liability company. The responsible politicians had deregistered the FRG on 3.10.1990 at the UNO as a state and had legally repealed the German Basic Law on 17.07.1990 by deleting its scope of application, article 23, on 17.07.1990. Without scope a law is void. The objection that this is now in the preamble is irrelevant, because the preamble is not part of the law.

The Federal Republic of Germany, the Bundestag and all its authorities, cities and municipalities are companies registered in commercial registers. During the last decades many state institutions have been transformed into private enterprises, in the health care system, the Federal Railway; the BRD-Finanz-GmbH" in Frankfurt was founded. The Unification Treaty[†††††††††††] and the 2+4 Treaty are invalid or not ratified. These privatisations as well as the fact that there is still no peace treaty with Germany also simplifies the transition of the BRD into the NWO. The fact that a peace treaty was not intended at all follows from the minutes of the French presidency of the negotiations on the 2+4 Treaty on 17 July 1990: *The FRG agrees with the declaration of the four powers and underlines that the events or circumstances mentioned in this declaration will not occur, i.e. that a peace treaty or a peace settlement is not intended. The GDR agrees to the declaration made by the FRG.* [541] This protocol clearly proves that the Germans, represented by the then Foreign Minister, Genscher, and the representative of the GDR, Meckel, prevented the peace treaty.

All this means that from a legal point of view, the foundation stone and the legal prerequisites for the planned transition of the FRG to the NWO were already created in the 1990s. And, as already mentioned, the Germans can no longer refer to their Basic Law, as they did during the numerous demonstrations during the Corona crisis (see Figures 51-57).

Thngs are likely to continue as described in the 'Weizsäcker quote': *For the sake of maintaining power, the world population will be reduced to a minimum. This will be achieved by means of artificially created illnesses, with bioweapons de-clarified as epidemics* ... (see Prologue – The Road to Tyranny). Covid 19 is only the beginning[††††††††††]. Further pandemic outbreaks will fol-

---

[†††††††††††] The Social Court of Berlin, in its judgement of an action for negation of 19.05.1992 (file number S 56 Ar 239/92), found that the so-called 'Einigungsvertrag' of 31.08.1990 (BGBl.1990, Part II, page 890) was invalid, since one could not join something that had already been dissolved on 17.07.1990.
[††††††††††] More precisely, the beginning actually came much earlier (see Are Ebola, AIDS, SARS and EHEC biological weapons?, chapter 6, 3)

low: real outbreaks as well as those hyped in the media. These will no doubt be blamed on those who demonstrated against the creeping erosion of Common Law[§§§§§§§§§§] and who thereby had the effrontery to undermine the 'protective measures' of global governments (see Figures 51-57). And the "second wave", which in prophetic prediction has been announced several times by some politicians, e.g. Söder, with threatening forefinger, in order to appease the critics, will come; it will be more dangerous than the "first wave", for which the exemption rules were issued at the end of March 2020. The "second wave" will coincide with the next seasonal wave of flu at the latest. More likely, however, it will come earlier, triggered by the widespread roll-out of 5G, for which 5G transmission masts have been installed in many conurbations since 2020 and hundreds of communications satellites have been launched into near-Earth space. Since the frequencies of the 5G bands are in the same frequency range as the frequencies in which human cells communicate with each other. 5G will massively interfere with our immune defences. The immune system, which also consists of cells, can be disturbed by this 5G radiation and as a result can no longer optimally combat invading viruses when the radiation intensity is sufficiently high. So if the people in charge of the 5G network start to use it across the whole area, people will become more susceptible to all kinds of germs, bacteria and viruses, including the Covid-19 virus. Everyone who is infected will have problems once 5G is up and running. The higher the level of radiation, the more dramatic their illness will be. The consequence will be that the morbidity and mortality rate in the population will increase compared to the "first wave". And then people will say "We have warned you. You did not hear. We have to tighten the exception rules again to save the population." But the fact that 5G is what makes the virus so dangerous will be ignored.

Eventually, a vaccine serum will be launched on the market that is supposed to protect people from Covid 19 and thus hold out the prospect of a return to normal. This serum for these epidemics will contain substances that are not good for people (see Glyphosate – a

---

[§§§§§§§§§§] Basic Law in Germany (SP)

cause of *genetic damage*, chapter 6, 8), may make them ill and even keep them in a state of sickness. It is also possible that a new strain of SARS covid ... virus, also produced in the laboratory, will be added to this serum, leading to a new influenza outbreak. This new vaccine will be of a new quality by intervening directly in the human genome, which is not the case with the classical vaccines used so far. For the first time in the history of vaccination, these so-called *"mRNA vaccines of the latest generation intervene directly in the hereditary substance, in the genetic material of the human/patient and thus change the individual genetic material in the sense of a genetic manipulation that has been forbidden, even criminal, up to now. This intervention can be compared with that of genetically manipulated food, which is also very controversial. Although the media and politicians are currently trivialising the issue, and are even unreflectively calling for a new type of vaccination in order to be able to return to normality, such a vaccination is problematic in terms of health, moral and ethical issues and also in terms of genetic damage, which, in contrast to the damage caused by previous vaccinations, will now be irreversible, irreversible and irreparable. "* [542]

This new vaccine could have devastating consequences for people in a similar way to the 1918 "Spanish flu" (see section "Vaccinated with glyphosate"). And this new flu outbreak ultimately serves to further tighten the emergency regulations. There will again be a two-class vaccine, one for ordinary people and one for the government, the members of the Bundestag and the state parliaments, just as was done in 2009 with the swine flu. [543] (see chapter 7. "How does the elite protect themselves from their own weapons?").

Many people will refuse this vaccination. These vaccination refusers can also be accused again of being responsible for the next "pandemic" outbreak. For those who have been vaccinated, the state of emergency will be eased, they will regain relatively normal living conditions and will be able to travel again. Those who refuse to be vaccinated will be denied this. For those who refuse to be vaccinated, the stricter conditions of the state of emergency will continue. The new "Corona App", which is automatically installed on the mobile phones, serves as a check and clearly allocates whether the mobile phone owner has been vaccinated or not. This makes it very easy to monitor whether the unvaccinated are meeting or participating in public events, etc. Even without this app this is already possible today, namely via an identification chip which is incorporated in every identity card and can be controlled via radio.

Thus, another component of **"divide and conquer"** will be applied on this "pandemic battlefield" (see page 5): **vaccinated people against vaccination refusers.** In this way, people will be concerned with themselves and will not recognize and hold responsible the real causers of the conditions. Many people will die, some as a result of the artificially created biological weapons, others as a result of the psycho-attrition war that accompanies them, others as a result of the economic catastrophe that has been brought about. All this will then lead to the great catastrophe of bare survival, in the struggle for daily bread. This is then "the real all-encompassing crisis" that Rockefeller had predicted as a prerequisite for the establishment of the "new world order". As a result, there will inevitably be a strong population reduction (see Agenda 2025, chapter 1).

The prescribed curfews serve another purpose. In the shadow of these measures, few people will notice how secretly, quietly and silently 5G antennas are being placed all over the country, sometimes hidden in chimneys, street lamps, in inconspicuous street posts, near schools, hospitals, sports fields, parking lots in front of large shopping malls and other central locations where many people live every day. Few people will register this, not only because of the initial restrictions, but because they are distracted and focused on "corona", which will remain the number one topic in the mainstream media. Virtually all the content of the hourly news, talk shows and entertainment programmes revolve around this one topic.*********** In parallel to the widespread installation of the 5G

*********** For UK citizens a similar situation existed around Brexit. For about three years Brexit dominated the political and media agenda to the detriment of far more important humanitarian issues in the UK and around the world – issues such as the refugee crisis, the survival of the NHS (National Health Service) in the face masts, hundreds of satellites will be launched by billionaire Elon Musk's private space company SpaceX to ensure 5G communications across the globe. Once 5G is fully operational, people will find themselves in a giant microwave oven, which will further weaken their health (see section "'5G' and transhumanism").

And then it will continue as outlined in the section. "The Nightmare". The year 2020 is an important year that will set the course, either in a direction as described here, i.e. towards the NWO and thus the enslavement of humanity, or towards the destruction of the Deep State, the driving force behind the Agenda 2025. (see end of chapter "8. The Final - Conclusion").

Bee and other insect death

Once the bee disappears from the earth, humans have only four years to live.
(Albert Einstein[†])

For several years, a massive death rate for bees and other insects has been registered. Worldwide 40% of species are undergoing dramatic rates of decline. In the UK the large shaggy bee (*Panurgus banksianus*), found along the Southern English and Welsh coast, has declined by more than 54% since 1980. The smooth-gastered furrow bee (*Lasioglossum parvulum*) has declined by 40% during the same period. The tree bumblebee (*Bombus*

---

of largely secret trade attacks made on it by the US and others; human rights failures everywhere (in Guantanamo Bay just for example); unrestrained pollution of land, sea, and air; spiralling homelessness; not forgetting the fact that a large number of the earth's population have insufficient food and dirty drinking water. It would now appear that for UK citizens Covid distraction continued where Brexit distraction left off. This is the not-so-new politics: the politics of perpetual distraction. (SP)

[†] This much-quoted statement by Einstein is certainly exaggerated, and it is not at all certain that Albert Einstein really said it. Nevertheless, a true core is contained in the fact that a large proportion of our supermarket food could no longer be offered if the bees ceased to pollinate the flowering plants

hypnorum), on the other hand, which colonised the UK as recently as 2001, has spread rapidly, though figures are not given; and the lobe-spurred furrow bee (*Lasioglossum pauxillum*) has experienced a five-fold increase. Generally, though, the situation has been described as an *extinction crisis*.[‡‡‡‡‡‡‡‡‡‡‡]

So who are the bee killers ...? [544]

In the media, various causes are discussed: for example, Varroa mites, brought into Germany from Asia, affect bees, but also the massive use of insecticides, herbicides, fungicides, and growth regulators. Some of these are suspected of disorienting the bees, disabling them from finding their way back to the hive. This could be a cause, but still it cannot be explained why beekeepers find so many bees dead in their beehives. Other causes discussed are the cultivation of monocultures and transport stress of bee colonies;[545] but the most frequent cited are poisons used as pesticides by farmers, such as the ant poison Fipronil and neonicotinoids that are now used increasingly[546] Even *loss of diversity in our landscapes*[547] was identified as a cause of bee death. However, one of the most likely major causes – the mass spraying of toxic substances via Chemtrails – is hardly discussed in the media.

I must take the plunge and say that bee and insect death *is* an indicator of how intensively toxic substances are sprayed via Chemtrails. Since dropping microscopically fine particles from Chemtrails can extend over long periods, sometimes up to a year, one must also take into account a time-lag effect on insects living near the ground, so that it would be difficult to clearly demonstrate the relationship between Chemtrails and insect deaths. But if these toxic substances are actually the main cause of bee and insect death, it should be clear that this would also have devastating effects on humans.

[‡‡‡‡‡‡‡‡‡‡‡] https://www.bbc.co.uk/news/science-environment-47698294.

In the German edition the preamble to this question would literally translate as: 'In Germany, beekeepers *lose between 10 and 30 percent of their colonies each year ... carried away by diseases and – by humans. If the bees die, most of the other crawlers die in the field and in beehives ...* (SP)[494]

Strong exposure to electromagnetic radiation can also have a negative impact on bees. For example, massive and sudden bee death has been documented, in real time, in the immediate vicinity of two 5G antennae when they were placed 10m apart.[548]

Glyphosate – a cause of *genetic damage*

Anyone who still has the idea that governments, or their own people, don't do this, is wrong.[549]

In the US the introduction of glyphosate, with a Pearson coefficient[§§§§§§§§§§§] *of 0.997, correlates with the occurrence of autism in children under 5 years of age, and therefore appears to play an important role in the genesis of autism.*[550] *Glyphosate is known to kill all but one of the pathogenic forms of colibacillus, compromising the gut's ability to eliminate toxins and absorb nutrients. Glyphosate also blocks choline before it can be absorbed through the stomach walls. Choline is important for the transport of nutrients, poisons and as a transport unit for neurotransmitters.*[551]

When experimenting with glyphosate the procedure was as follows:[552] *Two top politicians in Ecuador were paid relatively little money to allow entire areas of a town in Ecuador to be sprayed from the air with this agent, glyphosate. And then samples were taken in the population to see if it could cause permanent genetic damage. And the answer was: yes.*[553] *And what was the next step? In the US we have found clear biochemical evidence for larger cities having a mixture sprayed there in the sky,a mixture to which glyphosate was added. Small experiment in Equator, then*

[§§§§§§§§§§§] The Pearson Coefficient, or Pearson correlation coefficient (PCC), helps to reflect the correlation between two measures; it has the value +1 in the case of complete linear correlation, and the value 0 in the case of no correlation (JS/SP) *the application to your own people in the USA. The USA has the highest percentage of neurological diseases in the world today.*

The following can be read in an article titled 'Genetically Modified Plant Stock, Glyphosate and the Destruction (Decline) of Health in the United States of America' found in the *Journal of Organic Systems*, 2014:[554] *A huge increase in the spread and prevalence of Chronic diseases has been reported in the United States over the past 20 years. Similar increases have been noted globally. The herbicide glyphosate was introduced in 1974 and its use is accelerating with the introduction of herbicide-tolerant, genetically modified (GM) crops.*************Everything indicates that glyphosate interferes with metabolic processes in plants and animals, and glyphosate residues have been measured in both. Glyphosate disrupts the endocrine system and the balance of intestinal bacteria, damages DNA and is an influencing factor in mutations that lead to cancer...* Based on statistics published by the US government, the authors of this article find a pronounced correlation between glyphosate use and 22 serious chronic diseases. The Pearson coefficients determined for this are all very close to the maximum value R = +1.[555] Chronic diseases recorded include stroke, prediabetes, diabetes, obesity, Alzheimer's, senile dementia, Parkinson's, multiple schlerosis, autism, intestinal infections, end-stage kidney disease, acute kidney failure, thyroid cancer, bladder cancer, pancreatic cancer, kidney cancer and blood cancer. The authors of a YouTube video[556] come to a similar conclusion.

An interesting finding is that the number of deaths from lung cancer has risen sharply in the United States, despite the introduction of the general ban on smoking in public spaces.[557] So there has to be another smoking-independent cause that promotes the development of lung cancer.

*********** GM (Genetically Modified) crops and GE (Genetically Engineered) crops are effectively the same, except it could be said that the latter are a scientific but scarcely an ethical advance on the former (SP)

Vaccinated with glyphosate

A measles shot won't make kids autistic.
(Th Schmitz and S Siebert[558])

Vaccines have pathogenic side- effects, including autoimmune diseases, sudden infant death and autism.
(Andreas Moritz[559])

If you were born before 1989, the risk of a chronic disease, such as autoimmune diseases like diabetes, arthritis or lupus, or neurological diseases like ADHD, ADHD, tics, Tourette's syndrome, speech delays, necolepsy and autism, and allergic diseases like food allergies, anaphylaxis, asthma, eczema ... is 12%. And after 1989, with the vaccine regimen, the risk of chronic illness rose to 54%. And we know that's because of the vaccines. How do we know that? Because there's a two-place list of all these diseases One of them is the list of epidemic-like chronic diseases of this vaccination generation. And the second place is in the package inserts of the vaccines, in which the manufacturers have to list the side effects of these vaccines. These companies make 50 billion dollars a year selling vaccines, but they make 500 billion dollars a year selling the drugs to treat this epidemic of chronic disease. Drugs for diabetes, arthritis, epi-pens for food allergies, asthma inhalers, drugs for seizure disorders and many more. And they want to keep this market. So they are turning our children into commodities, they have taken control of our government agencies. They've hijacked the regulatory agencies. They conquered the courts, and they conquered the press. The only thing we have left against them is our democratic power. To unite with others and demand that we not be thrown into this abyss of pharmaceutical cartels. (Robert F. Kennedy Jr., 18.09.2019 [560])

In 2015 glyphosate was classified by the World Health Organization as *probably carcinogenic to humans, 'and the German government has decided not to react to this."*[561]

Consequently, in Brussels, on November 27th 2017, approval of glyphosate use in the EU was extended by another five years.

An article entitled 'CDC Confirmed: Glyphosate and Kidney Cells from Monkeys in Vaccines' states:[562] *Some vaccine ingredients are protected as a 'trade secret', perhaps just as well, since who would want to use vaccines containing kidney cells from African Green Monkeys or from aborted foetuses, or traces of glyphosate? Vaccines can contain not only glyphosate, but also formaldehyde, aluminium, thimerosal and polygeline.*[†] The following was an item on Pravda TV[563]: *But the outlook is different when one considers the components added to our vaccines – these would be: aluminium, mercury, formaldehyde and many other very questionable substances that are carcinogenic and lead to other serious illnesses ... Just imagine: formaldehyde is prohibited as furniture glaze, but may be injected into the bloodstream. Or else ADHD is caused by mercury compounds – ...*

Most of the above-mentioned ingredients are toxic and can cause serious side-effects and even disease.[564,565] Attacks on the autoimmune system may be included.

Aluminium, which is used to enhance effectiveness, is a nerve poison, the salts of which are suspected of causing cancer. Under the heading *Global shock: Cancer is transmitted in vaccines ...* the increase in the incidence of tumors in the past 50 years has been linked to a cancer virus being added to vaccines: *The company has admitted that Cancer virus has been inoculated*[‡] *by vaccines".*[566]

Thimerosal, a mercury compound, is used as a preservative. It is a contact allergen suspected of causing autism in children, just as polygeline is suspected of causing allergies. Formaldehyde

---

[†] For an update on thimerosal and polygeline, see *https://www.sciencedirect.com/topics/nursing-and-health-professions/polygeline* (SP)

[‡] Inoculation is the addition of an object capable of replication (eg a cell culture or pathogens such as viruses or prions) to a cell culture. (Wikipedia)

interferes with processes inside cells, which can lead to breast cancer, prostate cancer, and even brain damage.

Glyphosate could be the most important factor in the development of various chronic diseases that are spreading more and more in Westernized societies.[567]

The flu vaccination campaign, which in the UK, under the NHS (National Health Service) takes place once a year[§§§§§§§§§§§§§], is a typical example of the fear of the flu implanted in conventional medicine, and therefore the adult willingness to have a vaccination cocktail given regularly, although this can harm people and the benefits of this vaccination should be questioned. Let's not forget that flu is one of the body's methods for getting rid of pathogenic germs, whereby the parallel rising body temperature (called fever) serves a cleansing process, which can no longer take place when vaccination prevents it. This regular flu shot can also be seen as a business model for the pharmaceutical industry.[568]

Even before I had a closer look at the problems of vaccination, I had myself been vaccinated against swine flu in 2009 and went down with severe flu three days later, suggesting that the vaccination had triggered this flu. What I did not know at the time was that the outbreak of swine flu in 2009 was suspected to be due to a genetically engineered, human-made virus.[569,570] In line with this, my personal experience is described in an article entitled ***Vaccination – Decimation of Humanity***:[571] *The world's largest vaccination campaign was running in 2009/2010. Vaccines entered the market, the efficiency and safety of which were more than questionable. In addition, safety tests required for approval were sometimes not met. Furthermore, the manufacturers of these vaccines are legally excluded from any liability because the World Health Organization had declared a **level 6 pandemic**. This is despite the factual evidence that so-called swine flu is no more dangerous than ordinary, seasonal flu. Global casualties in no way justified the level 6 pandemic.*

[§§§§§§§§§§§§§] In Germany, the vaccination programme apparently takes place twice-yearly (SP)

An influenza outbreak is nothing exceptional since it recurs every year and was never previously classified a pandemic until just before the appearance of swine flu, when the WHO (World Health Organization) changed the criteria for what constitutes a pandemic. The older definition implied that there was a great danger to life and that very many deaths were to be expected. *This definition has been blatantly watered down so that this relatively normal and harmless swine flu virus could be turned into a worldwide panic and all measures for a pandemic could be initiated.*[572]

This was an example of the **World Health Organization** removing the final obstacle to the pharmaceutical companies' maximization of profit simply by designating the Pandemic a level 6, while at the same time eliminating their liability. Spanish Flu, on the other hand, was a real pandemic, which claimed an estimated 20 million fatalities from 1918 to 1920. Contrary to the widespread official version, however, Spanish Flu was apparently triggered by **mass vaccination**. *As far as is known, only vaccinated people get Spanish Flu. Those who refused the injections avoided the flu. So says the eyewitness Eleanora McBean: 'My family had refused all vaccinations, so we stayed fine all the time. We knew from the health teachings of Graham, Trail, Tilden and others that you cannot contaminate the body with toxins without causing illness. At the height of the epidemic, all shops, schools, companies and even the hospital were closed – even doctors and nurses had been vaccinated and were down with the flu. It was like a ghost town. We seemed to be the only family with no flu – we weren't vaccinated! So my parents went from house to house to take care of the sick. (...) But (still) they didn't get the flu and they didn't bring home any microbes that attacked us children. No one in our family had the flu. It was claimed that the epidemic killed 20 million people worldwide in 1918. But in reality they were killed by the doctors with their rough treatments and medication. This charge is tough, but correct – and attested by the success of naturopathic doctors.*[573]************

************ In the UK, despite there being a well-equipped private College of Naturopathic Medicine in West London, and the continued employment of some

The above-mentioned article[574] continued: *the only potential hazard of swine flu is that the virus is a human-developed virus. It was made in a **biological weapons** laboratory ... So why did international pharmaceutical companies and government agencies coordinate to generate a possibly enforced vaccination campaign of historic proportions? The past had already shown that there were always global élites who aimed to reduce the human population.* As we have already heard (but the context here begs for repetition) the same source adds: *For the sake of maintaining power, the world population will be reduced to a minimum. This will be achieved by means of artificially created illnesses, with bioweapons de-clarified as epidemics; but also by means of targeted famines and wars. The reason stems from the realization that once most people can no longer finance their own diet the rich will be forced to provide relief measures or risk a hugely dangerous potential for conflict.*[575]††††††††††††† (See Prologue – The Road to Tyranny, and Reducing World Population, chapter 2, 2)

So if the swine flu virus was developed in a bioweapons laboratory, it is part of the inhumane practice of developing bioweapons. Just like the swine flu project, it is possible that Coronavirus will again provide the pretext for a worldwide vaccination programme, at huge profit to the pharmaceutical industry. *The same globalists who own the patent for the virus and who were the first to predict and initiate the rise and spread of the virus have now announced that they will develop vaccines against the deadly Coronavirus. According to business insiders, 'a coalition backed by Bill Gates is funding biotechnology companies' that are trying to develop a vaccine against the*

---

naturopaths in NHS hospitals, naturopaths are frequently denounced by conventional medics as charlatans and quacks. Naturopathy goes unregulated, yet at the same time has been dropped from university courses since 2012 (*https://en.wikipedia.org/wiki/Naturopathy*; also *https://www.naturopathy-uk.com/contact/contact-details/*) [SP]

††††††††††††† As stated in the blog falsezitate.blogspot.com on May 1, 2018, this quote and the underlying 12 prophecies do not necessarily derive from Carl Friedrich von Weizsäcker, but from an unknown author, probably writing in 2007

coronary virus. What do you think? Is this all just a big coincidence?'[576] However, in the case of Coronavirus, there is effectively a toss-up between 'plague and cholera' – that is, a choice between the substances causing disease in the vaccine and the deadly Corona flu itself (see Are Ebola, AIDS, SARS and EHEC EHEC bioweapons?, chapter 6, 3).

As far as the *forced vaccination campaign* is concerned, there are indeed efforts today to enforce vaccinations by law. In this context there is an official media campaign to introduce a **mandatory vaccination obligation** for all people, which serves this purpose precisely.[577]

In 2019, German Health Minister Jens Spahn drafted a law on the obligation to vaccinate against measles, which provides for severe penalties for those who refuse.[578,579] This measles protection law has now been passed by the Bundestag (German Federal Parliament) and confirmed by the Bundesrat (German Federal Council), the State legisature, on December 20, 2019. It seeks to propose that those who refused to vaccinate could be fined €2,500 and their children excluded from daycare. This ignores grave evidence that Merck's (MMR) measles-mumps-rubella vaccine (as well as chickenpox, Pentacel‡‡‡‡‡‡‡‡‡‡‡‡‡, and all vaccines containing Hep-A) are manufactured using human foetal cell lines and there is a risk that these vaccines can cause autoimmune attacks.[580] Such a legal obligation to vaccinate is made out to be justified by the high risk of infection in measles, mumps and rubella.[581]

In 1987, an MMR vaccine with the trade name Trivirix[582] was used in Canada. Because this vaccine caused meningitis it was withdrawn from the market but licensed in the UK in the same month, changing the name to Pluserix. The vaccine also caused meningitis in the UK, but was nevertheless used for four years. Following protests the vaccine, no longer used in the UK, was

---

‡‡‡‡‡‡‡‡‡‡‡‡‡ Pentacel is a vaccine used to immunize against diphtheria, tetanus, pertussis, poliomyelitis, and against secondary infections caused by Haemophilus influenza
(https://www.fda.gov/vaccines-blood-biologics/vaccines/pentacel) [SP]

transferred instead to developing countries such as Brazil, where a meningitis epidemic occurred after a mass vaccination campaign. In a subsequent investigation, scientists found that the younger you were when you received the vaccine, the greater the risk of contracting meningitis.[§§§§§§§§§§§§§]

On November 28th, 19 an article appeared in the Ärzteblatt.[*************] *More than 5,000 measles dead in the Congo.*[583] There you can read: *Kinshasa – The measles epidemic in the Congo has claimed more than 5,000 lives since the beginning of the year. As the children's aid organization UNICEF announced yesterday, around 90 percent of the victims were children under the age of five. And on Welt.de you can read: 'The Democratic Republic of the Congo is currently fighting two epidemics: the second-largest Ebola outbreak in history and against measles. The "teething problem" has now claimed far more deaths than the feared Ebola.'*[584] A comment on one webpage[††††††††††††††] supplements these reports as follows:[585] *What happened BEFORE the violent measles outbreak? With a trustworthy search engine you can quickly obtain the information that the triple-vaccination campaign had already taken place. One of the organizations*

[§§§§§§§§§§§§§] This reminds me of the banning of asbestos in the UK, in 1985, which EGIS, the environmental group of which I was a member, celebrated as the winning of what had been a long-drawn-out campaign by many groups, including ours. Soon after, our office obtained a poster from an African country, where the use of asbestos was still legal, showing indigenous black workers actually throwing the stuff up in the air while 'joyfully' working with it. This publicity poster, produced by one of the companies whose asbestos operations had been banned in the UK, was intended to encourage African workers to dismiss all 'notions' of its dangers. I doubt that any of those workers featured in the poster, young as many of them were, lived another ten years. The best-known death from asbestos was that of the Hollywood star Steve McQueen (1930-80), who I seem to remember supported himself early in his career by working on the docks at San Francisco, where he regularly handled asbestos bales and unknowingly contracted pleural mesothelioma. But he himself thought he had contracted the disease when, as a Marine in the 50s, he had been ordered to remove asbestos lagging from a troop ship (*https://en.wikipedia.org/wiki/Steve_McQueen#Early_life*) [SP]

[*************] *Ärzteblatt* (literally, Doctor's Sheet or Medical Notes) is a weekly German medical magazine, published in German and English; the German version sometimes known as *Deutsches Ärzteblatt* (SP)

[††††††††††††††] *systematicgesund.de*

involved, Doctors Without Borders[‡‡‡‡‡‡‡‡‡‡‡‡‡‡]*, vaccinated more than 361,000 children against measles within 5 months. Incidentally, one learns that 223,000 people were vaccinated against Ebola. With an* **'experimental vaccine'**, *the use of which is controversial. So there are* **experiments with people in Africa**!!! ***A prankster who thinks of Ukraine at the measles outbreak.*** *In 2010 they had practically no measles and a vaccination rate of only 56%. The worst in Europe. In 2017 there was a large WHO vaccination campaign that brought the rate to 91% – and ensured that Ukraine had the most measles cases in Europe in 2018.* **But something like the risks and side-effects of vaccinations are often ignored and kept quiet.** *... Any reasonable person would expect the vaccination campaigns to stop immediately. Far from it, activities are intensified and donations are collected. Knowing the damaging consequences amounts to intentional grievous harm, if not to attempted murder!*

Contradicting these negative reports of vaccine effects, there are scientific studies that certify the safety of vaccines. These studies also serve to justify the usefulness of vaccinations. 'Plain text inoculation – An educational book to protect our health' by Schmitz and Siebert (2019) claims in large letters on the back of the cover: *Children do not become autistic from the measles vaccination ... facts versus misinformation....* And in chapter five it informs us that: ... *Melinda and Bill Gates*[§§§§§§§§§§§§§§] *are helping to reduce the number of children dying from preventable infectious diseases.* So vaccinating is not as dangerous as some vaccination sceptics would have us believe? In opposition to this view is 'The Vaccinated Nation: How Vaccination Hurts the Population. Why ADHD, autism, asthma and allergies are increasing dramatically', 2018, by A. Moritz. Some of its core statements are: *"Vaccines, not*

[‡‡‡‡‡‡‡‡‡‡‡‡‡‡] More often known, even in the UK, by the French name *Médecins Sans Frontières* (SP)

[§§§§§§§§§§§§§§] In terms of deposits, the **Bill & Melinda Gates Foundation** is by far the largest private foundation in the world (ahead of George Soros' Open Society Foundations). Both foundations have the common aim of advancing globalization. On the activities of Bill Gates in connection with the corona virus s. section "Are Ebola, AIDS, SARS and EHEC biological weapons?"

viruses, cause disease... Many vaccines are genetically engineered to cause disease and then invent 'preventative treatments' to save large populations from these 'killer diseases'. ... Vaccines have pathogenic side effects, including autoimmune diseases, sudden infant death and autism.[586] What is the truth? There are therefore two different points of view:"[587]

Perspective 1 – *pharmaceutical industry and monopoly media: Scientific studies supposedly prove there is no connection between MMR vaccination and autism!*

Perspective 2 - *Vaxxed Documentation:*[588] *Thousands of credible testimonies use practical experience to prove the connection between MMR vaccination and autism! Perspective 2 is the result* of the experience of 250,000 parents who responded to the request from an original couple of concerned parents.[589,590] *The practical experience of countless parents exposes the supposedly scientific studies as faulty or even manipulated!*

With the introduction of measles vaccination, the efforts of politicians seem to amount to introducing not only the obligation to vaccinate against these diseases, but a **general obligation to vaccinate.** One ignor *"that vaccinations can have dangerous side effects, e.g. Brain inflammation, paralysis, blindness, chronic ill-nesses."*[591,592] A general obligation to vaccinate opens the door to its abuse, which means that ... *the world population can be reduced to a minimum.*

Former Finnish Minister of Health Rauni-Leena Luukanen-Kilde openly stated that this whole vaccination craze mainly serves to reduce the world's population and, of course, to make the pharmaceutical mafia profitable.[593,594]

Conspiracy theory? Yes, of course! But with a high degree of truth: Bill Gates, to whom we have already referred in the section on Are Ebola, AIDS, SARS and EHEC biological weapons? (chapter 6, 3), is one of the main advocates of the widest possible coverage and high vaccination rates in the world, partly on the grounds that this would make it possible to slow down or reverse the unchecked growth of the world population. He propagates the thesis that if people are all vaccinated, they are healthier, and if they are healthier, they have fewer children.[595] Conversely, the world population, which has been growing faster and faster for about 50 years, and the associated increase in diseases such as heart attacks, diabetes, cancer, high blood pressure and obesity seem to confirm Bill Gates' thesis. For this reason, he calls for the comprehensive vaccination of all people. He is one of the main sponsors of the WHO, which is no longer independent and consequently supports high vaccination coverage.

I would like to add here: This compulsory vaccination also serves to weaken people's health. Weak people do not revolt; they are dealing with themselves.

The whole thing is bitterly serious, and the élites will enforce vaccination. This is done step by step, slowly, so that the population gets used to it. With the obligation to vaccinate, first against only one specific disease, measles, it starts. Gradually, other vaccinations will also be legally enforced, and finally a general obligation to vaccinate against all diseases that the élites will classify as dangerous. And this opens the door to its misuse, just as predicted in the above quotation.

At this point, it should also be mentioned that the pharmaceutical industry has a great interest in a mandatory vaccination, since it is another way to increase its profit. The fact that it is not just about profit, but also about the goal of reducing world population is substantiated in the section of the same name. If these tendencies are not stopped, there is a danger that the once beneficial discovery of vaccination against serious infectious diseases may be transformed into one of the most dangerous weapons against humanity.

This goal of reducing world population is therefore not only achieved through the disease-causing chemicals that are sprayed overhead (Chemtrails) and irradiation via beam weapons (including "5G"), but also through targeted vaccination campaigns. As discussed in Are Ebola, AIDS, SARS and EHEC bioweapons? (chapter 6, 3), AIDS was most likely brought about by a vaccination campaign.[596]

Vaccination campaigns can also be disguised and their failures often blamed on us as 'Trojan horses'. The article 'Vaccination - Decimation of Humanity'[597] presents a large number of concrete examples from past decades. Here are some key points:

- *"Secret sterilization through vaccination"* (Under the cover that the vaccination is a tetanus vaccination alone, millions of women in Nicaragua, Mexico and the Philippines aged 15 to 45 were sterilized in the 1990s.)
- *"Sterility from genetically modified maize"* ("Maize called MON 810 from Monsanto, a Rockefeller Foundation company, causes sterility and changes the immune system.")
- *"Sterilization using polio vaccination"* ("Some of the substances we found in the vaccines are dangerously toxic; and some also have a direct impact on the human reproductive system.")
- **Sterilisation by HPV vaccination:** *"In India, the Supreme Court is investigating Bill Gates: The Gates Foundation is funding trials of HPV vaccines which, according to official figures, have already cost dozens of people their lives. The trials were mainly carried out on girls from particularly poor Indian regions with low educational levels..."*[598] *"The main side effect of these HPV vaccines is infertility.*[599]

But lowering the birth rate is no longer the most perfect means of the oligarchs and élites. Additional funds were used to advance depopulation plans. And these are no longer 'just' aimed at people in third world countries. Each of us could be the victim of these measures today.[600] These depopulation measures extend to our diet. We are currently experiencing how genetically modified seeds are on the way to spreading all over the world. Even if many people believe that they are the arbiter in deciding whether to eat genetically modified food or not, this freedom of choice has long been an illusion; because such substances in industrially produced foods often reach our plates through ways that are difficult to understand or track logistically. For example, *Glyphosate reaches our plates via eggs, milk and meat, as does the additive polyethoxylated tallowamine (POEA) contained in glyphosate mixtures and the degradation product AMPA. Both are much more toxic than glyphosate itself ... POEA alone and in combination with glyphosate can cause cancer ... Current studies show serious health risks from glyphosate, POEA and AMPA even at the lowest concentrations. Indications of a hormonal effect are particularly worrying. Cancer, cell death, fertility problems, genetic damage, alterations to embryonic development, the liver and the kidneys are also among the consequences.*[601]

On Monsanto's website you can read:[602]
GMOs are Genetically Modified Organisms
One of the most important GMO facts is that GMOs are developed with beneficial traits that help them thrive in their environment. Think drought-tolerant corn, or pest-resistant soybeans that need less bug spraying. That helps farmers and better harvests benefit everyone, impacting what's available at the store...and what we can put on our plates.
Here a product range (including genetically modified maize and soy) is promoted as something positive. But the exact opposite is the case. In the article cited above, one can also read:[603] *Control of the food: Monsanto is the leader with GMO when it comes to controlling humanity. GMO alone could spread disease and death worldwide. However, Monsanto's seed programme involves seed that has already been developed to control the global food chain.*

Another attack on our health is the addition of fluorine or fluoride to our drinking water in various regions, particularly in the USA, on the grounds that it makes tooth enamel more resistant to caries. However, fluorine or fluoride is one of the strongest poisons[604] for the human organism and cannot practicably be removed from the body. *The addition of fluoride to the water supply has a direct correlation with the number of foetal deaths, children with Down syndrome, fragile teeth and enlarged dental root structures, spinal disorders, osteomalacia ... and osteoporosis ... Fluorination is the biggest case of scientific fraud, not just of this century, but perhaps of all time.*[605] A huge selection of toothpicks in Germany's supermarkets practically all contain fluoride as an extra; I couldn't find toothpaste without fluorine in any of the normal supermarkets. This is a deliberate attack on public health.[606] To get fluorine-free toothpaste, you have to go to specialty shops, for example those where you can only buy bioware. Urban drinking water may also contain traces of substances that do us no good: for example, residues of antibiotics, antidepressants and other drugs, which not have been completely filtered out – according to one source,[607] this is particularly the case in the USA.

In summary, it must be said that a huge programme for reducing world population is currently being implemented and realized through perpetual wars being waged by the USA and NATO, through the systematic poisoning of people by vaccination and via the food chain, the spraying of poisons in the air, and as a result of radioactive pollution.

It would appear that the majority of epidemics and infectious diseases of the last century have been invented in, or owe their origin to, viruses and bacilli developed in military laboratories and spread by mass vaccination. This is a money-making exercise: primarily from the nationwide (or indeed worldwide) vaccinations themselves and secondarily from the subscquent treatment of the sick – all with the aim of creating fear and stemming population growth. *We get dumbed down, we get sick, and we become infertile.*[608]

Covid19 vaccine - side effects

The main initiator and funder for the development of the future Covid19 vaccine is multi-billionaire Bill Gates. The UN estimates the total cost at 40 billion euros.[609] A large part of the necessary money will also be contributed by the donor conference of the heads of state and government at the beginning of May 2020: 7.4 billion euros. The development of the Covid19 vaccine is therefore a gigantic project that must not fail under any circumstances. Such statements that 700,000 victims (according to the estimation of the main initiator Bill Gates[610]) must be expected due to side effects can quickly fade into the background. However, in relation to the total number of people that Bill Gates wants to vaccinate, 7 billion,[611] this would only affect 0.1% of those vaccinated. What are the side effects? One can die or be permanently disabled, for example by paralysis.

What is so special about this novel vaccine? It is a so-called RNA vaccine in which the genes of the vaccinated person are altered - a kind of genetic manipulation in which the genetic material of the cells of the vaccinated person is altered.[612] It is therefore a new quality compared to the vaccines used up to now, in which weakened viruses are the main component of the vaccine against which the vaccination is intended to be effective.

In a letter, the physician Dr. Christin Gramsch describes the mode of action and the consequences of the planned new vaccine against Covid19 as follows[613]

"To all my patients:
Already now I would like to urgently draw your/your attention to important issues regarding an upcoming Covid-19 vaccination:
Over the last 20 years, I have had a number of patients come to me who have developed symptoms after being vaccinated, which I then had to treat. Of course, such artificially produced symptoms/diseases were always a special challenge in individual cases and somewhat more difficult to treat than the predominant diseases that arise from the nature of the patient, i.e. are of natural origin.
However, because the vaccination consequences were mainly based on the already frequently mentioned adjuvants with many side effects (active substance boosters, also called boosters), with whose excretion the body could not cope in individual cases and therefore developed a corresponding slight to severe symptomatology, a homeopathic therapy, in which the individual vital force was stimulated to eliminate the toxins from the body, was successful in the end and the vaccination consequences disappeared, even if often only after many months.

Due to the novel mode of action of the future coronavirus vaccine, however, such healing successes will no longer be possible in the future. For the first time in the history of vaccination, the so-called mRNA vaccines of the latest generation intervene directly in the genetic material of the person/patient and thus change the individual genetic material in the sense of a hitherto forbidden, even criminal genetic manipulation. This intervention can be compared with that of genetically manipulated food, which is also very controversial. Although the media and politicians are currently talking about it in a trivialised manner, and are even unreflectively calling for such a new type of vaccination in order to be able to return to normality, such a vaccination is just as problematic in terms of health, moral and ethical issues and also in terms of genetic damage, which, in contrast to the damage caused by previous vaccinations, will now be irreversible, irreversible and irreparable.

Dear patients, after such a novel mRNA vaccination, they will no longer be able to have the vaccination symptoms treated in an alternative way, they will have to live with the consequences, because they can no longer be treated simply by draining toxins from the human body, just as one cannot treat a person with a genetic defect (e.g. a cancer patient). e.g. trisomy 18 or 21, Klinefelter syndrome, Turner syndrome, genetic heart diseases, haemophilia, cystic fibrosis, Rett syndrome etc.), because the genetic defect remains once present forever!

In plain language this means: Should you develop a vaccination symptomatology after an mRNA vaccination, neither I nor any other therapist will be able to help you causally, because the vaccination damage will be genetically irreversible.

In my opinion, these novel vaccines represent a crime against humanity that has never been committed before in such a broad form in history."

As Dr. Wolfgang Wodarg, an experienced physician, put it: In fact this (for the vast majority of people) "promising vaccine" is a forbidden genetic manipulation!

7. How does the elite protect itself from its own weapons?

*Autumn 2009: The federal government, federal civil servants and soldiers of the Bundeswehr received a vaccine against swine flu **without enhancer**, but the population received a vaccine **with enhancer** (adjuvant***************).*[614]

In the section "Psychopaths" (chapter 2, 1) we had already pointed out that psychopaths also do things that can lead to their own destruction. Nevertheless, we can assume that the representatives of the Deep State take precautions and have already taken steps to protect themselves from the consequences of their actions. In times when the all-encompassing crisis (Rockefeller) has not yet broken out, they live in areas where no chemicals are sprayed and they have several places where they can be found. Furthermore, they have their own, non-public communication channels/facilities to inform each other when, where, what and how something is planned, a false flag operation by the secret services for example. And when the planned all-encompassing crisis begins (cross-country unrest, civil wars), they will not be "present". They have created safe havens for themselves in the form of huge underground tunnel systems, to which they can retreat for a long time to wait until the riots are over. These tunnel systems are hermetically sealed from the outside world, and their self-sufficient

---

**************Adjuvants are aluminium salts, such as aluminium hydroxide. Aluminium is the cause of many diseases, eg Alzheimer's. An adjuvant is allegedly 'a substance that strengthens the body's immune response (= ability to fight harmful substances, diseases, etc.'
(https://dictionary.cambridge.org/dictionary/english/adjuvant). The irony that an adjuvant might itself be harmful is so devious and insidious as to be almost overwhelming. (JS, SP)

supply (drinking water, food) is guaranteed for a long time. These tunnel systems are known only to the members of the Deep State and are accessible only to them. The realization and financing of these enormous tunnel systems is running and took place in the shadow and under the cover of other large projects (e.g. Denver Airport (USA), Berlin Airport, railway project "Stuttgart21"), which meant that their construction could take place relatively hidden and the neighboring residents had little knowledge of the actual construction goals and actual work. The enormous financial resources that these tunnel projects swallowed up in the Federal Republic of Germany were made available and invoiced via the major projects "Berlin Airport" and "Stuttgart21". With regard to Berlin's major airport BER, many people should have noticed by now that something could be wrong. After all, in more than eight (!) years since the first officially planned completion date (2012), German engineering must have succeeded in solving the technical problems that stand in the way of its release, especially since BER was a prestigious company from the very beginning. The unused Berlin airport costs the taxpayer about 1.3 million euros a day (!) (as of 2016). What are these enormous financial resources used for?

In Denver it was private investors who had financed and built the airport, but who are not officially known. [615]

The whistleblower du-Deborah Tavares also answers this question with an example, namely: how do the élite protect themselves from the illness-inducing influences from air, water and soil? *Some of the information we came across is: of course they have methods that are way ahead of those we have, such as cancer healing; they don't get cancer* ... To refute the protest against this "conspiracy theory," I would like to make the following comments on the topic of cancer prevention and treatment. Statistics show that nowadays one in two men and one in three women get cancer during their life and that this high probability of developing cancer is largely related to our way of life and the environmental toxins - environmental toxins such as pesticides, insect zide and synthetic products,[616] such as those used in agriculture for weed control or in the food industry for longer shelf life of food. *In 1850, only one in 2500 died of cancer, today every third dies of cancer."*[617] And a recent study found: *"Cancer is 100 percent a manmade disease ... after the Industrial Revolution, cancer cases skyrocketed, especially in children, where it is proven that this increase in cancer is not only due to a longer life expectancy ... There is practically nothing in nature that can cause cancer. Therefore, it has to be manmade, through pollution and changes in diet and lifestyle. The most important thing about our study is that it shows us this disease from a historical perspective. We can give clear information about cancer rates in different epochs and societies because we have a complete overview. We have studied thousands of years, not just the past 100 years, and we have countless data to fall back on.*[618]

Super-rich élites can easily escape these influences – which are harmful owing to our unhealthy lifestyle and the intake of environmental toxins – by living independently and eliminating these negative factors from their lives. And if they do happen to succumb there are proven anti-cancer drugs, the knowledge and distribution of which are not supported by the pharmaceutical industry, and are even suppressed and fought because these drugs cost too little and therefore do not make enough money. Being unpatentable, if these anti-cancer drugs got around, this would result in a huge loss of sales for the classic anti-cancer drugs (chemotherapy, radiology, super-expensive drugs). *Cancer therapies that cost little or nothing and are not patentable do not have the slightest political chance of approval. They are hushed up, suppressed, and made to look ridiculous and untrustworthy."*[619]

For example, one anti-cancer drug is a daily intake of natural vitamin C, taken as a high-dose therapy and supplemented by a healthy and balanced lifestyle that counteracts overacidification of human cells: a lot of physical exercise, correct or varied nutrition (lots of vegetables, if possible organic), sufficient sleep, sufficient sunlight, sufficient drinking, a positive attitude to life and a stress level that is not too high.[620]

Lack of light makes tumors grow. Why doesn't anyone know that a good dose of vitamin D, which is only produced in the skin by sunlight, can protect us from cancer? That people alternatively healed themselves with high-dose vitamins, oxygen therapy, deacidification and many other natural methods? It is suppressed to keep us addicted. Every day, thousands more victims have to go through the chemo-hell system ...[621]

The anti-cancer drugs mentioned here are not only the crucial means to prevent cancer, but possibly also to cure it; because cancer is not just the disease of a single organ, it is a disease of the whole body that first manifests itself in one of the organs. The author Lothar Hirneise[622] goes further: He says: If the stress level is too high for years, this leads to a permanent lowering of adrenaline levels in the cells, which in turn means that cells transglutinate, which once a certain sugar content is reached results in cell destruction. To avoid this destruction, evolution has set up the mechanism of switching to a so-called fermentation metabolism, which allows the cell to burn 20 times the amount of sugar than a normal cell. The cell thus changed is the cancer cell, which is therefore no longer in danger of over-sugering and dieing. That is, cancer is a good thing, because it allows survival by altering the metabolism. The disadvantage, however, is the unlimited cell division, which ultimately leads to death, if it fails to switch the cell metabolism back towards normal metabolism, which is possible by the supply of increased oxygen, accompanied by a change of life, towards a healthy lifestyle, i. e. detoxification of the body, change of diet and reduction of stress.

Cancer is a deficiency disease. Cancer occurs when a certain substance is missing from the body that was once part of the diet, but has now largely been bred away ... Similar to scurvy (vitamin C deficiency) or pelagra (vitamin B deficiency) or Rickets (vitamin D deficiency) causes cancer if it is not taken with food. Normally, our immune system is able to cope with the newly formed cancer cells every day. Only when the immune system is overloaded AND due to certain factors (radiation, malnutrition, stress and other carcinogenic factors) AND this substance is not present can cancer cells get out of hand and grow into a tumor.[623]

Here, too, we come across the fact that we repeatedly came across in the previous discourse, namely that the establishment, the élite, not only hides such positive insights but fights them. And it stirs up fear, a proven way to manipulate people. *This message, which programmes the human mind on: 'Diagnosis cancer, I die', has a very big effect on its fears. Since nothing is as vulnerable and manipulable as anything through fear, this report already involves them in the criminal spiral of the pharmaceutical industry.*[624]

The first to place "high-dose therapy" with natural vitamin C at the centre of cancer prevention and healing was the two-time Nobel Prize winner Linus Pauling, who received the *Nobel Prize* in Chemistry in 1954 and the *Nobel Peace Prize* eight years later. Pauling believed that most cancer research is fraudulent and that major cancer research organizations are committed to those who fund them.[625,626]

But since the élite were unable to refute Linus Pauling's findings on cancer prevention and treatment, he was insulted and tried to ridicule him as a "vitamin pope".[627] Linus Pauling has refuted this élite campaign by using his healing method on himself after receiving his own cancer diagnosis at the age of 60. He survived her by 33 years and died only at the age of 93 years. This cancer prevention and treatment has also been combated by the pharmaceutical industry in recent times, with the media being willing helpers in this fight. In 2011, the WDR broadcast a TV programme warning of dietary supplements; these would increase the risk of death and they were *highly harmful substances.*[628] This WDR broadcast was broadcast in close proximity to a series of lectures by Dr. Rath, a doctor who specializes in the role of vitamins in cancer prevention and cure. In the online version Bild.de you could read: *How dangerous are vitamin preparations? Women die sooner, men get prostate cancer more often,*[629] referring to a study from the USA, which was in fact not a clinical study, where vitamins are typically administered in one group of participants, while a second group, the control group, no vitamins receives. Instead, *the whole study was based on' questionnaires 'on' eating behavior 'and other aspects, where do you live, what level of education do you have, etc.*[630] And 80% of those who started this survey left it before completing it.

The representatives of these alternative medical approaches to combating cancer are experiencing opposition not only through the media, but also through lawsuits in court, where withdrawal of the license to practice medicine and even imprisonment can threaten.[631] In 2007, a pharmacist before the Lower Saxon Higher Administrative Court had reached a fundamental judgment[632] against the Chamber of Pharmacists, which passed on the passing on of amygdalin (also known as Amigdalina, Laetrile (Lätril), Mandelonitril or Vitamin B17) as an alternative means Prophylaxis and treatment of tumor diseases (cancer) or their symptoms wanted to ban.

A word about the "anti-cancer agent" vitamin C: *Artificial* vitamin C, ascorbic acid, also seems to be suitable for "high-dose therapy"; however, this should be supplemented by the parallel intake of other micronutrients, vitamins B1, B5, B12, B17 and others. The (pseudo-) vitamin B17 mentioned apparently plays a key role in the fight against cancer.[633] It is contained in a number of wild fruits,[†††††††††††††††] e.g. in apricot kernels in relatively high doses, but also in many other fruits that grow in our gardens. The bitter substances or the hydrocyanic acid content in these fruits play a decisive role. The advantage of the "B17 mechanism" is that it acts selectively against cancer cells and hardly destroys healthy tissue. Here there is even an analogy to the mode of action of penicillin in that penicillin also acts selectively, i.e. against bacteria, but does not attack human cells.[634] In contrast, chemotherapy destroys both cancer and healthy cells. This advantage alone would be reason enough for the pharmaceutical industry to invest billions of euros

---

[†††††††††††††††] In the modern forms of these fruits, some of these bitter substances are grown away, which is why they have lost part of their effectiveness as anti-cancer drugs.

in research into the scientific context of the "B17 mechanism", which it does not, however, instead relativizes previous findings or even discredits them.[635] In an article published by the German Pharmacist newspaper in 2012, the following could be read:[636] *Amygdalin, the ingredient in bitter almonds and in the kernels of apricots and apples, is a cytotoxic, apoptosis-inducing substance. Therefore, corresponding effects on tumor cells can generally be assumed, which, however, could not be confirmed in most animal studies nor in the few systematic studies available in cancer patients.* And the further text of this article read: *There are no controlled, randomized clinical studies with laetrile or amygdalin.* If so, how can you say that laetrile or amygdalin does not work against cancer? And again the question: why is the pharmaceutical industry not commissioning controlled, randomized clinical trials with laetrile or amygdalin? It's so incredible; there is a substance that is known to **selectively** kill cancer cells biochemically, but leaves normal cells undisturbed, and no research or study is commissioned on this.

In a video[637] entitled "Apricot Kernels against Cancer: Life-threatening Naturopathy", the example of a failed cancer therapy by the "B17 Therapy" is thematized in a patient and mixed with esoteric aspects (Bruno Groening, *the inventor of the divine healing current ... Horseshoe tin foil could increase the effect.*) and discredited alternative medicine. Another video[638] gives an answer. In an information leaflet, the unequal and unfair struggle between conventional medicine and alternative (new) medicine is summed up:[639] *Unfortunately, two measures are being used: If a single person dies in New Medicine, then a thunderstorm breaks out: 'He could still live, he would not have believed this nonsense.' On the other hand: Despite the many deaths in conventional medicine, it says here: 'We did our best, he could not be saved.'* Cancer patients often turn to an advanced stage of their cancer treatment into an alternative treatment, namely when conventional medicine can no longer help them, they are "out of therapy", so to speak. However, due to the loss of time and the additional cell damage during the previous treatments (chemotherapy, radiation, medication), the cancer is often well advanced, so that the chances of a cure with

B17 therapy are now poor. But even in the case of these "fully treated" cases, the B17 therapy is said to have worked in 15% of the cases.[640]

Because of this propaganda against alternative approaches to cancer therapy, here are some comments on B17 for those who are seriously looking for alternative treatments. While the oral intake of apricot kernels makes sense for **prevention** of cancer, this is often not sufficient in a therapy treatment because a considerable part of the effect is lost via the detoxification mechanism of the liver, but also during the intestinal passage, where the B17 Cores open and so the hydrogen cyanide is released there. Therefore, intravenous administration is preferable in **therapy**. Because Laetrile is prescription, you need to find an open-minded doctor (or dentist) who is willing to give you a (private) prescription for getting Laetrile. The next hurdle is to find a pharmacist who has Laetrile on offer. In the video[641] mentioned above, the Flora pharmacy in Hanover is mentioned as a reference source. The next hurdle is to find a medical practitioner to give you this drug intravenously. It is also important that, along with the B17 therapy, a healthy lifestyle is sought, as already described above in connection with vitamin C therapy. *Laetril is not a miracle cure, but it works, as empirically proven since 1834; there was the first clinically documented case. And since then, it has worked in hundreds of thousands of documented cases, on average, statistically in 85% of the cases, and in the case of overtreated patients who have been severely damaged and also abandoned by conventional medicine, 15% of all cases have been proven.*[642] Following Books give a good insight into the mechanism of action of B17 in relation to cancer cells:[643,644,645]

The representatives of the pharmaceutical industry are not interested in these alternatives or complementary therapies for cancer therapy because it would reduce their profit. ... *even expensive cancer drugs, which can cost € 20,000 a quarter, cannot promise a cure. All the more astonishing what a researcher from Ulm has found out: With methadone, a drug substitute, cancer cells can potentially be effectively combated, and that for just € 30 per quarter. Sounds good, but the pharmaceutical industry has no interest in scientifically examining this new method. ...*[646] On the contrary, such promising approaches are being kept silent or with arguments such as" there are no evidence-based studies".[647] Since the majority of medical studies are financed by the pharmaceutical industry, it is not surprising that no studies on such promising therapeutic approaches are launched.[648]

In addition to the cancer treatment therapies shown here, other promising natural science approaches should also be mentioned, which are also being combated by the pharmaceutical industry because these methods are not patentable and nothing can be earned, e.g. Graviola or GcMAF.[649] Hamers' approach to understanding cancer and its psychological causes such as shock and anxiety and the healing options derived from it should also be mentioned here.[650]

It is known that melancholy, worry, depressed mood can increase the risk of cancer, whereas optimistic, happy people are less likely to do so. In the latter, the serotonin level is obviously higher than in the former. This could be an indication, for example, that it is not the psychological component that is primary, but the biochemical cause behind it, the serotonin level; because the prerequisite for a positive mood is a high serotonin level. This in turn is only high if melatonin is also present in the body in sufficient quantities. Serotonin and melatonin are closely related in the human body. One is the prerequisite for the formation of the other. However, technically generated electromagnetic radiation can lead to a reduction in melatonin production, which weakens the cancer defense.[651] Melatonin is part of the cancer police in the body. This supports Hamer's approach to psychological causes such as shock and anxiety in the development of cancer.

Despite the slander of these "anti-cancer drugs" by the pharmaceutical industry and its henchmen, I assume that the élites will take advantage of this knowledge. However, the population should not benefit from it.

8. Summary and Conclusion

We put ourselves in danger when we get up. But we put our children and grandchildren in even greater danger if we don't. [652]

So, in the name of God, do something about it, do something for your own future, for example, by getting everyone to know what's going wrong here. [653]

The manipulation and dumbing down of people, which takes place simultaneously on different levels – through the media, education, distracting games, and diversion into scenarios of secondary importance - equate rather well with a **counter**-enlightenment, analogous to a **counter**-reformation. This describes a process comparable to Late Mediaeval endeavours by rulers of the Old World to dismantle the achievements of the Reformation initiated by Luther. Hence the **Counter-reformation**. The Reformation stood for progress towards liberation of the people from bondage to authority; Counter-reformation stood for its opposite, for regression, and that is exactly how it is panning out in our so-called enlightened times today.

We have been living in a (comparatively) enlightened society for a long time now, but through the reverse process that I would call **counter**-enlightenment the clock could easily be turned back to those darkest times when there was an incontrovertible will be an "authority" again, we call them "élite" or "secret world government" or "committee of the 300" or Illuminati. [654] The influence of the media and politicians on people's thinking plays a decisive role in this **counter**-enlightenment. It is a fight against the intellect, against independent, logical thinking. An example of this triumphal march of "restricted thinking" is the success in planting the idea that people are to blame for climate change and that the media and politicians have managed to get CO_2 into their heads as the identified villain plants, although CO_2 is only present in the air as a trace gas. Because the exact opposite is the case: CO_2 is vital for life because it is one of the prerequisites for life on our planet. With its help, the plants produce the oxygen that we humans and animals need to breathe. In the Middle Ages, critics of the dogmas of the church were stigmatized as heretics and, in the worst case, burned at the stake. Today, those people who contradict the thesis of human-made climate change through its CO_2 production are labeled as climate deniers and conspiracy theorists, whereby any contentual discussion is nipped in the bud.

Today, this process of **counter**-enlightenment, that is, pushing back the logical thinking ability of people, takes place in all social spheres, but also in science. In the social field, you can see that in gender mainstreaming, feminism, family destruction, replacing traditional terms such as father and mother with parents 1 and 2, Islamization, hostility to technology, inclusion in schools, mixed-age school classes, teaching in common school classes between German and migrant children, Turbo-Abitur.[655] Similar tendencies can be observed in the field of science: contradiction to the standard theories such as the *standard model of the elementary particles*, the cosmological theories of *parallel worlds* and *extra dimensions*, *bubble multiverse* are theories that most of the specialists today follow without contradiction, little or not at all not tolerated. Fundamental contradiction is barely allowed, partly fought by rejecting manuscripts that contradict the scientific mainstream. Research funding is preferred for research projects that follow the scientific mainstream. Dissenters or researchers who question or reject these "science dogmas" have a difficult time. A blatant example is the now deceased cosmologist Halton Arp, who found that there are contradictions between the Big Bang thesis and more recent observations. The consequence was that his manuscripts, which dealt with these contradictions, were no longer accepted by the scientific publishers and that he no longer received observation times on the large telescopes.[656] Gender mainstreaming, whose representatives argue that the human gender is a social construct, has meanwhile been scientifically accompanied by research from around 200 gender professors that exist in Germany. A professor of biology, author of the book "The Gender Paradox", who criticizes the *"fantasy teaching of gender mainstreaming"* and is upset about the ideological hypotheses of "gender researchers", is accused. *"Pretext: alleged incitement to act together with insult and defamation."*[657]

Human-made climate change is an invention of the élite, who pursue goals with this project entirely different from those that would stabilise the climate. Their main goal is to create a common project or topic that implicates the entire global community, with which all of humanity can identify. This commonality serves the élite who strive for One World Government. Their other objectives are:

- redistributing from bottom to top
- legalizing geoengineering (including Chemtrails)
- undermining the Western economy (the balance of living conditions within the EU)
- distracting from other political changes
- generating confusion and fear
- " Divide and conquer "
- accelerating the decline of democracy (in other words, promoting totalitarianism).

What we have been experiencing for several years is the celebration of a climate religion that has nothing to do with scientific facts, but has instead raised human-made climate change to the level of a dogma. The central claim of the representatives of human-made climate change is that human-made CO_2 accelerates global warming, the key phrase being greenhouse effect. Counter-arguments are either ignored by the political media or wiped off the table with the argument of a 'consensus among scientists' or a 'majority decision'. The majority decision that CO_2 contributes to global warming is ideologically motivated, not backed up by hard scientific facts.

However, human-made weather change actually exists if it includes the increase in frequency and intensity of weather phenomena, such as earthquakes, tsunamis, disturbance in the ecological balance of a region, changes in the weather (including cloud formation, cyclones, and tornados). But it is not the CO_2 that causes this human-made climate change: to a great extent it is the weather manipulations by HAARP in conjunction with the materials that are applied through Chemtrails. Chemtrails involve various aspects:

1)   spraying toxins such as barium, strontium, aluminium ...
2)   spraying components of a biological weapon (the Morgellon mushroom)
3)   creating a metallic layer over the surface of the earth, to enable the range of the HAARP activities over the entire globe‡‡‡‡‡‡‡‡‡‡‡‡‡‡‡
4)   spraying so-called nanobots (Smartdust) that implant in the human brain
5)   shielding solar radiation.

Fundamentally, technological progress is highly valuable, so long as it is not misused and is, above all, not used against people. But: *As long as the world is ruled by psychopaths, we unfortunately always have to assume the worst from experience: wars, weather manipulations, mind control.*[658] We are currently playing out the endgame and it looks as if the year 2025, which Three Documents (see Figures 1, 2 and 5) have in common, actually characterizes the checkmate following which the élite plan to take complete control over humanity, at least in the Western world. There is no other way of explaining how the same year is shown as climactic in these three documents.§§§§§§§§§§§§§§§   Technological   progress

---

‡‡‡‡‡‡‡‡‡‡‡‡‡‡‡ Where does this metallic layer go when the sky is blue and clear over several days? .(SP) The metal particles gradually sink and contaminate soil and water. This can take up to a year because the particle size is very small. How long this settling process takes also depends on the weather conditions. (JS)
§§§§§§§§§§§§§§§§§§§§§§§§§§§§§§§ I am not sure I agree with JS here. The habit among strategic planners to divide centuries up into quarters (rather like a macrocosm of the seasons) – or, to express it another way, to multiply upwards from traditional five-year plans – is well known (SP). However, the elite no longer has enough time as in past centuries. The reasons are the alternative media and the Internet, the dissemination of information, Wikileags, Edward Snowden, etc. In addition,

(geoengineering) in connection with the indoctrination of people by the media, politicians, NGOs and lobbyists, who act in the interests of the élite, serve this aim of taking power.***************
Why they all act in the interests of the élite seems incomprehensible, but must have something to do with the élite's vast monetary power.

The technological possibilities of geoengineering[659] already in use today include weather manipulation, triggering natural disasters such as earthquakes, tsunamis, hurricanes, darkening of the sky, deforestation (deforestation of the rainforests), poisoning of the air to breathe and pollution of the soil and water by Chemtrails.

Figure 58 gives an overview of what geoengineering can do and the consequences of its use for humans, animals and the environment. Behind geoengineering, a massive destruction project has been launched against humanity.

What is not yet included in this list are the efforts to introduce a compulsory vaccination and manipulate consciousness by spraying 'intelligent' nanoparticles/nanochips (Smartdust) as well as by creating microwave radiation via the 5G network, which has

---

national counter-movements have formed in recent years and are becoming in-creasingly strong. Furthermore, scientific and technical progress is advancing at an ever faster pace, especially artificial intelligence, bioengineering, 5G. Not to forget the Transhuman Agenda (Agenda 2045), which should lead to a dehumani-zation of the future slaves. If the elite waits any longer, it will become increasing-ly difficult for them to cloud their true goals. For today we live in a "Second Enlightenment" (JS).
*************** I agree with JS completely about indoctrination, but would place the indoctrinators in a different order of influence: the elite first (as controllers of corporations more powerful than most nation states); lobbyists second (by which I would mean corporate representatives especially – some of them representing corporations, and sponsored by them, unknowingly); politicians third (especially those in the pocket of corporations, but again some of them toeing the line un-knowingly); NGOs fourth (Non-Governmental Organizations being a classic Orwellian phrase); and the media fifth (bearing in mind that journalists of all hues – with the exception of freelance journalists – tend to be paid by corporations and feel commensurate gratitude, albeit misguided, towards their shady employers) (SP)

reached new heights of 'quality'. 5G's omnipresence will be something no longer avoidable or escapable.

Nanoparticles/nanochips can be introduced into our bodies in various ways without our becoming aware of them. By such means the brainwaves of every person can be read using the intelligent IoT (Internet of Things) grid, but also controlled, and even certain conscious states impressed, from the outside. *This is the ultimate enslavement from which there will be no escape, at least not by our own strength.*[660] This would amount to the perfection of tyranny.

This élite super-takeover[†††††††††††††††††] will be accompanied by great upheavals and civil wars, exacerbated by the mass migration[661] into Europe that has taken place in recent years, which will eventually lead to a population reduction. Another major population reduction will be achieved through the use of *chemtrails (or geoengineering), vaccines, irradiated food, GMOs (Codex Alimentarius), intelligent counters, 5G use ...*[662]

[†††††††††††††††††] The original German would simply translate as takeover, but since JS agrees that the élite are already in charge (though not totally without opposition) reference to a super-takeover, in which opposition would be ruled out, seems more apposite (SP)

Geoengineering is responsible for				
Weather-manipulation	**Blackout of the sky**	**Deforestation**	**Air-dirt**	**Pollution of the floors**
which causes the following				

Floods
Drought
Earthquake
Tsunami
violent storms
Natural Disasters
extremely cold
  Weather phases
	Investment losses for
	  solar and renewable
	  bare energies
	Vitamin D deficiency
	Rickets
	Depressions
	Paranoia
	Anxiety
		Bees and insects-
		  die
		Forest dieback
		Advantage of
		  Fungi and mould
		Oxygen reduction
		Death of the flora
		extinction of species (fau
			Increase in cancer
			Hay fever
			Influenza (Flu)
			Asthma
			Alzheimer
			Parkinson
			Multiple Sclerosis
			Autism
				End of the
				  Organic Farming
				Over saturation of the
				  Floors
				Death of the fauna
				Contamination of the
				  Water Cycle

and favors the following				

Banks
Energy companies
Real Estate Speculation
Manufacturer of
  stress-resistant
  Gene seeds
Weather change
  (Weather as a weapon)
	Energy companies
	pharmaceutical compani
	Nuclear Industry
	private health-
	  insurances
		Monsanto
		Agriculture with
		  Genetic Seed
		Reduction of the
		  World Population
			Pharmaceutical Industry
			private health-
			  insurances
				on genetic
				  modified seed
				  based land
				  economy
				aluminium resistant
				  Seeds

Figure 58: Overview of geoengineering capabilities and the consequences of their use for humans, animals and the environment‡‡‡‡‡‡‡‡‡‡‡‡‡‡‡‡

---

‡‡‡‡‡‡‡‡‡‡‡‡‡‡‡ *https://www.chemtrailsprojectuk.com*

Manipulation of consciousness does and will take place along classic lines also. Climate change propaganda and the Greta hype staged in the wake of it being a classic example, where the youth of today are incited against the adults, for which the FridayForFuture movement was launched, approved by governments and schools.§§§§§§§§§§§§§§§§§ *It is therefore easy to see where the new cultural revolution of people like Greta and Rezo is going. It should turn the power structure upside down, enforce climate dictatorship and disempower political and cultural élites ...*[663]

The apparent contradiction that these would be Communist ideas, which are actually committed to the struggle against the rule of capital, is in fact no contradiction, since the élite simply adopt these ideas and implement them. The 1966-78 Chinese Cultural Revolution was also initiated by the American establishment, brought about and financially supported by the offshoot of Yale University in China.[664,665] One important way for the élite to cement their position is by the divide and conquer principle; the cultural revolution was no different. This divisive principle also applies to the incitement of young against old in the FridayForFuture movement.

The subtitle of the 1st and 2nd edition of the present book, *A Child's Nightmare*, symbolised in the cover picture of the two children on the boulder, which is on the brink of falling, expresses how vulnerable our next generation is. For what will transpire will be a terror without end, if we fail to stop Agenda 2025. Once the NWO has been installed, all other globalist projects will continue, of which Mind Control and the Transhumanist Agenda will have the most devastating consequences for the continued existence of a civilized world, because, penetrating deeply into the Psyche and the Will, they will not only entail the total degradation of mental faculties, they will also interfere with the reproductive process. It is possible that our children will not even notice how their reality of

---

§§§§§§§§§§§§§§§§§ In the German original, government was in the singular, and though it may have been a spiritual singular, meaning all governments everywhere, I decided to pluralise it to make this clear (SP)

life is gradually changing, because change is occurring insidiously, in sync with (artificially designed) cognitive changes. ****************

The ultimate endgame objective is to remotely influence and control the population by overwriting and programming thoughts, controlling the feelings and actions of the masses, amounting to perpetual enslavement.

A fitting summary of our condition is given by a Facebook user, Alfred E Neumann, in the following farewell comment, posted on June 12, 2019:

Well, dear friends, my days on Fb are also numbered ... I've always tried to be neutral, avoiding hate and insults. Now that all of Fb has been scrutinized down to the very last bit, our state probably has no major problems other than punishing people who do not care or even consider the result of their policies to be dangerous, I see myself in my 'human dignity' so far impaired that even as a law-abiding citizen the presumption of innocence no longer applies, my freedom of expression is no longer possible without having to reckon with later reprisals and through the whole filter in image, sound and writing my right to information is so severely restricted that neutral information is impossible and my days here are over.
Until 2015, Germany was a strong country, but since then changes in direction have been so drastic that you can compare it to being inside a sack with its drawstrings pulled tight.
There are always new, unbelievable revelations that make you feel more like a laboratory rat than a human.

Whether **poisons in the air, water, soil, food, vaccinations, chemo etc.**

**************** A number of my writings express concern that an exchange process is going on between reality and virtual reality, so that what is now seen as real in an objective and external sense will all too soon be portrayed and regarded as virtual and unreal compared with what machines we wear on our heads tell us is real (SP)

Or companies, unions, employers, health insurance companies, lobbies, politics, school make more than worrying headlines, real estate bubble, bank rescue, euro crisis, Brexit, refugee crisis hover over our future like a sword of Damocles. International Law, Common Law†††††††††††††††††*, even almost all beliefs are no longer there for the good of the people .... one thing is certain for me ....*

All of this is not a national problem, but, I think, the historical moment when the global movers and shakers are exposed as wanting to keep us all like animals in a stable.

Even if someone like Trump stands up against chemtrails, you can see how it affects our occupiers (and they usually act like God ...

We are facing the big 'big bang', in which no one can confront the polluter.

One thing is certain, it will be ugly.

I hope that our children will forgive us. How could we let it get this far?

I wish you, your families and relatives all the best ...

The transition from freedom to enslavement is now entering its decisive phase: the endgame. The roadmap looks something like this:

1) Unleash a pandemic and create fear
2) Close off cities, stopping freight and passenger traffic
3) Proclaim a state of emergency, putting into force emergency ordinances
4) Take critics out of circulation and concentrate them in camps (the pretext: a quarantine to prevent further spread of the virus)
5) Mass vaccinate against the alleged pandemic (modelled on Spanish Flu)
6) Microchip humans via these vaccinations (the microchips controllable via 5G, with exitus option)
7) Abolish cash (justification: risk of infection)††††††††††††††††

---

††††††††††††††† The initial translation into English read 'the Basic Law' here, which in England equates with Common Law (SP)

†††††††††††††††† It has recently occurred to me that in the event of cash being abolished the homeless and other vulnerable sectors of the population would be in

8) Bring about a financial crash and the collapse of the world economy
9) Trigger off a famine with consequent civil wars and the basic struggle for survival
10) Reduce the population.

Points 1) to 3) we have already experienced in connection with Coronavirus.§§§§§§§§§§§§§§§§§§§. Here also the very long incubation period of 2 weeks was promulgated; because the longer the incubation period the more time available to the élite to implement the other points. Nothing should be left to chance.

The situation seems hopeless. As Karl Jaspers said, *Hopelessness is defeat anticipated.* Our only hope is to educate.******************
Educate so that as many people as possible become aware of the dangers and recognize them. Above all, they must unmask élitist strategy, which consists of enforcing the principle of 'divide and rule' with regard to the people. Because only if the government faces a powerful protest movement, which they can no longer control with the means at their disposal (the media, the police, the military, and the law), will it be possible to prevent the enslavement of humankind.

Clearing this mess up, though, is not so easy, because people's convictions, attitudes to life and political orientations have grown distorted over the years, through what is encapsulated in their personal environment – the influence of home, school, and work, and, of course, the daily propaganda and indoctrination streaming

---

danger of elimination – by which I do not mean that homes would be found for them. Vodafone is among those UK companies that recently became cashless (SP)

§§§§§§§§§§§§§§§§§The original English text, which I received on 19 February 2020, read: 'the corona virus in China 2019/20'. Clearly, JS knew about the Coronavirus outbreak before most of us did. In a short space of time 'the corona virus' became 'Coronavirus' in nearly all English publications. How rapidly language changes in times of crisis! (SP)

****************I see this dictum from JS as standing in direct opposition to Maurice Strong's (See the epigraph to Climate Change – a global topic, chapter 3) [SP] through radio, TV, and print media dominated by the élite. A person with convictions malformed over decades is often no longer able to correct his/her world view with new and sometimes contradictory information, let alone throw that world view overboard. This frequently dubious human quality is referred to in social psychology as cognitive dissonance. Cognitive dissonance creates psychological malaise, which people instinctively try to avoid by denying information or not perceiving it in the first place.[†] In this context media influence plays a crucial role, reinforcing the current world view daily inculcated in people's minds.[‡]

Whether it is still possible to overcome this hurdle (of not perceiving or of denying information) by educating the population is a question that may well determine the survival of human civilization. It is important to convince people of the guiding principle:
Do not believe everything, check everything yourself.[§]

Perhaps, as is so often the case in world history, surprising twists and turns could still prevent the enslavement of people and the total takeover of human thought, feelings and will by a self-proclaimed élite. The past teaches that the course of history is often largely determined by individuals in top positions and their character traits.[666] Negative examples are Hitler, Mao-Tse Tung and Pol Pot. In my opinion, positive examples are Trump and Putin. Trump has not yet started a war in his three-year term, unlike his predecessors. And Putin has withstood all provocations from the western 'community of values'.

[†] For extreme examples of cognitive dissonance, see the earlier footnote on the American natives encountered by the Conquistadors and 'the daylight moon' incident (SP)

[‡] But the media could, and indeed should, be used to reverse this insidious process (SP)

[§] We might refine this still further by proposing that all of us *Believe nothing without checking.* Relying entirely on one's own intuition would be going to the other extreme of ignorance (SP)

At present, Russia, the former bulwark of Socialism/Communism, and the Trump-led US seem to be the last and decisive bastions of hope that could avert the nightmare. The influence of Trump and Putin is discussed in a video.[667,668] There are people who put great hope in the US President and the QAnon movement. Both, so one hopes, have set themselves the task of unmasking the Deep State and rendering its backers harmless. One can read on Wikipedia: *QAnon, or Q for short, is the pseudonym of a suspected American person or group of people who spreads a right-wing extremist conspiracy theory on imageboards and pretends to have access to secret information about Donald Trump's presidency, his fight against a supposed 'Deep State', as well as being Trump's adversary. QAnon has now become a term for the widespread conspiracy theory itself.* Note that in this characterization the term 'conspiracy theory' is used once again, indicating that Wikipedia serves and is part of the Deep State, itself, belonging to the 4th circle within it (see Epilogue and Deep State Observations, next). To arrive at an independent perspective it is therefore advisable to consult independent sources.[*]

According to three documents triangulating on 2025 objectives (chapter 1, 1), 2025 seems to be the year in which the élite want to take over.[†] But it may well happen earlier, namely when Trump actually fights against the Deep State (as some predict), which puts that secret organization under such pressure as to try and pull off checkmate earlier.

---

[*] I agree with JS about independent sources; but since I make frequent unpaid contributions to Wikipedia myself – and everyone else has the opportunity to do so (so long as they can verify their sources) – I cannot see how his criticism of Wikipedia can stand (SP) My answer (JS): https://www.bing.com/videos/search?q=Unzicker&view=detail&mid=5730B95C57754687796D5730B95C57754687796D&FORM=VIRE , *"The decline of Wikipedia"*, 24.04.2019

[†] Doesn't this raise the question of who, if not the élite, is in charge now? (SP) My answer (JS): The elite (the Deep State) has gradually brought its followers or representatives into the leading positions of government, ministries, secret services, for example US Air Force, NASA, CIA, FBI, DARPA ..., or corrupted leading politicians with money and blackmail.

A first effective step against the total seizure of power by the Deep State in the direction of the NWO is the indictment against representatives of the Deep State cited on page 3. And it cannot be ruled out that in the course of the military "exercise" "Defender 2020" and the staged corona crisis, combined with curfews and assembly bans, a change of system is being prepared, which is intended to smash the international structures of the Deep State that have grown over decades. If this is true, we owe it to the Q-Anon movement and especially to the Trump administration. In 2016/17, Trump set out to smash the power of the Deep State and its media allies.

But it can also be quite different, namely that QAnon was installed by the Deep State to raise deceptive hope in those who already saw through the "game". Thus it could be achieved that the patriots fall into a wait and see mode and do not become active themselves to prevent the establishment of the NWO. However, the year 2020 is an important year that will set the course, either towards the NWO and thus the enslavement of humanity or towards the destruction of the Deep Staate. We will know it.

If Q and Trump should indeed actively fight the Deep State and also emerge victorious from it, then humanity would once again escape its greatest conceivable catastrophe. Then this book would be an authentic testimony of the danger she had run into. However, even then, humanity is not yet saved forever. It must continue to be vigilant and learn from it. For when people are full and have no more direct existential worries, they become lethargic and uninterested, and the dark forces may have learned from the "lost battle" and regain the upper hand. We remember, evil people and psychopaths with their special qualities (see section "Psychopaths") will always exist. So: Be alert!

Epilogue – Elite and Deep State

The western capitalist states today use particularly perfidious propaganda to market globalized capitalism under the label of democracy, freedom and 'western values' as the only conceivable economic and social order.
(Eugen Drewermann[669])

Those who decide are not elected, and those who are elected have nothing to decide.[670] This last sentence, a public utterance in 2010 of Horst Seehofer, a top German politician[‡], is an apt description of the current state of affairs. In so many words, some leading academics say the same in their researches into the current political situation in Germany: so-called democracy in the USA and in other states espousing 'western communal values' is, in reality, a complex nexus of mostly clandestine, or secret, underground rule, which eludes pubscrutiny. The term **Deep State** is sometimes used for this shadowy rule, but also other terms such as parallel government or secret government, from which the actual exercise of power is launched.

U Mies and J Wernicke[671] describe the 'visible state' as façade democracy, a play for the general public in front of the theatre curtain. The really important political decisions are made ... however, in the deep structures and 'parallel universes of power' behind the theatre curtain.[§] *These include all forms of power perversion such as surveillance, torture, robbery of the national wealth, secret service crimes, fear production to war preparations and the conduct of wars of aggression ... The Deep State organizes exploitation, looting and destruction and drives*

[‡] In 2010, Horst Seehofer (1949-) was Minister-President of Bavaria (2008-18) (SP)
[§] ... which is expressed by the covers of the two previous books; short summary at the end of this book.

militarization to extremes. The ruling élites installed their kleptomania as the centrepoint of arbitrary rule. They lack any moral compass; self-righteousness and mendacity are their essence.[672]

The cognitive scientist Professor Rainer Mausfeld uses the expression 'representative democracy'. What we are currently experiencing in politics, and in the influence of the masses by the media, epitomises neoliberalism, which for several decades now has devoured more and more space within Western democracies. Neoliberalism is a form of élite rule, with the word democracy serving as a cover-up. In reality, the élites redistribute from below to above, for which fig-leaf democracy is a useful camouflage. The following maxim applies to representative democracy: *Whoever owns the country should also govern it – representative democracy as a means of avoiding democracy.* This is according to a chapter heading in the book[673] *Why Do the Lambs Stay Silent******************* by Rainer Mausfeld. *If it does not want to eschew its democratic appearance, Neo-liberalism will increasingly be judged for being absolutely dependent on redistributive mechanisms from bottom to top and from public to private at all levels – from the EU to the municipalities.*[674] And legalization of this process further leads to laws that can then be put in place against democratic action (petitions, demonstrations, etc).

The transition from democracy to representative demo-democracy, with the aim of avoiding democracy altogether, has been fluid in recent decades. *In the UK, democracy is now limited to the regular elections to the House of Commons – with the House of Lords acting in an arbitrary fashion, sometimes democratically (as if by coincidence) and sometimes not.(SP)*†††††††††††††††††††† The élite, or

---

****************** In German, *Warum schweigen die Lämmer*
†††††††††††††††††††† The sentence in the German edition would translate as: *In Germany, democracy is now limited to the regular elections to the Bundestag and the state parliaments.* My copy-editing should make it clear that, in my view, the more or less identical situation re democracy applies in both countries. (SP)

Deep State, pull the strings behind the scenes. It is the élite that largely decide which politicians appear as candidates for election. This selection process is not made public, but, for example, *in the UK a candidate is selected by his political party's nominating officer*‡‡‡‡‡‡‡‡‡‡‡‡‡‡‡‡‡‡‡‡ *– ideally in some sort of consultation with the party office in the local constituency that the candidate is supposed to represent. For example, the Conservative Party's Nominating Officer at present is Victoria Carslake – someone very few British people have ever heard of, yet she, not us, is the person who determines the identity of our ruling MPs. If we do not like the idea of her having all this power we can always vote for another party to win the election, but our choice of MP is still limited to whatever, often quite unknown candidate that other party's equally anonymous Nominating Officer has chosen on our behalf (as if we were children who are never allowed the chocolate our parents might occasionally like to give us but can only choose a potentially poison apple selected by a family stranger). (SP)*

In Germany, candidates are decided on at the annual Bilderberg conferences, the results of which usually do not provide any information to the public.[675] It is the task of the media to rattle the drum for these candidates chosen by the élite, so that they win the upcoming election. In addition to heads of government, high financiers of Western Europe, the USA and Canada, leading industrialists, high-ranking military and intelligence officers, and the executive boards of the world's largest and best-known media companies all take part in the Bilderberg Conferences. It can therefore be assumed that the media also belong to the élite's narrow circle, and that media power and its propagandistic influence on the population make a decisive contribution to ensuring that candidates favoured by the Bilderbergers are chosen with a high degree of probability. If, contrary to expectations, it does not work out – for example in the election of Donald Trump to the Presidency of the USA or of Boris Johnson the Brexiteering

---

‡‡‡‡‡‡‡‡‡‡‡‡‡‡‡‡‡‡‡‡ The German edition similarly refers to the annual Bilderberg Conferences, the results of which do not usually provide any information to the public regarding the reasons for their choice of candidates for the German elections (SP)

Prime Minister (neither are élite preferences), an unprecedented media campaign is launched against these politicians who are characterized as displaying irrational traits. The same can be said in connection with the strengthening of the AfD (Alternative für Deutschland) in Germany: on a broad front, agitation and disparagement erupt against this young opposition party, both in the media and by politicians of the old parties, but also by other social forces, including representatives of the two Churches, foundations, (sponsored) artists, and NGOs.

To summarize, nowhere in the UK, Germany, or in the Western world in general do we live in a real democracy, where the sovereign people§§§§§§§§§§§§§§§§§§§§§§ determine what happens in the country; we live rather in a Representative Democracy, or Façade Democracy, where real power is exercised through the Deep State.

But who or what exactly is the Deep State? On this question the author B Hamm is summarized by U Mies:[676]

Based on the 'Power Structure Model' by C Wright Mills, Hamm describes the entire complex in the form of concentric circles:
*• In the inner circle we find the global élite, the richest individuals, families or clans with assets well in excess of one billion euros each.*********************
• The second circle consists of the CEOs of large transnational corporations and the largest international financial magnates. They are primarily concerned with increasing the wealth of the innermost circle and thus also their own.
• In the third circle are the most important international politicians, some in government positions, others in the background and in international institutions, as well as the leaders

---

§§§§§§§§§§§§§§§§§§§§§§ In German, der Souverän (SP)
******************** This inner circle is represented in particular by the Committee of 300, whose clear aim is world domination. In over 40 years of research, Dr. John Coleman has compiled a standard historical work in which he lists the goals and means of the Committee of 300 in 21 points (see Appendix 1 in the book *2025 - The penultimate act.*)

of the military. This political class in the narrower sense has two tasks: it has to organize the distribution of the social product in such a way that as much as possible is transferred to the two inner circles; and it must secure the political circus of a supposedly pluralistic democracy with the necessary legitimacy.
• In the fourth circle we find the top scientists, the media moguls, lawyers, sometimes also prominent writers, stars from film and music, artists, a few representatives of NGOs or the churches, a few top criminals – in short: everything that relatives of the inner circles appreciate for their decoration. They enjoy access to the powerful, are well paid and will do everything they can not to lose these privileges.

In conclusion, the United States can be seen as the central driver of Neoliberal Capitalism, perhaps more accurately described as Predatory Capitalism.

---

[1] https://www.dz-g.ru/19CV2407-CAB-AHG-vom-16-Dezember-2019 _Verbrechen-gegen-die-Menschheit , *"Why We Sued Big Tech for Artificial Intelligence Misuse & Contribution to Win for Humanity"*, 31.01.2020

[2] J. Sonntag, B. Lenoir and P. Ziolkowski, Electronic Transport in Alloys with Phase Separation (Composites). *Open Journal of Composite Materials,* 2019, 9, 21-56 https://www.scirp.org/Journal/PaperInformation.aspx?PaperID=90216

[3] https://www.youtube.com/watch?v=E8QsOz4u54M&t=14s *"Vermischung der Rassen auch mit Zwangsmaßnahmen - Französischer Ex-Präsident (2008)"*

[4] https://www.facebook.com/b.n.d.und.brid.machen.nur.noch.shit/videos/***united-nation-of-europe***-(une/1911800162465818/ „***UNITED NATION of EUROPE*** (UNE / NWO Umwandlung bis 2030/2050 ist bereits Vereinbart & Beschlossen worden)"*

[5] https://www.heise.de/forum/Telepolis/Kommentare/Ansichten-eines-Gutmenschen/Was-Carl-Friedrich-von-Weizsaecker-dazu-sagt/posting-24114785/show/

[6] https://www.youtube.com/watch?v=TFYHL8x16Y8 , *"Der bedrohte Friede 1983 Carl Friedrich von Weizsäcker"*, 04.12.2012.

[7] Joachim Sonntag, „*2025 - Der vorletzte Akt: Warum wir Heimat, Freiheit und Sicherheit verlieren*", CBX-Verlag München, 2019, pages 232ff

[8]
https://www.bing.com/videos/search?q=Unzicker&view=detail&mid=5730B95C57754687796D5730B95C57754687796D&FORM=VIRE
„Der Niedergang der Wikipedia", 24.04.2019

[9] Wikipedia-Eintrag, *„zuletzt am 17. April 2020 um 01:16 Uhr bearbeitet"*

[10] Wikipedia-Eintrag, *„zuletzt am 11. Mai 2020 um 19:51 Uhr bearbeitet"*

[11] Joachim Sonntag, *„2025 - Der vorletzte Akt: Warum wir Heimat, Freiheit und Sicherheit verlieren"*, CBX-Verlag München, 2019, pages 48ff

[12] as previously, Seiten 232ff

[13] https://www.youtube.com/watch?v=qhIIhokrZXo , *„Rechtsanwalt Steinhöfel über Heiko Maas, Zensur, Hate-Speech und Fake-News"*

[14] Oliver Janich: *Impossible Mission 9/11: Wie ein kleines Spezialkommando den größten Terroranschlag der Geschichte durchgeführt haben könnte* , CBX Verlag UG, 2018

[15] Joachim Sonntag, *„2025 - Der vorletzte Akt: Warum wir Heimat, Freiheit und Sicherheit verlieren"*, CBX-Verlag München, 2019, pages 48ff

[16] https://www.youtube.com/watch?v=tuVspN5RIoE *„NEWW!! ARD u ZDF zeigen Haarp und Chemtrails sind keineswegs eine Verschwörungstheorie UNFASSBAR!"*, am 03.01.2017 veröffentlicht

[17] https://new.euro-med.dk/20161121-haarp-wetter-manipulationdurch-nasa-satelliten-fotos-bewiwswn.php *„HAARP Wetter-Manipulation durch NASA-Satelliten-Fotos bewiesen"* , 21.11, 2016

[18] https://www.youtube.com/watch?v=WaudJgutsPw&t=1650s *„Doku: Der geheime Krieg - Solares Geoengineering - deutsch synchronisierte Version"* (Minute 5:25 im Video), veröffentlicht am 15.03.2016

[19] https://www.youtube.com/watch?v=5ZWAdpA6MHU
„Weather as a Force Multiplier: Owning the Weather in 2025 - PDF eBook - Air Force 2025", veröffentlicht am 07.07.2017

[20] Joachim Sonntag, *„2025 - Der vorletzte Akt: Warum wir Heimat, Freiheit und Sicherheit verlieren"*, CBX-Verlag München, 2019, page 14

[21] http://www.deagel.com/country/

[22] Joachim Sonntag, *„2025 - Der vorletzte Akt: Warum wir Heimat, Freiheit und Sicherheit verlieren"*, CBX-Verlag München, 2019, Kapitel PROLOG

[23] https://gloria.tv/video/kocXqyBeYEaG4QXzkK6TvdJdL , *„Kennedy und Eisenhower warnen vor einer monolithischen, ruchlosen, weltweiten Verschwörung!"*, 27. Juli 2013

[24] as previously

[25] https://www.oliverjanich.de/die-rede-die-john-f-kennedys-schicksal-besiegelte , Oliver Janich: *„Die Rede, die John F. Kennedys Schicksal besiegelte"*, 19. Juni 2013

[26] www.StopTheCrime.net

[27] http://euro-med.dk/?p=31327

[28] Joachim Sonntag, *„2025 - Der vorletzte Akt: Warum wir Heimat, Freiheit und Sicherheit verlieren"*, CBX-Verlag München, 2019, pages 11f

[29] https://www.youtube.com/watch?v=t4OwfkSEtlY *„Neue Prognosen von DEAGEL.com"*, am 28.04.2018 veröffentlicht

[30] https://www.youtube.com/watch?v=s_38tsQ4p0I&t=233s *"Silent Weapons For Quiet Wars Document - Full Read"*, veröffentlicht am 27.06.2013.

[31] www.newhorizonsstannes.com/pdfs/Silent_war_against_humanit... „Silent Weapons for a 'Quiet War' - New Horizons (St. Annes): *„The document "Silent Weapons for a Quiet War" was found by "co-incidence" in 1986 or even before, and it goes back to 1954 which also happens to be the year where the "nice think-tank" Bilderberg Group was founded – this world just happens to be full of "co-incidences" all the time :-)"*

[32] Joachim Sonntag, *„2025 - Der vorletzte Akt: Warum wir Heimat, Freiheit und Sicherheit verlieren"*, CBX-Verlag München, 2019, Back of the book

[33] https://www.activistpost.com/2017/10/nanochips-smart-dust-dangerous-new-face-human-microchipping-agenda.html , By Makia Freeman: *„Nanochips and Smart Dust: The Dangerous New Face of the Human Microchipping Agenda"*, October 20, 2017

[34] https://www.youtube.com/watch?v=cTp_1HzrCoo
Herbert Schott: *„ Chemtrails und Nanotechnologie zur Manipulation der Menschheit Teil 1 "*, am 16.03.2014 veröffentlicht

[35] https://internationalesforumblog.wordpress.com/2017/05/01/ueber-den-groessten-umweltverschmutzer-der-welt-wird-selten-gesprochen-er-ist-das-militaer-des-us-imperiums-und-darueber-wird-im-imperium-nicht-gern-gesprochen-die-gigantische-kriegsmaschinerie-is/?fbclid=IwAR3EPsPuoZpNJV3zl-tFbKcX2D-EDXpsJ7HvnJVAkppbb-iqfaZ--KhX6pQ , INTERNATIONALESFORUMBLOG:WORDPRESS:COM, David Swanson *"What I Said at the Peace Hub of the Climate March"*

[36]

https://www.youtube.com/watch?v=PLPLUKEmVRs&fbclid=IwAR1qhfvHLSG2nR6RbTf77f6WIlfhJqhCAE3NpFZAa1De_X7_vBvpycAbgkE *„MARKmobil Mittelpunkt - Die große Lage"*, veröffentlicht am 23.02.2019

[37] https://www.youtube.com/watch?v=5yoQUluPxv8 , *„Nuklearer Klimawandel? Über 2.100 Atombombentests seit 1945! | 27.04.2019 | www.kla.tv/14207"*

[38]

https://www.youtube.com/watch?v=PLPLUKEmVRs&fbclid=IwAR1qhfvHLSG2nR6RbTf77f6WIlfhJqhCAE3NpFZAa1De_X7_vBvpycAbgkE *„MARKmobil Mittelpunkt - Die große Lage"*, veröffentlicht am 23.02.2019, Minute 15:23

[39] as previously, Minute 14:33

[40] https://www.kleinezeitung.at/lebensart/nachhaltigkeit/5618082/Palmoel_Jede-Minute-verschwinden-30-Fussballfelder-an-Regenwald , *„Palmöl - Jede Minute verschwinden 30 Fußballfelder an Regenwald"*, 04. Juni 2019

[41]

http://webcache.googleusercontent.com/search?q=cache:8QuZTZquheYJ:www.planungsamt.bundeswehr.de/resource/resource/MzEzNTM4MmUzMzMyMmUzMTM1MzMyZTM2MzIzMDMwMzAzMDMwMzAzMDY4NzE2NjMwMzk3YTc5NjYyMDIwMjAyMDIw/Future%2520Topic%2520Geoengineering.pdf+&cd=1&hl=de&ct=clnk&gl=de&client=firefox-b-d

[42] as previously

[43] https://new.euro-med.dk/20161121-haarp-wetter-manipulationdurch-nasa-satelliten-fotos-bewiwswn.php *„NEW.EURO-MED.DK“*, 21.11. 2016

[44] https://www.n-tv.de/mediathek/videos/politik/Schulz-fordert-Vereinigte-Staaten-von-Europa-article20173119.html , Vertrag bis 2025: *„Schulz fordert Vereinigte Staaten von Europa“*, ntv, 31.12.2019

[45] http://www.anonymousnews.ru/2017/07/29/die-geplante-masseneinwanderung-angela-merkel-und-der-coudenhove-kalergi-plan/#comment-40328 *"Die geplante Zerstörung Europas: Angela Merkel und der Coudenhove-Kalergi-Plan"*

[46] Jörg Meuthen on 31.12.2019 in a post by AfD, distributed on Facebook

[47] Joachim Sonntag, *„2025 - Der vorletzte Akt: Warum wir Heimat, Freiheit und Sicherheit verlieren“*, CBX-Verlag München, 2019, Kapitel PROLOG, page 14

[48]   https://new.euro-med.dk/20161121-haarp-wetter-manipulationdurch-nasa-satelliten-fotos-bewiwswn.php , *„HAARP Wetter-Manipulation durch NASA-Satelliten-Fotos bewiesen“*, 21.11. 2016

[49] https://www.legitim.ch/home/author/Jan-Walter , Jan Walter: *„Geheime Agenda - Der wahre Grund für 5G ist 1000 Mal schlimmer als die Strahlung!“* , 8. April 2019

[50] https://www.contra-magazin.com/2017/09/wetterextreme-als-waffe-das-weltklima-als-versuchslabor-wurden-harvey-und-irma-kuenstlich-erzeugt/ , Eva-Maria Griese: *„Wetterextreme als Waffe: Das Weltklima als Versuchslabor – wurden Harvey und Irma künstlich erzeugt ?“* 13. September 2017.

[51] https://www.youtube.com/watch?v=2QZx3dOj4H0 , *„GRIPPEWELLE DURCH CHEMTRAILS ! SIE SPRÜHEN UNS KRANK 360p“*, am 10.10.2018 veröffentlicht, Minute 3:48

[52] https://www.youtube.com/watch?v=e2W-VeN0Glk&fbclid=IwAR1GxTTYStS1aNx2x_iBmv2bDEzF0HyD-LE3VTuYikGG95wF7LOtUCG1x54 , *„Was zur Zeit so abgeht (Stop 007)“*, 24.03.2019

[53] Markus Egert und Frank Thadeusz, Ein Keim kommt selten allein, Ullstein Buchverlage GmbH, 2018, page 145

[54] https://www.bild.de/ratgeber/gesundheit/krankenhaus-keime/krankenhaus-keime-jaehrlich-91000-tote-europa-studie-48335386.bild.html *„Alarmierende Zahlen: Jährlich ziehen sich insgesamt 2,6 Millionen Patienten Krankenhausin-fektionen zu, 91 000 sterben daran!“*, 18.10.2016

[55] Dieses Zitat stammt eigentlich von P.J. Dunning (1860), ist aber durch Karl Marx in einer Fußnote im „Kapital“ bekannt gemacht worden (s. Kapitel 4.)

[56] *https://www.youtube.com/watch?v=3MCaceXGYHw* „Die verschwiegene Wahrheit über Gifte und Krebs“, Veröffentlicht am 19.09.2018

[57] https://www.youtube.com/user/FMDsTVChannel

[58] https://www.youtube.com/watch?v=8qIAm1l-ZRA&t=391s
Dirk Steffens' Klima-Irrsinn ENTLARVT !!!

[59] *https://www.youtube.com/watch?v=6uNL7ygIias&t=38s*
Dirk Steffens' Klima-Irrsinn ENTLARVT !!! #2

[60] https://www.youtube.com/watch?v=ga-GdDknwxI&t=5s *"Arktis-Eis wird absichtlich geschmolzen! UNGLAUBLICH, aber WAHR!"*

[61] https://www.youtube.com/watch?v=EW-VPbtA2kg

62 https://www.bookrix.de/book.html?bookID=xnemesisx_1334144092.1235098839 Thomas Beschorner/ verschiedene Autoren, *"Wahrheitslügen"*

63 as previously

64 https://www.youtube.com/watch?v=EgczgWJUOLA *"Chemtrails und Haarp - Brigitta Zuber"*

65 https://www.youtube.com/watch?v=bli57XeXUt0 *"ES GIBT KEINE CHEMTRAILS ! - DU ALUHUTDEPP ! DAS ULTIMATIVE BEWEISVIDEO"* (ddb Netzwerk)

66 https://news-for-friends.de/wie-wird-die-agenda-21-weltweit-umgesetzt/?fbclid=IwAR2uFUSfj_8zESyEV2wn_-OU00kKYJfphcGGxkWOqhD-J-mJq6NYKy_hYYQ , *„Wie wird die Agenda 21 weltweit umgesetzt?"*, 7.April 2019

67 Joachim Sonntag, *„2025 - Der vorletzte Akt: Warum wir Heimat, Freiheit und Sicherheit verlieren"*, CBX-Verlag München, 2019, pages 14ff and 102ff

68 Netzfund

69 https://www.heise.de/forum/Telepolis/Kommentare/Ansichten-eines-Gutmenschen/Was-Carl-Friedrich-von-Weizsaecker-dazu-sagt/posting-24114785/show/

70 Joachim Sonntag, *Deutschland im freien Fall – Wie die milliardenschweren Finanzeliten unsere freiheitliche Demokratie zerstören und unsere Politiker und öffentlichen Medien zu deren Werkzeugen wurden*, 2. erweiterte Auflage, BoD-Verlag, 2017, Anlage K, pages 189ff

71 https://www.youtube.com/watch?v=W8Ifp_O9oRA&t=10s *„MILLIONEN TOTE BIS 2025 Deagel Die erschreckende Prognose!"*, veröffentlicht 22.02.2015.

72 https://www.konjunktion.info/2017/03/zum-tod-von-david-rockefeller/

73 https://www.youtube.com/watch?v=t4OwfkSEtlY *„Neue Prognosen von DEAGEL.com"*, am 28.04.2018 veröffentlicht

74 https://www.youtube.com/watch?v=W8Ifp_O9oRA&t=10s *„MILLIONEN TOTE BIS 2025 Deagel Die erschreckende Prognose!"*, veröffentlicht 22.02.2015.

75 https://www.youtube.com/watch?v=c2quPTsPy8o *„GLADIO - Die NATO-Geheimarmeen"*, veröffentlicht am 25.03.2014 veröffentlicht

76 https://www.youtube.com/watch?v=t4OwfkSEtlY *"Neue Prognosen von DEAGEL.com"*, am 28.04.2018 veröffentlicht, Minute 4:50

77 https://kopp-report.de/amerikas-bauern-stehen-vor-der-schwersten-krise-seit-einer-generation-und-das-naechste-monstroese-unwetter-ist-bereits-im-anmarsch/ , Michael Snyder: *„Amerikas Bauern stehen vor der schwersten Krise seit einer Generation – und das nächste monströse Unwetter ist bereits im Anmarsch"*, 11.06. 2019

78 http://endoftheamericandream.com/archives/u-s-farms-are-facing-their-worst-crisis-in-a-generation-and-now-here-comes-another-monster-storm , Michael Snyder: *„U.S. Farms Are Facing Their Worst Crisis In A Generation – And Now Here Comes Another Monster Storm"*, June 6, 2019

[79] Joachim Sonntag, *Deutschland im freien Fall – Wie die milliardenschweren Finanzeliten unsere freiheitliche Demokratie zerstören und unsere Politiker und öffentlichen Medien zu deren Werkzeugen wurden*, 2. erweiterte Auflage, BoD-Verlag, 2017, pages 28ff

[80] https://www.youtube.com/watch?v=IqH--Yi2CI4&t=833s Hartmut Bachmann: *„Der Ursprung der Klimalüge"*, 07.12.2016, Minute 14:15

[81] https://www.welt.de/kultur/plus204357014/Ein-Mann-ein-Wort-Wie-die-Linke-lernte-den-Notstand-zu-lieben.html , Matthias Heine: *„Wie die Linke lernte, den Notstand zu lieben"*, 16.12.2019

[82] www.euractiv.de/section/energie-und-umwelt/news/eu-parlament-ruft-klimanotstand-aus/ , Peter Esser: *„EU-Parlament ruft 'Klimanotstand' aus"*, 28.11.2019

[83] https://www.sueddeutsche.de/politik/eu-klimanotstand-parlament-beschluss-1.4701180 , Süddeutsche Zeitung, *„Resolution:Europäisches Parlament ruft Klimanotstand aus"*, 28.11.2019

[84] *as previously*

[85] https://www.spiegel.de/wissenschaft/mensch/european-green-deal-wie-die-eu-zum-klimaschutz-kontinent-werden-will-a-1300723.html , Susanne Götze: *„Von der Leyen präsentiert Plan für grünes Europa"*, 11.12.2019

[86] https://www.tagesschau.de/ausland/eu-klima-greendeal-101.html , *„Klimaschutz der EU Was sich der 'Green Deal' vornimmt"*, 11.12.19

[87] https://www.legitim.ch/post/enth%C3%BCllt-prayfortheamazon-ist-fake-von-a-bis-z , Jan Walter: *„Enthüllt: #PrayForTheAmazon ist FAKE! (von A bis Z)"*, am 29.08.19, aktualisiert am 31.08.19

[88] https://www.welt.de/debatte/kommentare/article13466483/Die-CO2-Theorie-ist-nur-geniale-Propagan-da.html?wtmc=socialmedia.facebook.shared.web&fbclid=IwAR1oTewiEL7F4sV NOnN__WB2Ss-f39J0ce1JbsRTFF2mJ5PLmGKpb08lRJ0

[89] https://www.youtube.com/watch?v=IqH--Yi2CI4&t=833s Hartmut Bachmann: *„Der Ursprung der Klimalüge"*, 07.12.2016, Minute 14:05

[90] https://www.youtube.com/watch?v=5xSHYWyJtQ4&t=801s , *„Volksverdummung vom deutschen CO2 als monokausaler Erwärmungsursache – Boehringer Klartext (82)"*, veröffentlicht am 08.12.2019, Minute 3:30.

[91] https://www.youtube.com/watch?v=Ls07THzlL9M , *„Dirk Müller - "One World": Darum ist den Eliten das Klima plötzlich so wichtig!"*, am 24.05.2019 veröffentlicht

[92] https://www.handelsblatt.com/politik/deutschland/gutachten-benzin-und-heizoel-koennten-teurer-werden-merkels-berater-fordern-co2-steuer/24042222.html?ticket=ST-425900-D23uZ1hoAzoprK407X16-ap1 , Gutachten: *„Benzin und Heizöl könnten teurer werden: Merkels Berater fordern CO2-Steuer"*, 27.02.2019

[93] https://www.wahrheiten.org/blog/klimaluege/ , *„Die Klima-Lüge"*

[94] https://www.spiegel.de/wissenschaft/technik/extinction-rebellion-gruender-roger-hallam-wenn-eine-gesellschaft-so-unmoralisch-handelt-wird-demokratie-

irrelevant-a-1286561.html , SPIEGELONLINE : *"Wenn eine Gesellschaft so unmoralisch handelt, wird Demokratie irrelevant"*; 13.09.2019

[95] https://www.watson.de/deutschland/die%20gr%C3%BCnen/791308473-die-afd-sagt-robert-habeck-wuensche-sich-eine-diktatur-das-steckt-dahinter , Felix Huesmann: *„Die AfD behauptet, Robert Habeck wolle eine Diktatur – das steckt dahinter"*, 20.06.19

[96] https://www.youtube.com/watch?v=kbnX7yG91R0 "Klimawandel: #kurzerklärt kurz aufgeklärt", veröffentlicht 06.08.2017

[97] https://www.youtube.com/watch?v=GL3AEKIKtN4&fbclid=IwAR3ifX8QhdA1d Lxdk2Ug7fa34zDSP0zdbTWc80jRuwbG7_0wcA8WAD_UIrI&app=desktop , *„Cook-Studie widerlegt: Weniger als 1% machen Menschen für Klimawandel verantwortlich!"*, 04.01.2020

[98] https://www.youtube.com/watch?v=kbnX7yG91R0 "Klimawandel: #kurzerklärt kurz aufgeklärt", veröffentlicht 06.08.2017

[99] https://kaltesonne.de/wp-content/uploads/2019/09/signature-list.pdf , *„There is noclimate emergency"*, 26.09.2019

[100] https://www.youtube.com/watch?v=GL3AEKIKtN4&fbclid=IwAR3ifX8QhdA1d Lxdk2Ug7fa34zDSP0zdbTWc80jRuwbG7_0wcA8WAD_UIrI&app=desktop , *„Cook-Studie widerlegt: Weniger als 1% machen Menschen für Klimawandel verantwortlich!"*, 04.01.2020

[101] as previously, ab Minute 1:20

[102] https://www.youtube.com/watch?v=kbnX7yG91R0 "Klimawandel: #kurzerklärt kurz aufgeklärt", veröffentlicht 06.08.2017

[103] https://www.epochtimes.de/umwelt/ueber-31-000-wissenschaftler-unterzeichnen-petition-hypothese-der-vom-menschen-verursachten-globalen-erwaermung-ist-falsch-a2323579.html?fb=1&fbclid=IwAR0kPp8vhCiibZbaM7zlidcObC_VezpzdsFnLs ZjkpUv-g5bm-qUH7YE7YDw „Über 31.000 Wissenschaftler unterzeichnen Petition: Hypothese der *vom Menschen verursachten globalen Erwärmung ist falsch"*, 17.Januar 2018

[104] http://diekaltesonne.de/category/news/ , *„90 italienische Wissenschaftler unterzeichnen Petition gegen Klimaalarm"*, 5. Juli 2019

[105] https://kaltesonne.de/wp-content/uploads/2019/09/signature-list.pdf , *„There is noclimate emergency"*, 26.09.2019

[106] https://kaltesonne.de/fritz-vahrenholt-wir-haben-aber-keinen-klimanotstand/ , Fritz Vahrenholt: *„ Wir haben keinen Klimanotstand"*, 8. Oktober 2019

[107] as previously

[108] https://www.klimafakten.de/behauptungen/behauptung-31000-wissenschaftler-oregon-petition-hypothese-klimawandel-menschgemacht-erderwaermung-falsch?fbclid=IwAR0LBGWyJg8In852u6lxRTk-JdcdDwQW9ItrghguSWEblakq3_4tzljSHDo , G. P. Wayne/Michael: *„Behauptung: „Über 31.000 Wissenschaftler unterzeichnen Petition - Hypothese der vom Menschen verursachten globalen Erwärmung ist falsch"*, August 2010; zuletzt aktualisiert: Juni 2018

[109] https://www.eike-klima-energie.eu/2017/11/09/desinformation-der-klimafakten-de-in-was-sagt-die-afd-zum-klimawandel-was-sagen-die-anderen-parteien-und-was-ist-der-stand-der-wissenschaft/ , *Horst-Joachim Lüdecke: „Desinformation der Klimafakten.de in 'Was sagt die AfD zum Klimawandel? Was sagen die anderen Parteien? Und was ist der Stand der Wissenschaft?'"* , 9.November 2017

[110] www.easy-wetter.de/Klimazustandsbericht%202016.pdf *„Klimazustandsbericht 2016"* der UN-Klimakonferenz im November, vorgelegt von Marc Morano, Climate Depot und dem Committee for a Constructive Tomorrow CFACT

[111] https://www.youtube.com/watch?v=IoXxrZG-_eU *„DER KLIMASCHWINDEL - DOKU in voller Länge"*

[112] http://news-for-friends.de/mit-haarp-zum-tornado-mit-dem-tornado-zur-co2-steuer/ *"Mit HAARP zum Tornado, mit dem Tornado zur CO2-Steuer....."* Von nfriends, 20. Juli 2017

[113] https://www.youtube.com/watch?v=ZYXrGlYAZOg&feature=share , *„Tricksen, Täuschen, Fabulieren - Der Klimaschwindel / Neu!",* am 13.07.2019 veröffentlicht

[114] LOWELL PONTE: *"THE COOLING – Has the next ice age already begun? Can we survive it?"* (zitiert in https://www.youtube.com/watch?v=ga-GdDknwxI&t=5s *"Arktis-Eis wird absichtlich geschmolzen! UNGLAUBLICH, aber WAHR!")*

[115] http://www.spiegel.de/spiegel/print/d-41002273.html *„FORSCHUNG - Steine verweht -* Klima-Forscher haben die Hauptursache der Eiszeiten erkannt: Unregelmäßigkeiten im Lauf der Erde um die Sonne. Die gegenwärtige Wärmeperiode, sagen sie vorher, geht zu Ende." Veröffentlicht 10.01.1977

[116] https://www.welt.de/debatte/kommentare/article13466483/Die-CO2-Theorie-ist-nur-geniale-Propaganda.html ; Günter Ederer: *„Die CO2-Theorie ist nur geniale Propaganda"* , Veröffentlicht am 04.07.2011

[117] https://www.youtube.com/watch?v=KFu9oJJXgdQ *"Sonneborn rettet die EU (VI): Golf mit Präsident Chulz"*

[118] as previously

[119] as previously

[120] https://www.facebook.com/peter.boringer.7/videos/2445566389013759/ Peter Boeringer: *„Wer mauert hat's nötig: Altparteien bewehren sich gegen die Folgen der eigenen Politik – Peter Boehringer spricht Klartext (67)",* am 23.7.2019

[121] http://news-for-friends.de/mit-haarp-zum-tornado-mit-dem-tornado-zur-co2-steuer/ *"Mit HAARP zum Tornado, mit dem Tornado zur CO2-Steuer....."* Von nfriends, 20. Juli 2017

[122] as previously

[123] https://www.youtube.com/watch?v=8qIAm11-ZRA&t=391s *Dirk Steffens' Klima-Irrsinn ENTLARVT !!!*

[124] https://qpress.de/2015/05/03/prima-klima-katastrophe-glaubensgrundsaetze-der-klimareligion-versinken-im-meer-der-zweifel/ *"Prima Klima-Katastrophe, Glaubensgrundsätze der Klimareligion versinken im Meer der Zweifel"* , 03.05.2015

[125] Das_Skeptiker-Handbuch_3.0_kurz_96dpi.pdf
[126] as previously
[127] https://de.wikipedia.org/wiki/Eine_unbequeme_Wahrheit Davis Guggenheim und Al Gore: „*Eine unbequeme Wahrheit*" („*An Inconvenient Truth*")
[128] https://www.wahrheiten.org/blog/klimaluege/ , „*Die Klima-Lüge*"
[129] https://www.youtube.com/watch?v=w_9DUPoI_WU , Naomi Seibt: „*KLIMAWANDEL - Alles nur heiße Luft..? - Teil 1!*, Am 01.07.2019 veröffentlicht
[130] https://www.swr.de/swr2/wissen/co2-ist-schwerer-als-luft/-/id=661224/did=6081902/nid=661224/1aj2o8i/index.html , „CO2 ist schwerer als Luft. Wie soll es dann in die obere Atmosphäre aufsteigen und den Treibhauseffe *1000 Antworten - Frag den Paal. SWR2 Impuls vom 4.3.2010*"
[131] https://www.pravda-tv.com/2018/12/haarp-geoengineering-in-deutschland-die-hitzewelle-2018-video/?fbclid=IwAR1RWT9A6K_FPPseisuP76063wpFCWvZzIzTZGN1SKPf8qH DfKAC-jBYETU , „*HAARP: Geoengineering in Deutschland - die Hitzewelle 2018 (Video)*", 18. 12.2018
[132] Chris Haderer und Peter Hiess, „Chemtrails – Wettermanipulation am Himmel? – Wettermanipulation unter den Augen der Öffentlichkeit", Copyright by V. F. SAMMLER, Graz 2005, page 9
[133] https://www.eike-klima-energie.eu/2010/01/20/nur-00004712-prozent-bund-aktivist-weiss-nicht-wieviel-co2-von-deutschland-in-die-luft-abgegeben-wird/#comment-202403 *"Nur 0,0004712 Prozent!! BUND Aktivist weiss nicht wieviel CO2 von Deutschland in die Luft abgegeben wird!"* , 20.01.2010
[134] https://www.youtube.com/watch?v=IqH--Yi2CI4 „*Der Ursprung der Klimalüge*", veröffentlicht am 06.12.2016
[135] Hartmut Bachmann: „*Die Lüge der Klimakatastrophe: ...und wie der Staat uns damit ausbeutet. Manipulierte Angst als Mittel zur Macht*", Kurzbeschreibung, entnommen aus https://docplayer.org/43335841-Die-luege-der-klimakatastrophe.html , „*Die Lüge der Klimakatastrophe - Version 15*"
[136] https://www.youtube.com/watch?v=OBdRittlo8w&t=46s , „*Die Zerstörung der Klima-Hysterie!!? * Klimawandel-Kommentar*", 07.09.2019
[137] https://www.youtube.com/watch?v=uhz9XGU2D-4 , Maximilian Pütz: „*Klimawandellüge vor Gericht entlarvt- Jetzt ist es offiziell !!!*", 03.09.2019
[138] as previously
[139] https://www.spiegel.de/wissenschaft/natur/klimaforschung-streit-um-die-hockeyschlaeger-grafik-a-886334.html , Axel Bojanowski: *"Vorwürfe gegen Klimaforscher Wahn der Weltverbesserer, Teil 2*", 14.03.2013
[140] Committee on Surface Temperature Reconstructions for the Last 2,000 Years, National Research Council (2006): *Surface temperature reconstructions for the last 2,000 years*. Washington, D.C.: National Academies Press
[141] P.D. Jones und M.E. Mann (2004): *Climate Over Past Millennia*, in: Review of Geophysics, Vol. 42, No. 2, RG2002
[142] https://www.klimafakten.de/behauptungen/behauptung-die-beruehmte-hockeyschlaeger-kurve-ist-eine-faelschung , John Cook/klimafakten.de, „*Fakt ist:*

Die Aussage der oft kritisierten 'Hockeyschläger'-Kurve wird durch viele unabhängige Studien bestätigt", Juli 2010; zuletzt aktualisiert: Dezember 2014

[143] https://www.youtube.com/watch?v=OBdRittlo8w&t=46s , *„Die Zerstörung der Klima-Hysterie!!? * Klimawandel-Kommentar"*, 07.09.2019

[144] https://www.eike-klima-energie.eu/2019/09/28/die-manipulation-von-temperaturdaten-ist-der-groesste-wissenschafts-skandal-jemals/ , *„Die Manipulation von Temperaturdaten ist der größte Wissenschafts-Skandal jemals"*, 28.09.19

[145] Hartmut Bachmann: *„Die Lüge der Klimakatastrophe: ...und wie der Staat uns damit ausbeutet. Manipulierte Angst als Mittel zur Macht"*, Kurzbeschreibung, entnommen aus https://docplayer.org/43335841-Die-luege-der-klimakatastrophe.html , *„Die Lüge der Klimakatastrophe - Version 15"*

[146] https://mail.google.com/mail/u/0/#category/updates/FMfcgxwChSKsjNJTMfHLpjKDFbSzqcxC, Chris Frey: *„Adjustierte „unadjustierte" Daten: NASA nutzt den „Zauberstab" des Frisierens und erzeugt Erwärmung dort, wo es nie eine gab"*, 28.Juni 2019

[147] https://notrickszone.com/2019/06/25/adjusted-unadjusted-data-nasa-uses-the-magic-wand-of-fudging-produces-warming-where-there-never-was/ , P Gosselin "Adjusted "Unadjusted" Data: NASA Uses The "Magic Wand Of Fudging", Produces Warming Where There Never Was", on 25. June 2019

[148] https://data.giss.nasa.gov/cgi-bin/gistemp/show_station.cgi?id=501941200004&ds=1 , *"GISS Surface Temperature Analysis, Station Data: Darwin Airpor (12.4 S,130.9 E)"*

[149] https://data.giss.nasa.gov/cgi-bin/gistemp/stdata_show_v4.cgi?id=ASN00014015&ds=14&dt=1 , *"GISS Surface Temperature Analysis (v4) <, Station Data: Darwin Airport (12.4239S, 130.8925E)"*

[150] https://sciencefiles.org/2019/07/23/die-seltsame-erwarmung-der-schweiz-in-den-daten-der-nasa/ , "Die seltsame Erwärmung der Schweiz in den Daten der NASA - Manipuliert die NASA Klimadaten?", 23. Juli 2019

[151] https://mail.google.com/mail/u/0/#category/updates/FMfcgxwChSKsjNJTMfHLpjKDFbSzqcxC, Chris Frey: *„Adjustierte „unadjustierte" Daten: NASA nutzt den „Zauberstab" des Frisierens und erzeugt Erwärmung dort, wo es nie eine gab"*, 28.Juni 2019

[152] as previously

[153] https://data.giss.nasa.gov/cgi-bin/gistemp/show_station.cgi?id=501941200004&ds=1 , *"GISS Surface Temperature Analysis, Station Data: Darwin Airport (12.4 S,130.9 E)"*

[154] https://data.giss.nasa.gov/cgi-bin/gistemp/stdata_show_v4.cgi?id=ASN00014015&ds=14&dt=1 , *"GISS Surface Temperature Analysis (v4) <, Station Data: Darwin Airport (12.4239S, 130.8925E)"*

[155] https://www.youtube.com/watch?v=ZYXrGlYAZOg&feature=share , *„Tricksen, Täuschen, Fabulieren - Der Klimaschwindel / Neu!"*, am 13.07.2019 veröffentlicht

[156] as previously

[157] https://realclimatescience.com/2019/06/nasa-data-tampering-not-just-for-temperatures/ , *„NASA Data Tampering – Not Just For Temperatures"*, Posted on June 26, 2019 by tonyheller, In 1982, NASA's James Hansen showed that sea level rise slowed to almost a halt after 1950. That 30 year hiatus in sea level rise has since been erased."

[158] as previously

[159]

https://mail.google.com/mail/u/0/#category/updates/FMfcgxwChSKsjNJTMfHLpj KDFbSzqcxC, Chris Frey: *„Adjustierte „unadjustierte" Daten: NASA nutzt den „Zauberstab" des Frisierens und erzeugt Erwärmung dort, wo es nie eine gab"*, 28.Juni 2019

[160] http://www.sauberer-himmel.de/2015/02/01/wer-steckt-hinter-den-chemtrails-eine-verschwoerung-oder-gar-ein-weltimperium/ , *„ Wer steckt hinter den Chemtrails? Eine Verschwörung? Eine Weltverschwörung? Oder gar ein Weltimperium?"*, 01.02.2015

[161] as previously

[162]

https://mail.google.com/mail/u/0/#search/Ingrid/QgrcJHsTkxvNtzMKDCHknRW xbVFLZWVHZjB?projector=1 *„Grüner Hass: Hetzen Spaß-Youtuber die Jugend auf? - Gerhard Wisnewski im Gespräch"*, am 05.06.2019 veröffentlicht

[163]

https://mail.google.com/mail/u/0/#inbox/FMfcgxwBVzwnZddlMHKxGHqsGbW bdzst, Axel Robert Göhring: *„Gretas deutsche „Adjutantin" ist erfahrene Vielfliegerin – mit 22"*, 10. März 2019

[164] https://www.youtube.com/watch?v=Ls07THzlL9M , *„Dirk Müller - "One World": Darum ist den Eliten das Klima plötzlich so wichtig!"*, am 24.05.2019 veröffentlicht

[165]

https://www.facebook.com/dawid.snowden/videos/vb.345142656089183/4147186 92710144/?type=2&theater , *„Die Masse wird zu hörigen Lemmingen erzogen"*, 3.Juni 2019

[166] https://www.youtube.com/watch?v=_G9GQvwsfT4 , „Grüner Hass: Hetzen Spaß-Youtuber die Jugend auf? - Gerhard Wisnewski im Gespräch", am 05.06.2019 veröffentlicht

[167] https://www.youtube.com/watch?v=_G9GQvwsfT4 , „Hetzen Spaß-YouTuber die Jugend auf? (Gerhard Wisnewski im Gespräch) | 08.06.2019 | www.kla.tv/14393", klagemauerTV , am 08.06.2019 veröffentlicht

[168] http://www.wisnewski.ch/rezo-kulturrevolution-2-0/

[169] https://www.youtube.com/watch?v=qtu2hbPkzm4 , *„Die grüne Kulturrevolution: Wie viele Tote wird sie fordern? Debattiert!"*, Am 01.06.2019 veröffentlicht

[170] https://www.youtube.com/watch?v=jA6Oit-4sKY&fbclid=IwAR25A73-XS-yoanG30l7rA25s9MVac0NPOw3qD3uUI8Bxx87u3CvUv9i4eU , „WDR 2 Comedy Kinderchor: *"Meine Oma ist ne alte Umweltsau"*, 27.12.2019

[171] https://www.youtube.com/watch?v=jA6Oit-4sKY&fbclid=IwAR25A73-XS-yoanG30l7rA25s9MVac0NPOw3qD3uUI8Bxx87u3CvUv9i4eU , „WDR 2 Comedy Kinderchor: *"Meine Oma ist ne alte Umweltsau"*, 27.12.2019

[172] https://www.youtube.com/watch?v=_G9GQvwsfT4 , „Grüner Hass: Hetzen Spaß-Youtuber die Jugend auf? - Gerhard Wisnewski im Gespräch", am 05.06.2019 veröffentlicht

[173] as previously

[174] https://www.youtube.com/watch?v=IqH--Yi2CI4   *„Der Ursprung der Klimalüge"*, veröffentlicht am 06.12.2016

[175] Joachim Sonntag, *Deutschland im freien Fall – Wie die milliardenschweren Finanzeliten unsere freiheitliche Demokratie zerstören und unsere Politiker und öffentlichen Medien zu deren Werkzeugen wurden*, 2. erweiterte Auflage, BoD-Verlag, 2017, pages 23ff

[176] https://www.pravda-tv.com/2018/12/haarp-geoengineering-in-deutschland-die-hitzewelle-2018-

vi-

deo/?fbclid=IwAR1RWT9A6K_FPPseisuP76063wpFCWvZzIzTZGN1SKPf8qH DfKAC-jBYETU , *„HAARP: Geoengineering in Deutschland - die Hitzewelle 2018 (Video)"* ; veröffentlicht 18.12.2018

[177] http://news-for-friends.de/mit-haarp-zum-tornado-mit-dem-tornado-zur-co2-steuer/ *"Mit HAARP zum Tornado, mit dem Tornado zur CO2-Steuer....."* Von nfriends, 20. Juli 2017

[178] https://de.scribd.com/doc/3436120/UN-1976-Weather-Weapon-Treaty

[179] https://www.youtube.com/watch?v=5blrkhKucIQ   *„Hitze Dürre - Haarp Wetterwaffen töten 300 Menschen pro Tag."*; veröffentlicht 09.08.2018

[180] https://www.youtube.com/watch?v=pCWJ027U8SI *„Geo-Engineering, Wettermanipulation HAARP 2018 in Deutschland"* ; veröffentlicht 14.08.2018

[181] as previously

[182] https://www.youtube.com/watch?v=5blrkhKucIQ   *„Hitze Dürre - Haarp Wetterwaffen töten 300 Menschen pro Tag."*

[183] *https://www.youtube.com/watch?v=pCWJ027U8SI „Geo-Engineering, Wettermanipulation HAARP 2018 in Deutschland"* , from minute 6:20; veröffentlicht 14.08.2018

[184] https://www.youtube.com/watch?v=5blrkhKucIQ   *„Hitze Dürre - Haarp Wetterwaffen töten 300 Menschen pro Tag."*, from minute 2:25; veröffentlicht 09.08.2018

[185] https://www.youtube.com/watch?v=VaiNlH51lOM *„Die größte Waffe, welche die Welt je gesehen hat! - Deutsche Untertitel"* , veröffentlicht: 13.08.2018

[186] https://www.youtube.com/watch?v=Y80h1B-_DL4

"Manipulation des Wetters und des Bewusstseins Geo Engeneering"

[187] https://www.youtube.com/watch?v=DFVi6DYMnMY&t=276s *"JEDER MUSS DAS WISSEN BEVOR ES GELÖSCHT WIRD !!! Seht was sie euch verschweigen!"*

[188] https://www.youtube.com/watch?v=NRbVZo9v5I4 *„Bürgeranwalt Dominik Storr zu Chemtrails - Todestreifen am Himmel"*, am 03.04.2019 veröffentlicht

[189] https://www.weather-modification-journal.de/nsa-whistleblower-snowden-enth%C3%BCllt-schockierende-wahrheit-hinter-den-chemtrails/ *„Wetter-Modifikation = Wetteränderung durch toxische Chemikalien"*
[190] https://www.youtube.com/watch?v=Dt46HlnRLkM *„Das Märchen von den Chemtrails - Erklärungen und Hintergründe"*
[191] https://www.youtube.com/watch?v=U2FWU_Nx4Uc *„Chemtrails gibt es nicht - die spinnen, die Verschwörungstheoretiker"*
[192] https://www.youtube.com/watch?v=0rNpHKSjIdQ *"Gibt es Chemtrails? | Harald Lesch"*
[193] *https://www.youtube.com/watch?v=BrIKAI5snFk*
„CHEMTRAILS - das sind die Beweise! - Bundeswehr gibt sprühen zu! Geoengineering" Hier wird die Existenz von Chemtrails geleugnet.
[194] https://www.augsburger-allgemeine.de/landsberg/Woher-kommen-die-Kreise-am-Himmel-id43014186.html Augsburger Allgemeine, 19.10.18 *„Woher kommen die Kreise am Himmel?"*
[195] https://www.tz.de/muenchen/stadt/nanu-sind-etwa-chemtrails-ueber-muenchen-sagen-experten-9553863.html *„Seltsame Ringe über München: Jetzt ist die Ursache für das Phänomen geklärt"*
[196] https://www.youtube.com/watch?v=A_Ix6rP0M78 *„heute show: Deutschland Deine Irren: Chemtrails mit Lutz van der Horst"*
[197]

https://www.youtube.com/watch?v=OUuUwe85ZlU&fbclid=IwAR15ZmlVCEiOrCaF8dhfWrNR8d3BzxanRdeJMaufi6Pwlj27MXLnyKQaNqY *„OVERCAST Klimaexperiment am Himmel (Chemtrail/Geoengineering Doku)"*, veröffentlicht am 13.12.2017
[198] https://www.mimikama.at/allgemein/nie-gesehene-fotos-von-chemtrails-flugzeugen/?fbclid=IwAR1WNQ1HeWlB4rWfZ3MCZQUnBI5Sn-oYQuB7uWYQY1fLtupOViHfQRfL5fA , MIMIKAMA *„Nie gesehene Fotos von Chemtrails-Flugzeugen? – Ehm… doch!"*
[199] https://www.youtube.com/watch?v=HitwJhUJrT4 *„Mammatus Wolken aus dem Labor?"*, am 04.01.2018 veröffentlicht
[200] as previously
[201] https://www.youtube.com/watch?v=Dt46HlnRLkM *„Das Märchen von den Chemtrails - Erklärungen und Hintergründe"*
[202] https://www.youtube.com/watch?v=0rNpHKSjIdQ *"Gibt es Chemtrails? | Harald Lesch"*
[203] https://www.youtube.com/watch?v=U2FWU_Nx4Uc *„Chemtrails gibt es nicht - die spinnen, die Verschwörungstheoretiker"*
[204] https://www.youtube.com/watch?v=8RPlQ8jsXSs&feature=youtu.be *"NDR Regenwasser voller Nanopartikel"*
[205] https://gesundmagazin.com/chemtrails-sind-verantwortlich-fuer-krankheiten-sie-zerstoeren-unser-immunsystem-mit-video/ , *„Chemtrails sind verantwortlich für Krankheiten Sie zerstören unser Immunsystem (mit Video)"*, 21. Februar 2019
[206] *„Von Klimawandel, Geisterwolken, und Chemtrails"*, 2008, DVD, Skadi-Media Bochum

[207] https://www.youtube.com/watch?v=-OwxcaoZECA *"Aerosol Crimes - Clifford E. Carnicom [Deutsch]"*, am 23.10.2013 veröffentlicht

[208] https://www.youtube.com/watch?v=HitwJhUJrT4 *„MammatusWolken aus dem Labor?"*, am 04.01.2018 veröffentlicht

[209] https://www.youtube.com/watch?v=FW9gVpzvSZo *„Piloten, Ärzte & Wissenschaftler berichten über Chemtrails"*

[210] https://www.youtube.com/watch?v=_8o4xgSVcyg *"Chemtrails Trojanische Wolken Doku (full length)"*

[211] www.bmbf.de/pubRD/Infografik_climate_engineering.pdf

[212] https://www.youtube.com/watch?v=8RPlQ8jsXSs&feature=youtu.be *"NDR Regenwasser voller Nanopartikel"*, am 17.07.2016 veröffentlicht

[213] https://www.youtube.com/watch?v=Xot1EI4s6j0 *"ZDF heute-journal 14.01.2009 Wetter – Chemtrails"*

[214] https://www.youtube.com/watch?v=tuVspN5RIoE *„NEWW!! ARD u ZDF zeigen Haarp und Chemtrails sind keineswegs eine Verschwörungstheorie UNFASSBAR!"*, am 03.01.2017 veröffentlicht

[215] https://www.youtube.com/watch?v=Xot1EI4s6j0 *"ZDF heute-journal 14.01.2009 Wetter – Chemtrails"*

[216] https://www.youtube.com/watch?v=tuVspN5RIoE *„NEWW!! ARD u ZDF zeigen Haarp und Chemtrails sind keineswegs eine Verschwörungstheorie UNFASSBAR!"*, am 03.01.2017 veröffentlicht

[217] https://www.youtube.com/watch?v=sEWe-EBcx1k *„Dr. med D. Klinghardt === ✈ Chemtrail Fallout ist die wichtigste Vergiftungsursache!"*, am 29.08.2018 veröffentlicht

[218] https://www.youtube.com/watch?v=UCIZT05hfjc *„#ARD & #ZDF zeigen #Haarp und #Chemtrails Es gibt sie wirklich 2017."*

[219] https://www.legitim.ch/single-post/2017/08/07/Die-NASA-gibt-zu-Lithium-und-andere-Chemikalien-in-die-Atmosph%C3%A4re-zu-sprayen Jan Walter: *"Die NASA gibt zu Lithium und andere Chemikalien in die Atmosphäre zu sprayen"*, 7 Aug 2017

[220] as previously

[221] DIE WELT – Nr. 254 – Dienstag, 31. Oktober 1978

[222] https://www.politikforen.net/showthread.php?155157-Die-90-Dezimierung-der-Menschheit-wird-mit-Nano *„Die 90%-Dezimierung der Menschheit wird mit Nano-Waffen erfolgen!"* ,11.08.2014

[223] as previously

[224] http://saga4ever.blogspot.com/ , *„Bayern: Katastrophale Konzentration von Aluminium, Barium und Arsen in der Atemluft amtlich bestätigt"*, 18. November 2016
saga4ever.blogspot.com

[225] Joachim Sonntag, *Deutschland im freien Fall – Wie die milliardenschweren Finanzeliten unsere freiheitliche Demokratie zerstören und unsere Politiker und öffentlichen Medien zu deren Werkzeugen wurden*, 2. erweiterte Auflage, BoD-Verlag, 2017, Anlage 3

[226] https://www.weather-modification-journal.de/nsa-whistleblower-snowden-enth%C3%BCllt-schockierende-wahrheit-hinter-den-chemtrails/ *„Wetter-Modifikation = Wetteränderung durch toxische Chemikalien"*

[227] as previously

[228] http://www.bund-rvso.de/chemtrails.html *„Chemtrails 2019: Kritische BUND-Stellungnahme zu Verschwörungstheorien, Industrieinteressen & postfaktischen Debatten"*

[229] https://www.youtube.com/watch?v=-OwxcaoZECA *"Aerosol Crimes - Clifford E. Carnicom [Deutsch]"*, Am 23.10.2013 veröffentlicht, das Zitat s. Minute 22:10 im Video.

[230] as previously, das Zitat s. Minute 26 im Video.

[231] http://www.sauberer-himmel.de/untersuchungen/ *„Untersuchungen von Regenwasser, Polymerfasern etc. & wissenschaftliche Grundlagen"*

[232] https://www.youtube.com/watch?v=_8o4xgSVcyg *"Chemtrails Trojanische Wolken Doku (full length)"*

[233] as previously

[234] George Orwell, *1984*, Ungekürzte Ausgabe im Ullstein Taschenbuch, 38. Auflage 2015, page 115

[235] https://www.facebook.com/ursula.l.mayer/posts/2116799428344036

[236] as previously

[237] https://www.politikforen.net/showthread.php?155157-Die-90-Dezimierung-der-Menschheit-wird-mit-Nano *„Die 90%-Dezimierung der Menschheit wird mit Nano-Waffen erfolgen!"* ,11.08.2014

[238] https://www.facebook.com/marigny.degrilleau/posts/1018294345016824

[239] Zitiert aus einer Rezension (2015) bei Amazon.de: zum Buch *„Kriegswaffe Planet Erde"* von Rosalie Bertell

[240] https://www.youtube.com/watch?v=_8o4xgSVcyg *"Chemtrails Trojanische Wolken Doku (full length)"*

[241] as previously

[242] https://www.youtube.com/watch?v=7oTa9CZVw6c *„Neue Wolkenarten - Die Presse bestätigt Chemtrails!"*, veröffentlicht am 25.03.2017

[243] http://www.chemtrail.de/wp-content/uploads/2013/12/art1.pdf *„Piloten, Ärzte und Wissenschaftler packen aus! – Chemtrails"*

[244] https://www.youtube.com/watch?v=PW9wF5gI5dg *„Dr. Klinghardt (Deutsch/English) - subtitulado en Castellano"* , veröffentlicht am 13.12.2018

[245] as previously

[246] https://www.youtube.com/watch?v=NRbVZo9v5I4 *„Bürgeranwalt Dominik Storr zu Chemtrails - Todestreifen am Himmel"*, am 03.04.2019 veröffentlicht

[247] *„Von Klimawandel, Geisterwolken, und Chemtrails"*, DVD, Skadi-Media,Friederikastr. 107, D-44789 Bochum, 2008

[248] https://www.youtube.com/watch?v=ofXyRV73xaw *„Dr. Klinghardt zu Geoengineering, Impfungen + Entgiftung (Kurzversion)"*, veröffentlicht am 05.12.2017

[249] https://www.weather-modification-journal.de/

[250] https://www.zeit.de/wissen/umwelt/2019-09/geoengineering-klimawandel-ccs-ozeanduengung-kohlendioxid-strahlungsbilanz , *„Geoengineering: Da hilft nur noch, am Klima zu klempnern"*, 28.09.2019

[251] https://www.youtube.com/watch?v=bli57XeXUt0 *"ES GIBT KEINE CHEMTRAILS ! - DU ALUHUTDEPP ! DAS ULTIMATIVE BEWEISVIDEO"* (ddb Netzwerk)

[252] Joachim Sonntag, *Deutschland im freien Fall – Wie die milliardenschweren Finanzeliten unsere freiheitliche Demokratie zerstören und unsere Politiker und öffentlichen Medien zu deren Werkzeugen wurden*, 2. erweiterte Auflage, BoD-Verlag, 2017, Anlage 3

[253] Gabriele Schuster-Haslinger, *„verraten verkauft verloren"*, Amadeus Verlag GmbH & Co. KG, 2015, pages 45ff

[254] https://www.youtube.com/watch?v=_8o4xgSVcyg *"Chemtrails Trojanische Wolken Doku (full length)"*

[255] https://www.youtube.com/watch?v=Bs-_BOFdbpM , *„Bewusst.tv – Morgellons und Transhumanismus"*, Am 05.02.2014 veröffentlicht

[256] https://www.youtube.com/watch?v=39hqrLPsSt8 , *„HAARP und die NSA - Geheime Wetterexperimente in Alaska? | ExoMagazin"*, veröffentlicht am 25.12.2013

[257] https://www.youtube.com/watch?v=P9dc3Plo7MA&feature=share&fbclid=IwAR20JzMaRVbxTaTLok4AYCaCROY27ceAYPsbSf7R0h43NLFKTD-PxHZAfHU , *„Der wahre Grund für 5G ist 1000 Mal schlimmer als die Strahlung"*, Am 12.04.2019 veröffentlicht

[258] https://www.youtube.com/watch?v=WaudJgutsPw&t=1650s *„Doku: Der geheime Krieg - Solares Geoengineering - deutsch synchronisierte Version"* (Minute 5:25 im Video), veröffentlicht am 15.03.2016

[259] Chris Haderer und Peter Hiess, „Chemtrails – Wettermanipulation am Himmel? – Wettermanipulation unter den Augen der Öffentlichkeit", Copyright by V. F. SAMMLER, Graz 2005, page 25

[260] as previously

[261] as previously

[262] https://www.youtube.com/watch?v=_8o4xgSVcyg *"Chemtrails Trojanische Wolken Doku (full length)"*

[263] Gabriele Schuster-Haslinger, *„verraten verkauft verloren"*, Amadeus Verlag GmbH & Co. KG, 2015, pages 45ff

[264] https://gesundmagazin.com/chemtrails-sind-verantwortlich-fuer-krankheiten-sie-zerstoeren-unser-immunsystem-mit-video/ , *„Chemtrails sind verantwortlich für Krankheiten Sie zerstören unser Immunsystem (mit Video)"*, 21. Februar 2019

[265] https://www.youtube.com/watch?v=GA3Gvr_ApL0 *„Wie wir vergiftet werden - Dr. Dietrich Klinghardt"*

[266] http://www.chemtrail.de/wp-content/uploads/2013/12/art1.pdf *„Piloten, Ärzte und Wissenschaftler packen aus! – Chemtrails"* veröffentlicht: 25.03.2017

[267] https://www.youtube.com/watch?v=8RPlQ8jsXSs&feature=youtu.be

"NDR Regenwasser voller Nanopartikel"
[268] https://www.youtube.com/watch?v=brkm2QoXWsM
„Werner Altnickel: Geoengineering, Chemtrails, SRM & HAARP"
[269] https://www.stuttgarter-nachrichten.de/inhalt.bosch-chef-diesel-reinigt-die-luft-vom-feinstaub.79ed306c-f509-4b21-ad8a-7f512891004a.html , Klaus Köster: *„Bosch-Chef - Diesel reinigt die Luft vom Feinstaub"*, 27.01.2016
[270] https://www.youtube.com/watch?v=brkm2QoXWsM
„Werner Altnickel: Geoengineering, Chemtrails, SRM & HAARP"
[271] https://gesundmagazin.com/chemtrails-sind-verantwortlich-fuer-krankheiten-sie-zerstoeren-unser-immunsystem-mit-video/ *„Chemtrails sind verantwortlich für Krankheiten Sie zerstören unser Immunsystem (mit Video)"*, 21. Februar 2019
[272] https://www.n-tv.de/wissen/COPD-haeufiger-als-Krebs-article4271976.html , *„Hohes Risiko für Lungenleiden COPD häufiger als Krebs"*, 11.9. 2011
[273] https://gesundmagazin.com/chemtrails-sind-verantwortlich-fuer-krankheiten-sie-zerstoeren-unser-immunsystem-mit-video/ *„Chemtrails sind verantwortlich für Krankheiten Sie zerstören unser Immunsystem (mit Video)"*, 21. Februar 2019
[274] https://www.youtube.com/watch?v=PW9wF5gI5dg *„Dr. Klinghardt (Deutsch/English) - subtitulado en Castellano"* , veröffentlicht am 13.12.2018
[275] https://www.focus.de/gesundheit/werden-menschen-duemmer-umwelthormone-eine-gefahr-fuer-das-menschliche-gehirn_id_7847170.html , FOCUS-Online-Gastautorin Pia Jaeger
18.02.2018, 18:30
[276] https://www.youtube.com/watch?v=8RPlQ8jsXSs&feature=youtu.be
"NDR Regenwasser voller Nanopartikel"
[277] https://www.youtube.com/watch?v=_8o4xgSVcyg *"Chemtrails Trojanische Wolken Doku (full length)"*
[278] http://www.chemtrail.de/wp-content/uploads/2013/12/art1.pdf *„Piloten, Ärzte und Wissenschaftler packen aus! – Chemtrails"*
veröffentlicht: 25.03.2017
[279] Jugend TV – CH – St.Gallen: *„Giftige Chemtrails – Ein Geschäft auf Kosten der Umwelt"* (am Ende des Videos *"Chemtrails Trojanische Wolken Doku (full length)"* wiedergegeben.
[280] https://www.youtube.com/watch?v=Y80h1B-_DL4&t=48s
"Manipulation des Wetters und des Bewusstseins Geo Engeneering"
[281] Ulrich Heerd, *HAARP PROJEKT – über Mobilfunk zur Strahlenwaffe*, 2. Auflage, Edition HAARP, MICHAELS VERLAG, 2012, page 17
[282] https://zeit-zum-aufwachen.blogspot.de/2014/08/haarp-rostock-marlow-grote-anlage-der.html
[283] as previously
[284] https://www.youtube.com/watch?v=DFVi6DYMnMY&t=276s *"JEDER MUSS DAS WISSEN BEVOR ES GELÖSCHT WIRD !!! Seht was sie euch verschweigen!"*
[285] https://www.chemtrailsprojectuk.com/new-world-survival-tips/ *"Chemtrails Project UK - Campaign to Ban Chemtrails and Geoengineering"*

286 https://www.youtube.com/watch?v=39hqrLPsSt8 , *„HAARP und die NSA - Geheime Wetterexperimente in Alaska? | ExoMagazin"*, veröffentlicht am 25.12.2013, Minute 4:07

287 https://www.youtube.com/watch?v=dmTT9HN-sOw *„HAARP SPIEGELT sich auf OSTSEE! WIE VIELE Beweise wollt IHR noch?"*, veröffentlicht am 16.04.2018, Minute 1:31

288 Ulrich Heerd, *HAARP PROJEKT – über Mobilfunk zur Strahlenwaffe*, 2. Auflage, Edition HAARP, MICHAELS VERLAG, 2012, pages 19ff

289 https://www.youtube.com/watch?v=39hqrLPsSt8 *„HAARP und die NSA - Geheime Wetterexperimente in Alaska? | ExoMagazin"*, veröffentlicht am 25.12.2013

290 Ulrich Heerd, *HAARP PROJEKT – über Mobilfunk zur Strahlenwaffe*, 2. Auflage, Edition HAARP, MICHAELS VERLAG, 2012, page 66

291 https://www.youtube.com/watch?v=39hqrLPsSt8 *„HAARP und die NSA - Geheime Wetterexperimente in Alaska? | ExoMagazin"*, veröffentlicht am 25.12.2013

292 https://www.youtube.com/watch?v=dmTT9HN-sOw *„HAARP SPIEGELT sich auf OSTSEE! WIE VIELE Beweise wollt IHR noch?"*, veröffentlicht am 16.04.2018

293 https://www.youtube.com/watch?v=UCIZT05hfjc *„#ARD & #ZDF zeigen #Haarp und #Chemtrails Es gibt sie wirklich 2017."*

294 http://www.ostsee-zeitung.de/Nachrichten/Das-Geheimnis-im-Wald-von-Marlow *„Das Geheimnis im Wald von Marlow – Die Deutsche Marine betreibt im Recknitz-Städtchen eine Sendestation. Um die Anlage ranken sich wüste Verschwörungstheorien."*

295 https://futurezone.at/meinung/haarp-todesstrahlen-aus-alaska/286.909.761

296 http://www.europarl.europa.eu/sides/getDoc.do?pubRef=-//EP//TEXT+REPORT+A4-1999-0005+0+DOC+XML+V0//DE#Contentd374406e958 , Bericht über Umwelt, Sicherheit und Außenpolitik, Ausschuß für auswärtige Angelegenheiten, Sicherheit und Verteidigungspolitik, 14.01.1999

297

https://www.facebook.com/search/top/?q=chemtrails%20in%20verbindung%20mit%20haarp%20benutzt%20werden.&epa=SEARCH_BOX

298 https://www.youtube.com/watch?v=DFVi6DYMnMY&t=276s *"JEDER MUSS DAS WISSEN BEVOR ES GELÖSCHT WIRD !!! Seht was sie euch verschweigen!"*

299 https://www.youtube.com/watch?v=a9g5LIFc8Y4&t=73s *„Bester Chemtrail-Vortrag von Werner Altnickel"*

300 https://www.youtube.com/watch?v=a9g5LIFc8Y4&t=73s *„Bester Chemtrail-Vortrag von Werner Altnickel"*

301 https://www.youtube.com/watch?v=dmTT9HN-sOw *„HAARP SPIEGELT sich auf OSTSEE! WIE VIELE Beweise wollt IHR noch?"*, veröffentlicht am 16.04.2018

302 https://www.youtube.com/watch?v=7oTa9CZVw6c *„Neue Wolkenarten - Die Presse bestätigt Chemtrails!"*, veröffentlicht am 25.03.2017

---

303 https://www.youtube.com/watch?v=Y80h1B-_DL4&t=48s
„Manipulation des Wetters und des Bewusstseins Geo Engeneering"
304 https://www.youtube.com/watch?v=Cl_IR_qxi34 *"Globalisierung Fakten"*
305 as previously
306 https://www.youtube.com/watch?v=a9g5LIFc8Y4&t=73s *„Bester Chemtrail-Vortrag von Werner Altnickel"*
307 as previously
308 as previously
309 as previously
310 www.stopthecrime.net
311 https://www.youtube.com/watch?v=a9g5LIFc8Y4&t=73s *„Bester Chemtrail-Vortrag von Werner Altnickel"*
312 http://www.arbeiterfotografie.com/naturgewalten-als-waffe/index-naturgewalten-als-waffe-0001.html , Anneliese Fikentscher und Andreas Neumann: *"Naturgewalten als Waffe - Hiroshima, Nagasaki, Fukushima – Japan 11-03-11 – Analyse zur Entstehung des Erdbeens in Japan am 11.3.2011"*, 25.3.2011
313 https://www.youtube.com/watch?v=a9g5LIFc8Y4&t=73s *„Bester Chemtrail-Vortrag von Werner Altnickel"*
314 as previously
315 https://www.youtube.com/watch?v=dmTT9HN-sOw&t=245s
„HAARP SPIEGELT sich auf OSTSEE ! WIE VIELE Beweise wollt IHR noch?"
316 https://www.youtube.com/watch?v=EgczgWJUOLA *„Chemtrails und Haarp - Brigitta Zuber"*
317 https://www.youtube.com/watch?v=dmTT9HN-sOw&t=245s
„HAARP SPIEGELT sich auf OSTSEE ! WIE VIELE Beweise wollt IHR noch?"
318 as previously
319 http://www.arbeiterfotografie.com/naturgewalten-als-waffe/index-naturgewalten-als-waffe-0001.html , Anneliese Fikentscher und Andreas Neumann: *"Naturgewalten als Waffe - Hiroshima, Nagasaki, Fukushima – Japan 11-03-11 – Analyse zur Entstehung des Erdbeens in Japan am 11.3.2011"*, 25.3.2011
320 as previously
321 https://bilddung.wordpress.com/2014/12/26/war-dieser-tsunami-menschgemacht/ BilDung für das Volk *„War dieser Tsunami menschgemacht ?"*
322 http://www.stopthecrime.net
323 https://bilddung.wordpress.com/2014/12/26/war-dieser-tsunami-menschgemacht/ BilDung für das Volk *„War dieser Tsunami menschgemacht ?"*
324 as previously
325 Ulrich Mies (Hg.), *Der Tiefe Staat schlägt zu – Wie die westliche Welt Krisen erzeugt und Kriege vorbereitet*, Promedia Verlag, Wien, 2. Auflage 2019, page 132
326 as previously
327 as previously
328 http://news-for-friends.de/mit-haarp-zum-tornado-mit-dem-tornado-zur-co2-steuer/ *"Mit HAARP zum Tornado, mit dem Tornado zur CO2-Steuer....."* Von nfriends, 20. Juli 2017

[329] https://gumshoenews.com/2017/08/31/manmade-hurricane-harvey-the-military-can-steer-a-hurricane/

[330] https://gumshoenews.com/2017/07/10/the-breaking-of-the-levees-in-new-orleans-gentrification-and-jewish-law/ *„The Breaking of the Levees in New Orleans, "Gentrification," and Jewish Law"*, July 10, 2017

[331] as previously

[332] https://www.contra-magazin.com/2017/09/wetterextreme-als-waffe-das-weltklima-als-versuchslabor-wurden-harvey-und-irma-kuenstlich-erzeugt/ , Eva-Maria Griese: *„Wetterextreme als Waffe: Das Weltklima als Versuchslabor – wurden Harvey und Irma künstlich erzeugt ?"*, 13. September 2017.

[333] https://www.globalisierung-fakten.de/ozonloch/ozonloch-entwicklung/

[334] Rosalie Bertell, *„Kriegswaffe Erde"*, j-k-fischer-verlag, Gelnhausen/Roth, 3. Auflage 11/2016, page 256

[335] https://www.youtube.com/watch?v=YmL7mJExaFQ *„Der OZON-SCHWINDEL- Wissenschaftler Entdeckten die Wahre Ursache des Ozonlochs!"*, veröffentlicht am 24.02.2018

[336] https://www.youtube.com/watch?v=YmL7mJExaFQ *„Der OZON-SCHWINDEL- Wissenschaftler Entdeckten die Wahre Ursache des Ozonlochs!"*, veröffentlicht am 24.02.2018

[337] Marion Schimmelpfennig, *„Giftcocktail Körperpflege: Der schleichende Tod aus dem Badezimmer"*, J.K.Fischer-Verlag, 2017

[338] Thomas Klein, *Sonnenlicht – Das größte Gesundheitsheimnis – Sonnenmangel und seine schwerwiegenden Folgen, Hygeia-Verlag, 2010*

[339] https://www.youtube.com/watch?v=Ll6i6M64On8&t=14s *"Waldbrände = Waffentests? Äußerst verdächtiges 'Brandverhalten'"*

[340] *https://www.facebook.com/photo.php?fbid=1577984245580731&set=pcb.1997665910447245&type=3&theater Günter Stellmaszek: Reale Verschwörungen! 14. Oktober 2017*

[341] https://www.youtube.com/watch?v=8RT9BReqSag&t=141s *„ENERGIEWAFFEN-TEST am eigenen Volk! 'Waldbrände' in Kalifornien 2017! Laserwaffen, Mikrowellen, NWO"*, Minute 1:50

[342] https://www.youtube.com/watch?v=lMIoBdQxKHY , *„Boeing YAL-1 Airborne Laser Testbed Lethal Intercept"*, Minute 2:15 – 2:29

[343] https://www.youtube.com/watch?v=8RT9BReqSag&t=141s *„ENERGIEWAFFEN-TEST am eigenen Volk! 'Waldbrände' in Kalifornien 2017! Laserwaffen, Mikrowellen, NWO"*, Minute 3:30

[344] https://www.legitim.ch/post/enth%C3%BCllt-prayfortheamazon-ist-fake-von-a-bis-z , Jan Walter: *„Enthüllt: #PrayForTheAmazon ist FAKE! (von A bis Z)"*, am 29.08.19, aktualisiert am 31.08.19

[345] http://www.faszination-regenwald.de/info-center/zerstoerung/index.htm , *„Faszination-regenwald - Zerstörung tropischer Regenwälder"*

[346] https://www.regenwald.org/themen/palmoel/fragen-und-antworten , *„Fakten über Palmöl"*

[347] https://www.youtube.com/watch?v=Ahcc-Gr55WA , *„Waldbrände in Südamerika - die ganze Wahrheit!"*, am 25.08.2019 veröffentlicht

[348] https://www.youtube.com/watch?v=hzWKNUQfG_4 *„Aus der „Feuerhölle" Südamerikas - aktueller Bericht"*, Am 25.08.2019 veröffentlicht

[349] https://www.legitim.ch/post/enth%C3%BCllt-prayfortheamazon-ist-fake-von-a-bis-z , Jan Walter: *„Enthüllt: #PrayForTheAmazon ist FAKE! (von A bis Z)"*, am 29.08.19, aktualisiert am 31.08.19

[350] F. William Engdahl, *„Geheimakte NGOs"*, Kopp-Verlag, 2017

[351] https://www.youtube.com/watch?v=lJ-rXRf88sA , *„Feuer in Australien: Was hinter den Buschbränden steckt"*, 15.11.2019

[352] https://www.youtube.com/watch?v=lYA6ErMN9RM&t=34s *„Warum brennt Australien? Von wegen Klimawandel!"*, 12.01.2020

[353] https://www.youtube.com/watch?v=5ZRwpKrVlKw *„Brandstiftung in Australien: Gretas Klima-Schwindel aufgedeckt"*, 10.01.2020

[354] as previously, Minute 3:30

[355] https://www.youtube.com/watch?v=lYA6ErMN9RM&t=34s *„Warum brennt Australien? Von wegen Klimawandel!"*, 12.01.2020, Minute 2; 4:50

[356] https://www.mimikama.at/allgemein/hochgeschwindigkeitsbahnen-ausloeser-der-braende-in-australien-und-kalifornien/ *„Hochgeschwindigkeitsbahnen: Auslöser der Brände in Australien und Kalifornien?"*, 11.01.2020

[357] https://www.youtube.com/watch?v=lYA6ErMN9RM&t=34s *„Warum brennt Australien? Von wegen Klimawandel!"*, 12.01.2020, Minute 7:30

[358] https://www.zeit.de/gesellschaft/zeitgeschehen/2020-01/australien-braende-hitze-feuerwehr-evakuierung-victoria *„240.000 Menschen zur Evakuierung aufgefordert"*, 10. Januar 2020

[359] as previously, Minute 3:30

[360] https://www.zeit.de/gesellschaft/zeitgeschehen/2020-01/australien-braende-hitze-feuerwehr-evakuierung-victoria *„240.000 Menschen zur Evakuierung aufgefordert"*, 10. Januar 2020

[361] as previously

[362] Joachim Sonntag, *„2025 - Der vorletzte Akt: Warum wir Heimat, Freiheit und Sicherheit verlieren"*, CBX-Verlag München, 2019, Anhang 1, pages 212ff

[363] https://www.youtube.com/watch?v=lYA6ErMN9RM&t=34s *„Warum brennt Australien? Von wegen Klimawandel!"*, 12.01.2020, Minute 10:15

[364] https://mail.google.com/mail/u/0/#inbox/FMfcgxwHMjvMCNTNCbSTthQbB MxZljvh , *„LAURA EISENHOWER PACKT AUS !!!"*, Legitim.ch, 13.4.20

[365] https://www.youtube.com/watch?v=L2ziG1GKVsg&t=188s „16. AZK: „Digitalisiert in eine strahlende Zukunft – todsicher!" - Anke Kern | www.kla.tv/13437" , veröffentlicht am 01.12.2018

[366] https://www.youtube.com/watch?v=sX3QSsG6_64 *"DIE DRECKIGE WAHRHEIT ÜBER DEIN HANDY !!! WILLST DU GESUND BLEIBEN ? BITTE VERBREITEN !!!"*

[367] as previously

[368] as previously

[369] https://www.kla.tv/5g-mobilfunk/10543&autoplay=true , *„Baumschäden durch Mobilfunkstrahlung"*, www.kla.tv/10543 , 21.05.2017

[370] as previously

[371] https://zeit-zum-aufwachen.blogspot.de/2014/08/haarp-rostock-marlow-grote-anlage-der.html

[372] https://www.youtube.com/watch?v=KFV51crLwQE *"Heiße Abschreckung: US-Armee testet Mikrowellenwaffe"*

[373] https://www.youtube.com/watch?v=Cl_IR_qxi34
„Mobilfunk als Mikrowellenwaffe- Barrie Trower"

[374] https://www.youtube.com/watch?v=KFV51crLwQE *"Heiße Abschreckung: US-Armee testet Mikrowellenwaffe"*

[375] https://www.youtube.com/watch?v=8RT9BReqSag&t=141s
„ENERGIEWAFFEN-TEST am eigenen Volk! 'Waldbrände' in Kalifornien 2017! Laserwaffen, Mikrowellen, NWO"

[376] https://www.youtube.com/watch?v=L2ziG1GKVsg&t=188s „16. AZK: „Digitalisiert in eine strahlende Zukunft – todsicher!" - Anke Kern | www.kla.tv/13437", veröffentlicht am 01.12.2018

[377] as previously

[378] as previously

[379] https://www.youtube.com/watch?v=vqFKhjXl1Cw *"Aufrüstung der Polizei mit Mikrowellenwaffen"*

[380] http://google.com/patents/US6506148
(zitiert in http://www.globale-evolution.de/showthread.php/4025-Mind-Control-(Gedanken-Kontrolle)/page7 vom 26.01.2016)

[381] https://www.youtube.com/watch?v=pjy6yWBzwpE *„MK Ultra - Das Gehirnwäscheprogramm der CIA [ZDF/Phoenix Doku]"*, am 03.09.2016 veröffentlicht

[382] https://www.spiegel.de/netzwelt/netzpolitik/5g-mobilfunkfrequenzen-versteigert-firmen-bezahlen-6-6-milliarden-euro-a-1272131.html ,
„Mobilfunkfrequenzen 5G-Auktion bringt Deutschland knapp 6,6 Milliarden Euro", 12.06.2019

[383] https://www.spiegel.de/netzwelt/web/5g-gefaehrlich-was-experten-zum-thema-5g-und-gesundheit-sagen-a-1257267.html#js-article-comments-box-pager ,
„Neuer Mobilfunkstandard Gefährdet 5G die Gesundheit?",11.03.2019

[384] https://www.jungewelt.de/artikel/368178.fortschritt-kontra-gesundheit-versuchskaninchen-f%C3%BCr-5-g.html , Ralf Wurzbacher: *„Versuchskaninchen für »5 G«"*, 5.12.2019

[385] https://www.tagesschau.de/inland/5g-gefahren-115.html , Wulf Rohwedder, tagesschau.de: *„Neue Mobilfunktechnik - Ist 5G gefährlich?"*, 12.06.2019

[386] Offenlegungsschrift DE 10253 433 A1 2004.05.27, Bundesrepublik Deutschland, Deutsches Patent- und Markenamt, Anmeldetag: 11.11.2002

[387] https://www.youtube.com/watch?v=qVG5wwO1PDI *„AUF • GEKLÄRT - TRANSHUMANISMUS | SMART-DUST UND AGENDEN 21, 2030 & 2045"*, am 18.11.2017 veröffentlicht

[388] https://www.youtube.com/watch?v=fDk960sQIvw&t=1236s
„Gedankenkontrolle mit 5G – Patente", am 11.04.2019 veröffentlicht

[389] https://www.youtube.com/watch?v=fDk960sQIvw&t=1236s
„Gedankenkontrolle mit 5G – Patente", am 11.04.2019 veröffentlicht

[390] https://www.youtube.com/watch?v=L2ziG1GKVsg&t=188s „16. AZK: „Digitalisiert in eine strahlende Zukunft – todsicher!" - Anke Kern | www.kla.tv/13437" , veröffentlicht am 01.12.2018

[391] https://www.google.com/search?q=Harald+Kautz-Vella+%C3%BCber+5G+%26+die+Hintergr%C3%BCnde&ie=utf-8&oe=utf-8&client=firefox-b , *„Harald Kautz-Vella über 5G & die Hintergründe"*, am 10.11.2018

[392] **Dr. Klaus Scheler: *„Polarisation: Ein wesentlicher Faktor für das Verständnis biologischer Effekte von gepulsten elektromagnetischen Wellen niedriger Intensität"*** (Sonderbeilage 3-2016 | 29. Jahrgang, „umwelt – medizin – gesellschaft")

[393] as previously

[394]

https://www.youtube.com/watch?v=P9dc3Plo7MA&feature=share&fbclid=IwAR20JzMaRVbxTaTLok4AYCaCROY27ceAYPsbSf7R0h43NLFKTD-PxHZAfHU , *„Der wahre Grund für 5G ist 1000 Mal schlimmer als die Strahlung"*, am 12.04.2019 veröffentlicht

[395] https://www.youtube.com/watch?v=eZmRom81nQo , *„RFID Chip muss nicht mehr implantiert werden. Chippen ohne es zu wissen – Cyborg"*, 18.05.2016, Minute 0:36

[396] as previously

[397] https://www.kla.tv/ErichHambach Erich Hambach: „16. AZK: Bühnen-Interview mit Erich Hambach zum Thema *'Auslaufmodell Mensch? – Transhumanismus und künstliche Intelligenz wollen uns ersetzen'"*

[398] https://www.legitim.ch/home/author/Jan-Walter , Jan Walter: *„Geheime Agenda - Der wahre Grund für 5G ist 1000 Mal schlimmer als die Strahlung!"* , 8. April 2019

[399] https://www.mines-kreativstuebchen.de/blog/digitalisierung-5g-smartphone#gsc.tab=0 , Jasmin Reichel: *„Digitalisierung, 5G, Smartphone, Nanotechnologie, Smartdust und Phased Array - was wirklich dahinter steckt"*, 21.5.2019

[400] https://marbec14.wordpress.com/2019/09/10/kalifornien-passant-filmt-wie-leblose-bienen-zwischen-zwei-5g-antennen-auf-den-boden-klatschen/ , *„Kalifornien: Passant filmt, wie leblose Bienen zwischen zwei 5G-Antennen auf den Boden klatschen!"*, 10. September 2019

[401] https://www.t-online.de/digital/smartphone/id_85555326/5g-netz-versuche-in-genf-und-bruessel-wegen-strahlung-gestoppt.html?fbclid=IwAR1f9jo7ppPx97QPjxW9-FAnakfl4rY0cMWjFFTAAYwF5uRnbiqBlUi74Gg , *„Bedenken wegen Strahlung - 5G-Versuche in Genf und Brüssel gestoppt"*, am 12.04.2019

[402] https://www.t-online.de/digital/smartphone/id_85555326/5g-netz-versuche-in-genf-und-bruessel-wegen-strahlung-gestoppt.html?fbclid=IwAR1f9jo7ppPx97QPjxW9-FAnakfl4rY0cMWjFFTAAYwF5uRnbiqBlUi74Gg , *„Bedenken wegen Strahlung - 5G-Versuche in Genf und Brüssel gestoppt"*, am 12.04.2019

[403] https://www.google.com/search?q=Harald+Kautz-Vella+%C3%BCber+5G+%26+die+Hintergr%C3%BCnde&ie=utf-8&oe=utf-8&client=firefox-b , *„Harald Kautz-Vella über 5G & die Hintergründe"*, am 10.11.2018

[404] *https://www.youtube.com/watch?v=S-NiZqNzerg* „5G Experiment misslingt und hunderte Vögel sterben in Den Haag,wie gefährlich ist 5G für den Mensch" (Text unter dem video),am 06.11.2018 veröffentlicht

[405] *https://www.youtube.com/watch?v=S-NiZqNzerg* „5G Experiment misslingt und hunderte Vögel sterben in Den Haag,wie gefährlich ist 5G für den Mensch" (Text unter dem video),am 06.11.2018 veröffentlicht

[406] Faltblatt *„Gender Mainstreaming – Kinderseelen werden gebrochen. Empörte Bürger wehren sich"*, heraugegeben von „Junge Freiheit", 11.Auflage, Stand September 1016

[407] Interview mit Prof. Dr. Ulrich Kutschera, COMPACT Spezial Magazin, Sonderausgabe Nr. 12, pages 40ff.

[408] Fachtagung *„Frühkindliche Sexualerziehung in der KiTa"*, *herausgegeben von der HAG (Hamburgische Arbeitsgemeinschaft für Gesundheitsförderung e.V.)*

[409] https://www.youtube.com/watch?v=G1FtXKR5jic&feature=youtu.be *„Der Krieg gegen Kinder - Sexualpädagogik der Vielfalt (CSE Agenda)"*

[410] as previously

[411] https://www.kla.tv/9603 , *„Pädagogik der Geschlechter- und Familienvielfalt führt zur Auflösung des traditionellen Familienbildes (2 von 3)"*, 23. Dezember 2016

[412] http://www.gender-mich-nicht.de/?gclid=CjwKEAjw9MrIBRCr2LPek5-h8U0SJAD3jfhtOwx0tL3UkYpbq-VNz2jHgXAp4W8h1Qb_lkfU_QN5ghoCfpjw_wcB

[413] Faltblatt *„Gender Mainstreaming – Kinderseelen werden gebrochen. Empörte Bürger wehren sich"*, heraugegeben von „Junge Freiheit", 11.Auflage, Stand September 1016

[414] George Orwell, *1984*, Ungekürzte Ausgabe im Ullstein Taschenbuch, 38. Auflage 2015, pages 131ff

[415] https://www.legitim.ch/post/agenda-21-einst-florierende-industrienationen-stehen-am-rande-des-kollaps , Jan Walter: *„AGENDA 21 - Einst florierende Industrienationen stehen am Rande des Kollaps!"*, 04.07.2019

[416] https://www.mobilegeeks.de/news/implantierte-rfid-chips-in-schweden-mehr-als-nur-ein-trend/ , Carsten Drees: *„Implantierte RFID-Chips: In Schweden mehr als nur ein Trend"*, 25.10.2018

[417] https://www.youtube.com/watch?v=eZmRom81nQo , *„RFID Chip muss nicht mehr implantiert werden. Chippen ohne es zu wissen – Cyborg"*, 18.05.2016, Minute 0:36

[418]
https://www.youtube.com/watch?v=P9dc3Plo7MA&feature=share&fbclid=IwAR20JzMaRVbxTaTLok4AYCaCROY27ceAYPsbSf7R0h43NLFKTD-PxHZAfHU , *„Der wahre Grund für 5G ist 1000 Mal schlimmer als die Strahlung"*, Am 12.04.2019 veröffentlicht

[419] https://traugott-ickeroth.com/liveticker/ , Traugott Ickeroth Blog, „Der Sturm ist da – Liveticker". 19.06.2020

[420] https://www.auswaertiges-amt.de/de/aussenpolitik/themen/abruestung-ruestungskontrolle/uebersicht-bcwaffen-node/verbotbiowaffen-bwue-node „Übereinkommen über das Verbot biologischer Waffen (BWÜ)", „Das Übereinkommen über das Verbot der Entwicklung, Herstellung und Lagerung bakteriologischer (biologischer) Waffen und von Toxinwaffen sowie über die Vernichtung solcher Waffen (BWÜ) trat am 26. März 1975 in Kraft und enthält ein umfassendes Verbot biologischer Waffen."

[421] https://vitzlisneuer.wordpress.com/2019/04/07/die-deutsche-luegenpresse-schweigt-eisern-das-labor-des-todes/ „Die deutsche Lügenpresse schweigt … eisern. Das Labor des Todes.", 7.4.2019

[422] as previously

[423] as previously

[424] as previously

[425] https://vitzlisneuer.wordpress.com/2019/04/07/die-deutsche-luegenpresse-schweigt-eisern-das-labor-des-todes/ „Die deutsche Lügenpresse schweigt … eisern. Das Labor des Todes.", 7.4.2019, Minute 9:25

[426] https://vitzlisneuer.wordpress.com/2019/04/07/die-deutsche-luegenpresse-schweigt-eisern-das-labor-des-todes/ „Die deutsche Lügenpresse schweigt … eisern. Das Labor des Todes.", 7.4.2019, Minute 8:53

[427] as previously, Minute 19:31

[428] as previously, Minute 18:50

[429] as previously, Minute 17:54

[430] as previously, Minute 25:25

[431] as previously

[432] as previously

[433] https://www.youtube.com/watch?v=byXgus2Cksk&feature=youtu.be , „Die Eugenik-Agenda der Elite und Transhumanismus", Min 34:24, am 02.08.2014 veröffentlicht

[434] https://steemkr.com/deutsch/@saamychristen/geographie-026-biowaffen-in-georgien , „Geographie 026 - Biowaffen in Georgien?", 01. Oktober 2018

[435] Frank-Rüdiger Halt: „Volk im Wachkoma", Frieling-Verlag Berlin, 2016, page 23

[436] https://www.youtube.com/watch?v=8RPlQ8jsXSs&feature=youtu.be "NDR Regenwasser voller Nanopartikel"

[437] https://www.legitim.ch/single-post/2017/08/07/Die-NASA-gibt-zu-Lithium-und-andere-Chemikalien-in-die-Atmosph%C3%A4re-zu-sprayen Jan Walter: "Die NASA gibt zu Lithium und andere Chemikalien in die Atmosphäre zu sprayen", 7 Aug 2017

[438] https://www.youtube.com/watch?v=8RPlQ8jsXSs&feature=youtu.be "NDR Regenwasser voller Nanopartikel"

[439] http://www.spiegel.de/gesundheit/diagnose/morgellons-krankheit-schlimmes-hautleiden-beruht-wohl-auf-einbildung-a-836099.html ; 6.6.2012

[440] http://www.spiegel.de/gesundheit/diagnose/morgellons-krankheit-schlimmes-hautleiden-beruht-wohl-auf-einbildung-a-836099.html ; 6.6.2012

[441] https://www.youtube.com/watch?v=NR0m_ADZ4JA ; *„Morgellons 'Krankheit' Chemtrails"*

[442] https://daserwachendervalkyrjar.wordpress.com/2015/03/11/morgellons-die-buchse-der-pandora-ist-geoffnet/ *„Morgellons: Die Büchse der Pandora ist geöffnet"*, 11/03/2015

[443] as previously

[444] http://www.wakenews.tv/watch.php?vid=16d2ed12d *"Morgellons"*

[445] https://www.youtube.com/watch?v=cTp_1HzrCoo ; Herbert Schott: *„Chemtrails und Nanotechnologie zur Manipulation der Menschheit Teil 1"*

[446] https://www.youtube.com/watch?v=NR0m_ADZ4JA ; *„Morgellons 'Krankheit' Chemtrails"*

[447] https://www.youtube.com/watch?v=8eoNuIDOaVg *"Dr. med. Manfred Doepp, Thema 'Morgellons' "*

[448] http://www.wakenews.tv/watch.php?vid=d27522d26 *"Morgellons sind Biowaffen (Borellien übrigens auch)"*

[449] http://www.wakenews.tv/watch.php?vid=16d2ed12d *"Morgellons"*

[450] http://www.wakenews.tv/watch.php?vid=dcddf6e34 *„erschreckend ! "Morgellons" (Nanorobots, synthetische Würmer, Biowaffen) bewegen sich"*

[451] http://www.wakenews.tv/watch.php?vid=f047d398f *"Morgellons in Karotte"*

[452] http://www.wakenews.tv/watch.php?vid=9911df782 *„Chemtrails + Morgellons (Fasern) in Nordrhein Westfahlen Deutschland !"*

[453] http://www.wakenews.tv/watch.php?vid=eb30896d8 *„Erschreckend !!! Morgellons schon überall, sogar in BIO-Bananen !"*

[454] https://daserwachendervalkyrjar.wordpress.com/2015/03/11/morgellons-die-buchse-der-pandora-ist-geoffnet/ *„Morgellons: Die Büchse der Pandora ist geöffnet"*, 11/03/2015

[455] www.morgellons-research.org

[456] Gabriele Schuster-Haslinger, *„verraten verkauft verloren"*, Amadeus Verlag GmbH & Co. KG, 2015

[457] as previously , pages 50ff

[458] https://www.youtube.com/watch?v=cTp_1HzrCoo ; Herbert Schott: *„Chemtrails und Nanotechnologie zur Manipulation der Menschheit Teil 1"*

[459] https://www.youtube.com/watch?v=Do9lehJNg88 ; Herbert Schott: *„Chemtrails und Nanotechnologie zur Manipulation der Menschheit Teil 2"*, am 17.03.2014 veröffentlicht

[460] https://www.youtube.com/watch?v=cTp_1HzrCoo ; Herbert Schott: *„Chemtrails und Nanotechnologie zur Manipulation der Menschheit Teil 1"*, am 16.03.2014 veröffentlicht

[461] as previously

[462] Weiterführende Literatur bezüglich der Schnittstelle zwischen Funksignal und dem menschlichen Biophotonenhaushalt findet man auf http://www.aquarius-technologies.de/veroeffentlichungen.html.

[463] https://www.youtube.com/watch?v=cTp_1HzrCoo ; Herbert Schott: *„Chemtrails und Nanotechnologie zur Manipulation der Menschheit Teil 1"*, am 16.03.2014 veröffentlicht

[464] https://www.youtube.com/watch?v=Do9lehJNg88 ; Herbert Schott: *„Chemtrails und Nanotechnologie zur Manipulation der Menschheit Teil 2"*, am 17.03.2014 veröffentlicht

[465] https://www.youtube.com/watch?v=Do9lehJNg88 ; Herbert Schott: *„Chemtrails und Nanotechnologie zur Manipulation der Menschheit Teil 1"* , am 16.03.2014 veröffentlicht

[466] https://www.youtube.com/watch?v=NR0m_ADZ4JA ; *„Morgellons 'Krankheit' Chemtrails"*

[467] https://www.youtube.com/watch?v=5blrkhKucIQ *„Hitze Dürre - Haarp Wetterwaffen töten 300 Menschen pro Tag."* : ab 20:42

[468] https://www.youtube.com/watch?v=rQA_Jf8svPc&t=29s   *" 'Ihr Thema ...':* *Geo-Engineering ein unkalkulierbares Risiko für Mensch und Natur"*

[469] https://www1.wdr.de/fernsehen/aktuelle-stunde/startseite/nsu-prozess-zeugen-sterben-100.html ; Jan Hofer, Matthias Goergens: *„Das reihenweise Sterben der NSU-Zeugen"*

[470] https://www.youtube.com/watch?v=cTp_1HzrCoo ; Herbert Schott: *„Chemtrails und Nanotechnologie zur Manipulation der Menschheit Teil 1"*

[471] http://www.aquarius-technologies.de/veroeffentlichungen.html ; Harald Kautz-Vella: *„Fakten zum Thema Geoengineering"*

[472] https://www.youtube.com/watch?v=Bs-_BOFdbpM , *„Bewusst.tv - Morgellons und Transhumanismus"*, am 05.02.2014 veröffentlicht

[473] https://www.youtube.com/watch?v=NR0m_ADZ4JA ; *„Morgellons 'Krankheit' Chemtrails"*

[474] https://www.youtube.com/watch?v=Bs-_BOFdbpM *„Bewusst.tv - Morgellons und Transhumanismus"*

[475] as previously

[476] https://www.zentrum-der-gesundheit.de/codex-alimentarius-ia.html?fbclid=IwAR17zPrh9oKnPMo5k2sQKdoti8jglrDXC5c-rFD8yNcKwcR_mTeTDifCTtA#toc-gesundheitliche-selbstbestimmung-ist-bedroht

[477] as previously

[478] https://www.youtube.com/watch?v=Bs-_BOFdbpM , *„Bewusst.tv - Morgellons und Transhumanismus"*, Minute 26:40, am 05.02.2014 veröffentlicht

[479] *https://gesundmagazin.com/chemtrails-sind-verantwortlich-fuer-krankheiten-sie-zerstoeren-unser-immunsystem-mit-video/* „Chemtrails sind verantwortlich für Krankheiten Sie zerstören unser Immunsystem (mit Video)", 21. Februar 2019

[480] Gabriele Schuster-Haslinger, *„verraten verkauft verloren"*, Amadeus Verlag GmbH & Co. KG, 2015, pages 48

[481] https://patents.google.com/patent/US20120251502

[482] http://de.wikimannia.org/Kanzlerakte

[483] https://www.youtube.com/watch?v=XtA9o6IQSo4 Augenöffner! Die Unterwerfung der BRD-Kanzler, am 09.10.2012 veröffentlicht

[484] https://www.planet-wissen.de/gesellschaft/krankheiten/ehec/ehec-epidemie 100.html ,

„Bakterien. Die Ehec-Epidemie von 2011 – ein Rückblick", planet wissen, 24.03.2017

[485] http://www.spiegel.de/wirtschaft/service/ehec-epidemie-2011-die-infektionsquelle-wurde-nie-gefunden-a-923249.html SPIEGEL ONLINE, Nicolai Kwasniewski: *„Neue Erkenntnisse zur Epidemie 2011 Der Ehec-Skandal, der nie aufgeklärt wurde"*, 20.09.2013

[486] http://www.spiegel.de/wirtschaft/service/ehec-epidemie-2011-die-infektionsquelle-wurde-nie-gefunden-a-923249.html SPIEGEL ONLINE, Nicolai Kwasniewski: *„Neue Erkenntnisse zur Epidemie 2011 Der Ehec-Skandal, der nie aufgeklärt wurde"*, 20.09.2013

[487] Wolfgang Eggert u.a. , *„Die geplanten Seuchen AIDS, SARS und die militärische Genforschung"*, 2003

[488] http://euro-med.dk/?p=23140 *„Chemtrails "Offiziell": Bakterielle Und Chemische Kriegsführung Unter Dem Vorwand Der Inexistenten Globalen Erwärmung"*, 3. Juni 2011

[489] http://chronos-medien.de/texteinblicke6.html#seuchen , Interview mit der illustrierten Zeitschrift "BOX"

[490] Markus Egert, *"Ein Keim kommt selten allein"*, Verlag: Ullstein extra, 2018

[491] http://www.spiegel.de/gesundheit/diagnose/ebola-kommt-das-virus-aus-dem-labor-a-997610.html , Holger Dambeck *„Stammt das Ebolavirus aus einem Geheimlabor?"*, 17.10.2014

[492] http://chronos-medien.de/texteinblicke6.html#seuchen , Interview mit der illustrierten Zeitschrift "BOX"

[493] https://www.amanita.at/interessantes/artikel?id=21&fbclid=IwAR3IfzvtTX-JdVyWRyt2EbrdWiRjS-rM72S_gIA2KZtbcIbGIDd_LkT2bRE *„Kriegszyklen & der Schweinegrippe-Völkermord"* (ohne Datum, jedoch aus dem Text kann man schließen, dass der Artikel aus dem Jahre 2009 stammt)

[494] https://www.focus.de/politik/deutschland/soeder-prescht-voran-merkel-deutete-sie-nur-an-warum-sich-deutschland-mit-ausgangssperre-so-schwertut_id_11789268.html?obref=outbrain-f100-web&cm_ven=f100_outbrain , Henriette Jedicke: *„Merkel deutet an, Söder drohtWarum sich Deutschland mit Ausgangssperre so schwertut"*, 19.03.2020

[495]

https://www.facebook.com/100015405430664/posts/768076520382522/?comment_id=768094813714026 , Min.1:53

[496] as previously

[497]

https://www.facebook.com/nach.denker.9/posts/609796002929040?comment_id=609864572922183 , *„Ist das Coronavirus im Labor entstanden?"*, 08.02.2020, , Min.9:15

[498] https://www.youtube.com/watch?v=dGx9MPSBWPY , *„WUHAN - Was geht in China vor sich?"*, 02.02.2020", Min.12:50

[499] as previously, Min.3:35

[500] as previously, Min.7:05

[501] https://www.zeit.de/news/2020-01/30/coronavirus-und-bill-gates-falschbehauptungen-im-umlauf , Faktencheck: Coronavirus und Bill Gates: Falschbehauptungen im Umlauf, 30. Januar 2020

[502] as previously, Min.5:10

[503] as previously, Min.11:10

[504] https://www.anonymousnews.ru/2020/01/26/bill-gates-stiftung-corona-virus/ , „*Bill Gates Stiftung prognostizierte 65 Millionen Tote durch Corona-Virus – vor 3 Monaten*", 26.01.2020

[505]

https://www.youtube.com/watch?v=j3BSN6kCZkE&feature=share&fbclid=IwAR1qZSHfIVG2T4OeKVYXFmyRK4PUVpDI0TGW4Nb53SIpB9lIZfdjc7FHs3M , „*Amazing Polly - deutsch - Die globale Pandemie Event 201*", 14.03.2020, Minute: 0:38

[506] as previously, Minute: 3:17

[507] as previously

[508] https://www.independent.ie/opinion/comment/fear-is-more-contagious-than-any-virus-39045195.html , Donald Lynch: "*Fear is more contagious than any virus*", 15.03.20

[509]

https://mail.google.com/mail/u/0/#search/legitim/FMfcgxwHMZLFPhksLCBXFSdhCphNklrV , LEGITIM - Newsletter (27.3. 2020), „***Trump will Notstand lockern: Massnahmen sollten nicht schlimmer als das Problem selbst sein!***"

[510]

https://heidenzorn.omasiso.de/stuff/wordpress/index.php/2020/04/04/kommentar-eines-facharztes-dr-juergen-mueller-zu-prof-bhakdi/ „*Kommentar eines Facharztes – Dr. Jürgen Müller zu Prof Bhakdi*", 4. April 2020

[511]

https://www.youtube.com/watch?v=2sZUS3SAWzk&fbclid=IwAR3SvNf3Z5Uz3MN6lj3pNK5kIDYkMPzc_lzAxcqA-ss_8K3WZqBN8ohwo9o
„*Corona ist eine Inszenierung: Padologe sagt: Corona ist eine Inszenierung und gibt es so gar nicht!*", 23.04.2020

[512] https://splitter-pfe.ch/pdf/home/200502_rubikon_wodarg_der-pandemie-krimi.pdf , Wolfgang Wodarg: „*Der Pandemie-Krimi - Covid-19 ist ein Fall für Medizin-Detektive.*", 02.05.2020

[513] as previously

[514] as previously

[515] as previously

[516] as previously

[517] as previously

[518] https://www.youtube.com/watch?v=Vaw_3F3Kq50 , „*RUBIKON: Im Gespräch: „Ein Menschheitsverbrechen*" (Wolfgang Wodarg und Jens Lehrich)", 31.05.2020, Minute 14:50

[519] https://www.tagesschau.de/inland/fernsehpreis-corona-berichterstattung-101.html

[520] *https://www.freiewelt.net/nachricht/covid-19-in-der-endphase-ist-wie-ertrinken-nur-langsamer-10080673/ , „Qualvoller Tod durch das Coronavirus - COVID-19 in der Endphase ist wie Ertrinken, nur langsamer", 16.03.2020*
[521]
https://www.facebook.com/anonline.darktribefashion/videos/2591724261142684/ , Demokratischer Widerstand Berlin I Pressekonferenz 07.05.2020, Minute 0 - 2
[522] https://splitter-pfe.ch/pdf/home/200502_rubikon_wodarg_der-pandemie-krimi.pdf , Wolfgang Wodarg: *„Der Pandemie-Krimi - Covid-19 ist ein Fall für Medizin-Detektive. ",* 02.05.2020
[523] as previously
[524] *https://www.youtube.com/watch?v=PfYot63f7Kg&t=2349s ,* „Herman & Popp Bombe im Bundesinnenministerium geplatzt! (Reupload)", 12.05.2020, Minute 20:53
[525] as previously, Minute 4:57
[526] https://traugott-ickeroth.com/liveticker/ , Traugott Ickeroth Blog, *„Der Sturm ist da – Liveticker".* 19.06.2020
[527]
https://mail.google.com/mail/u/0/#inbox/FMfcgxwHNVtkckTkRcpmDZtrRSnRJcJ C , „Das BUNDESAMT für STATISTIK widerlegt den BUNDESRAT !!! (KEINE PANDEMIE)" , ©2020 LEGITIM | NEWSLETTER, 18.05.20
[528] as previously, Minute 19:05
[529] https://www.house-of-light.gr/de/_/1./corona-virus-hoax-defender-2020.html *„Corona-Virus-Hoax & - DEFENDER 2020"*
[530] https://www.youtube.com/watch?v=JBB9bA-gXL4&feature=youtu.be&fbclid=IwAR0us-GU9kbG9yBXoTXPJlsT4wuoJZJx2UYIlYJP2EEsBQkzvseJRt3wouQ : *„Corona-Krise: Prof. Sucharit Bhakdi erklärt warum die Maßnahmen sinnlos und selbstzerstörerisch sind"* , 19.3.20, Minute 9
[531] https://www.youtube.com/watch?v=gpdIUunAPys&t=166s , *„Herbert Kickl zieht Bilanz: 'Kanzler Kurz hat Menschen bewusst in Angst und Schrecken versetzt!' ",* 22.04.2020
[532] https://www.youtube.com/watch?v=BBsET-tUzzM&t=732s , *"18 - Das Corona Kartenhaus zerstört ! Überraschung! schnell gucken*
18 - Das Corona Kartenhaus zerstört ! Überraschung! schnell gucken", 27.04.2020
[533] https://www.youtube.com/watch?v=MQGAtnDfeWM , *„Corona-Diktatur und Impfzwang: Hier wächst der Widerstand – Die Woche COMPACT",* 26.04.2020
[534]
https://m.youtube.com/watch?v=f6ikWIVpkv0&feature=share&fbclid=IwAR2X QT9Sf5XkZOVbVeuT9rwxCqeE_qmfKcWX1ziTcfMlOOsG_AsMnVfOMEU
[535] net find
[536] https://www.heidelberg24.de/heidelberg/coronavirus-heidelberg-klage-anwaeltin-bahner-regeln-gericht-massnahmen-corona-verordnung-verbot-13640822.html , *„Polizei ermittelt gegen sie - Wegen Corona-Verordnungen: Anwältin aus Heidelberg macht ernst",* 10.04.20

537
https://www.facebook.com/photo.php?fbid=1353132768225118&set=a.58555939
8315796&type=3&theater
538
*https://www.youtube.com/watch?v=wwXYbCQNVZA&feature=youtu.be&fbclid=I
wAR1KzXlrUdOYUUbJUH-LBBB-3leBPk9hEmlT00UZqY2mCi5cRi6jFBP3ASo*
„Rechtsanwältin Beate Bahner verhaftet und in Psychiatrie (Sprachnachricht)“,
13.04.2020
539 https://www.youtube.com/watch?v=HNZgXpVNXIg *„Broders Spiegel:
Generalprobe für den Notstand?“*, 06.04.2020
540 https://www.youtube.com/watch?v=W186IQ3ljC8 , Ken Jebsen *„Gates kapert
Deutschland! #GibGATESkeineChance
#WIRWOLLENUNSERERECHTEWIEDER“*, 06.52020, Minute 2
541 Dr. Klaus Maurer, *Die „BRD“-GmbH oder zur völkerrechtlichen Situation in
Deutschland und den sich daraus ergebenden Chancen für ein neues Deutschland*, Dritte Auflage, Sunflower-Verlag, 2016, page 40
542 https://viennnna.blogspot.com/2020/05/die-*neuenmrna-impfstoffe*.html , *“DIE
NEUEN mRNA-IMPFSTOFFE - viennnna.blogspot.com“*, 24.05.2020
543 https://www.sueddeutsche.de/politik/schweinegrippe-aufregung-um-zwei-
klassen-impfung-1.36055 Süddeutsche Zeitung: *„Aufregung um "Zwei-Klassen-
Impfung"*, 19.Oktober 2009
544 Stern Nr.22, 24.5.2018, Norbert Höfler und Jonas Wresch: *„ WIR BRAUCHEN
EUCH!“* page 27
545 https://www.planet-
wissen.de/natur/insekten_und_spinnentiere/bienen/pwiebienensterben100.html
Planet wissen: *„Bienensterben“*
546 Stern Nr.22, 24.5.2018, page 27
547 https://www.zeit.de/wissen/umwelt/2018-04/bienensterben-ursachen-pestizide-
imker-klimawandel Gunther Willinger: *“Bienensterben: Rettet die Bienen, aber
nicht so!”*
548 https://marbec14.wordpress.com/2019/09/10/kalifornien-passant-filmt-wie-
leblose-bienen-zwischen-zwei-5g-antennen-auf-den-boden-klatschen/ ,
*„Kalifornien: Passant filmt, wie leblose Bienen zwischen zwei 5G-Antennen auf
den Boden klatschen!“*, 10. September 2019
549 https://www.youtube.com/watch?v=a9g5LIFc8Y4&t=73s *„Bester Chemtrail-
Vortrag von Werner Altnickel“*
550 Nancy L. Swanson, Andre Leu, Jon Abrahamson and Bradley Wallet (2014),
Genetically engineered crops, glyphosate and the deterioration of health in the
United States of America. *Journal of Organic Systems* 9, Number 2, page 6
551 http://www.aquarius-technologies.de/veroeffentlichungen.html ;
Harald Kautz-Vella: *„Fakten zum Thema Geoengineering - 2. Faserkrankheit,
Pseudo-Darmparasiten, eingebildete Parasitose & Autismus. Die vielen Gesichter
der Morgellon'schen Erkrankung.“*
552 https://www.youtube.com/watch?v=GA3Gvr ApL0
„Wie wir vergiftet werden - Dr. Dietrich Klinghardt“
553 http://www.scielo.br/pdf/gmb/v30n2/a26v30n2.pdf

[554] Nancy L. Swanson, Andre Leu, Jon Abrahamson and Bradley Wallet (2014), Genetically engineered crops, glyphosate and the deterioration of health in the United States of America. *Journal of Organic Systems* 9, Number 2, page 6
[555] as previously
[556] https://www.youtube.com/watch?v=FW9gVpzvSZo
„Piloten, Ärzte & Wissenschaftler berichten über Chemtrails"
[557] https://www.youtube.com/watch?v=GA3Gvr_ApL0
„Wie wir vergiftet werden - Dr. Dietrich Klinghardt"
[558] Th. Schmitz und S. Siebert, *Klartext Impfen – Ein Aufklärungsbuch zum Schutz unserer Gesundheit,* HarperCollins Germany GmbH, Hamburg, 2019
[559] A. Moritz, *Die geimpfte Nation: Wie Impfen der Bevölkerung schadet Warum ADHS, Autismus, Asthma und Allergien dramatisch zunehmen,* Narayana Verlag GmbH, 2018
[560] https://cc.bingj.com/cache.aspx?q=Robert+F.+Kennedy+Jr.+-+Vereint+gegen+den+Impfzwang!&d=4520500498137245&mkt=de-DE&setlang=de-DE&w=xh2rtqV-lE4Hr4b6Qy6NkheC1GmgpFuX , *„Robert F. Kennedy Jr. - Vereint gegen den Impfzwang!",* 18.09.2019
[561] as previously
[562] https://www.die-gesunde-wahrheit.de/2017/12/02/impfstoffen/ *„CDC bestätigt: Glyphosat und Nierenzellen von Affen in Impfstoffen"*
[563] https://www.pravda-tv.com/2017/02/die-groesste-luege-dieser-welt-impfungen-und-das-masern-virus/ *„Die größte Lüge dieser Welt: Impfungen und das Masern-Virus",* 8. Februar 2017 aikos2309
[564] as previously
[565] https://www.pravda-tv.com/2017/02/die-groesste-luege-dieser-welt-impfungen-und-das-masern-virus/ 8. Februar 2017 aikos2309
[566] https://news-for-friends.de/ *„Globale Schock: Krebs wird in Impfstoffen übertragen, gibt das Unternehmen zu"* 26. Mai 2018
[567] https://www.die-gesunde-wahrheit.de/2017/12/02/impfstoffen/ *„CDC bestätigt: Glyphosat und Nierenzellen von Affen in Impfstoffen"*
[568] http://www.wakenews.tv/watch.php?vid=387f43076 *"Parasiten und Würmer im Körper - Eine Gefahr für die Gesundheit? QuantiSana.TV 12.06.2017"*(ab Minute 13:45)
[569] https://www.zentrum-der-gesundheit.de/dezimierung-der-menschheit-ia.html *"Impfung - Dezimierung der Menschheit"* (aktualisiert: 06.03.2018)
[570] A. Moritz, *Die geimpfte Nation: Wie Impfen der Bevölkerung schadet Warum ADHS, Autismus, Asthma und Allergien dramatisch zunehmen,* Narayana Verlag GmbH, 2018
[571] https://www.zentrum-der-gesundheit.de/dezimierung-der-menschheit-ia.html *"Impfung - Dezimierung der Menschheit"* (aktualisiert: 06.03.2018)
[572] https://www.youtube.com/watch?v=Sfm1oXpvkTA&t=833s ,
„COVID-19 , Aktuelle Informationen zum COVID-19 von der BZgA. - Heiko Schöning: #Corona - Kriminelle Zusammenhänge verstehen. #Coronavirus" , 27.03.2020

[573] https://www.pravda-tv.com/2013/12/eine-jahrhundertluge-spanische-grippe-wurde-durch-massenimpfungen-ausgelost/ *„Eine Jahrhundertlüge: Spanische Grippe wurde durch Massenimpfungen ausgelöst"*, 4. Dezember 2018

[574] https://www.zentrum-der-gesundheit.de/dezimierung-der-menschheit-ia.html *"Impfung - Dezimierung der Menschheit"* (aktualisiert: 06.03.2018)

[575] https://www.heise.de/forum/Telepolis/Kommentare/Ansichten-eines-Gutmenschen/Was-Carl-Friedrich-von-Weizsaecker-dazu-sagt/posting-24114785/show/

[576] https://www.anonymousnews.ru/2020/01/26/bill-gates-stiftung-corona-virus/ , *„Bill Gates Stiftung prognostizierte 65 Millionen Tote durch Corona-Virus – vor 3 Monaten"*, 26.01.2020

[577] http://www.s-und-g.info *„Stimme Gegenstimme S & G"*, Ausgabe 15/2017

[578] https://www.spiegel.de/politik/deutschland/jens-spahn-legt-gesetz-zur-impfpflicht-gegen-masern-vor-a-1265812.html , *„Gesundheitsminister Spahn legt Vorschläge zur Impfpflicht gegen Masern vor"*, 05.05.2019

[579] 9-Uhr-Nachrichtensendung am 5.5.2019 im WDR4

[580] https://vaccineimpact.com/ , *„Fetal DNA Contaminants Found in Merck's MMR Vaccines"*, May 21, 2019

[581] https://www.tagesschau.de/kommentar/impfpflicht-103.html

[582] https://systematischgesund.de/gesundheit/impfen/kindersterblichkeit/ als Video eingebettet (kla.tv/14793), Minute 19:19 bis 21:13

[583] //www.aerzteblatt.de/nachrichten/107757/Schon-mehr-als-5-000-Maserntote-im-Kongo?rt=8659a0b86d7e4097af5151b41fcf0ba4 , *"Masernimpfung erhöht Kindersterblichkeit dramatisch"*, 28.11.2019

[584] https://www.welt.de/vermischtes/article200979632/Kinderkrankheit-im-Kongo-Toedlicher-als-Ebola.html , *„Tödlicher als Ebola"* , veröffentlicht am 26.09.2019

[585] https://systematischgesund.de/gesundheit/impfen/kindersterblichkeit/ *"Masernimpfung erhöht Kindersterblichkeit dramatisch"*, 2.12.2019

[586] A. Moritz, *Die geimpfte Nation: Wie Impfen der Bevölkerung schadet Warum ADHS, Autismus, Asthma und Allergien dramatisch zunehmen,* Narayana Verlag GmbH, 2018

[587] https://www.youtube.com/watch?v=dbRCARZlzhc , *„Dringender Weckruf 2: Halten Impfunbedenklichkeitserklärungen einem Praxistest stand?"* | 21.09. 2019, Minute 1:02 - 1:28

[588] https://systematischgesund.de/gesundheit/impfen/kindersterblichkeit/ als Video eingebettet (kla.tv/14793)

[589] as previously, Minute 1:46

[590] https://www.youtube.com/watch?v=tsArJHgBoCg , *„VAXXED | Trailer deutsch german [HD]"*, 03.03.2017

[591] Daniel Prinz, *Wenn das die Menschheit wüsste ...,* Amadeus Verlag GmbH & Do KG, 2017, pages 251ff

[592] http://www.s-und-g.info *„Österreich: Kein Job ohne Impfung – Vorbote allgemeiner" Impfpflicht?"*, zitiert in *„Stimme Gegenstimme S & G"*, Ausgabe

15/2017, www.krone.at/oesterreich/graz-wer-nicht-geimpft-ist-bekommt-keinen-job-strenge-regelung-story-548460
[593] https://www.youtube.com/watch?v=nTgyakGAddM , „La Dra Rauni Kilde habla sobre la Conspiración de la Gripe Porcina" ("Dr. Rauni Kilde spricht über die Schweinegrippe-Verschwörung"), Am 31.08.2009 veröffentlicht
[594] https://www.amanita.at/interessantes/artikel?id=21&fbclid=IwAR3IfzvtTX-JdVyWRyt2EbrdWiRjS-rM72S_gIA2KZtbcIbGIDd_LkT2bRE „*Kriegszyklen & der Schweinegrippe-Völkermord*" *(*ohne Datum, jedoch aus dem Text kann man schließen, dass der Artikel aus dem Jahre 2009 stammt)
[595] https://www.youtube.com/watch?v=Z8jgOa1vw4w , „*Corona Virus - Fakten ! keine Verschwörung! Was ist die WAHRHEIT ? Coach Cecil*", 02.02.2020, Min.16
[596] http://chronos-medien.de/texteinblicke6.html#seuchen , Interview mit der illustrierten Zeitschrift "BOX",
[597] https://www.zentrum-der-gesundheit.de/dezimierung-der-menschheit-ia.html *"Impfung - Dezimierung der Menschheit"* (aktualisiert: 06.03.2018)
[598] https://www.epochtimes.de/politik/welt/toedliche-menschenversuche-mit-hpv-impfungen-indische-aerzte-verklagen-bill-gates-a1291203.html, „*Tödliche Menschenversuche mit HPV-Impfungen: Indische Ärzte verklagen Bill Gates*", 11.12.2015
[599] https://www.youtube.com/watch?v=Z8jgOa1vw4w , „*Corona Virus - Fakten ! keine Verschwörung! Was ist die WAHRHEIT ? Coach Cecil*", 02.02.2020, Min.20:30 – 22:40
[600] https://cgconsult.jimdo.com/2013/10/27/dezimierung-der-menschheit/ , „*Dezimierung der Menschheit*", 27. Oktober 2013
[601] http://www.umweltinstitut.org/themen/landwirtschaft/pestizide/glyphosat.html „*Glyphosat - Das meistverkaufte Pflanzengift der Welt*"
[602] https://monsanto.com/innovations/biotech-gmos/articles/gmo-facts/
[603] https://www.zentrum-der-gesundheit.de/dezimierung-der-menschheit-ia.html *"Impfung - Dezimierung der Menschheit"* (aktualisiert: 06.03.2018)
[604] Thomas Klein, *Fluor – Vorsicht Gift! Die schwerwiegenden Folgen der Fluoridvergiftung, Hygeia-Verlag, 2012*
[605] https://news-for-friends.de/ „*Warum vergiften sie uns?*" 26. Mai 2018
[606] Thomas Klein, *Fluor – Vorsicht Gift! Die schwerwiegenden Folgen der Fluoridvergiftung, Hygeia-Verlag, 2012*
[607] https://news-for-friends.de „*Warum vergiften sie uns?*" 26. Mai 2018
[608] https://www.youtube.com/watch?v=_8o4xgSVcyg „*Chemtrails Trojanische Wolken Doku (full length)*"
[609] https://www.zdf.de/nachrichten/politik/die-welt-verbuendet-sich-milliarden-fuer-corona-impfstoff-100.html , „*Corona-Geberkonferenz - 7,4 Milliarden gegen das Virus*", 04.05.2020
[610] https://www.youtube.com/watch?v=9inOYVK7Bj8 , „*Gates rechnet mit 700.000 Impfgeschädigten! Interview * Kommentar*", 26.05.2020
[611] https://www.youtube.com/watch?v=083VjebhzgI , Interview Bill Gates im ARD, 12.04.2020

[612] https://www.youtube.com/watch?v=Vaw_3F3Kq50 , *„RUBIKON: Im Gespräch: „Ein Menschheitsverbrechen" (Wolfgang Wodarg und Jens Lehrich)",* 31.05.2020, Minute 8:50

[613] https://viennnna.blogspot.com/2020/05/die-*neuenmrna-impfstoffe*.html , *"DIE NEUEN mRNA-IMPFSTOFFE - viennnna.blogspot.com",* 24.05.2020

[614] https://www.sueddeutsche.de/politik/schweinegrippe-aufregung-um-zwei-klassen-impfung-1.36055 Süddeutsche Zeitung: *„Aufregung um "Zwei-Klassen-Impfung",* 19.Oktober 2009

[615] https://www.youtube.com/watch?v=-rD9M-M8GIo Norman Investigativ *„Denver Illuminaten Airport - Ist an den Gerüchten was dran?",* 30.10.2019

[616] https://www.youtube.com/watch?v=3MCaceXGYHw *„Die verschwiegene Wahrheit über Gifte und Krebs",* Veröffentlicht am 19.09.2018

[617] https://www.youtube.com/watch?v=6ccUAQHdUGo&t=4s , *„ Vitamin B17 gegen Krebs - Die Wirkung von bitteren Aprikosenkernen",* am 28.10.2012 veröffentlicht

[618] https://www.alternativ-report.de/2019/06/09/neue-studie-beweist-krebs-ist-zu-100-prozent-eine-vom-menschen-gemachte-krankheit/ , *„Neue Studie beweist: Krebs ist zu 100 Prozent eine vom Menschen gemachte Krankheit",* 9.Juni 2019

[619] https://dieblauehand.info/chemotherapie-eine-mta-med-techn-assistentin-packt-aus/ Andrea Viertl: *„Chemotherapie – Eine MTA (med. techn. Assistentin) packt aus!",* 10.7.2018

[620] https://www.youtube.com/watch?v=pwkLXPhOTQI&feature=youtu.be&t=782 *„KenFM im Gespräch mit: Lothar Hirneise ("Chemotherapie heilt Krebs und die Erde ist eine Scheibe")",* Am 14.05.2019 veröffentlicht

[621] https://dieblauehand.info/chemotherapie-eine-mta-med-techn-assistentin-packt-aus/ Andrea Viertl: *„Chemotherapie – Eine MTA (med. techn. Assistentin) packt aus!",* 10.7.2018

[622] as previously

[623] Amazon.de: Aus einer Rezension von Uwe Hiltmann zum Buch: G Edward Griffin: „Eine Welt ohne Krebs: Die Geschichte des Vitamin B17 und seiner Unterdrückung" 2005

[624] https://dieblauehand.info/chemotherapie-eine-mta-med-techn-assistentin-packt-aus/ Andrea Viertl: *„Chemotherapie – Eine MTA (med. techn. Assistentin) packt aus!",* 10.7.2018

[625] as previously

[626] https://www.youtube.com/watch?v=HI7DOgj1sJI&t=261s *"Was Ihr über Krebs nicht wissen sollt..."*

[627] https://quer-denken.tv/biologische-krebsvorsorge-krebstherapie-i-linus-pauling-und-vitamin-c/ von Michael Friedrich Vogt in Querdenken-TV: *„Biologische Krebsvorsorge & Krebstherapie I: Linus Pauling und Vitamin C",* 27. Mai 2017

[628] https://www.youtube.com/watch?v=DuidG6hNCrk&t=1726s *"Krebs - Das Ende einer Volkskrankheit Dr. Matthias Rath - Das Ende einer Volkskrankheit 20.10.2011"*

[629] as previously

[630] as previously

[631] https://www.youtube.com/watch?v=6ccUAQHdUGo&t=4s
„vitamin b17 gegen krebs - die wirkung von bitteren aprikosenkernen"
[632] http://webcache.googleusercontent.com/search?q=cache:73-ZWpyDUZkJ:www.ralf-kollinger.de/wp/wp-content/uploads/2014/01/Akte-Vitamin-B-17-Amygdalin-Urteil-Laetril.pdf+&cd=1&hl=de&ct=clnk&gl=de&client=firefox-b
„Akte Vitamin B 17 Amygdalin Urteil – Laetril - Ralf Kollinger"
[633] https://www.youtube.com/watch?v=6ccUAQHdUGo&t=4s
„vitamin b17 gegen krebs - die wirkung von bitteren aprikosenkernen"
[634] Markus Egert und Frank Thadeusz, *Ein Keim kommt selten allein*, Ullstein Buchverlage GmbH, 2018, page 148
[635] https://www.deutsche-apotheker-zeitung.de/daz-az/2012/daz-46-2012/vitamin-b17-bei-krebs *"'Vitamin B17' bei Krebs? - Wie Amygdalin zu beurteilen ist"*
[636] *https://www.deutsche-apotheker-zeitung.de/daz-az/2012/daz-46-2012/vitamin-b17-bei-krebs* , Dr. Ulrike König: *„Fragen aus der Praxis - 'Vitamin B17' bei Krebs? - Wie Amygdalin zu beurteilen ist"*
[637] https://www.youtube.com/watch?v=H0Whdt1DBpc&t=314s
"Aprikosenkerne gegen Krebs: Lebensgefährliche Naturheilkunde"
[638] https://www.youtube.com/watch?v=MJ23O_fV5b4 *"Vitamin B17: Die größte Vertuschung über Krebs in der Geschichte oder doch alles Lüge?"*
[639] *Gesundheit und Krankheit verstehen – Eine neue Medizin auf Basis der 5 Biologischen Narurgesetze – entdeckt von Dr. med. Mag. Theol. Tyke Geerd Hamer,* 11. Auflage, Verantwortlicher Autor: Björn Eybl, Traunstr. 23, A-4600 Wels:
[640] https://www.youtube.com/watch?v=6ccUAQHdUGo&t=4s
„vitamin b17 gegen krebs - die wirkung von bitteren aprikosenkernen"
[641] as previously
[642] as previously
[643] Brigitte Helene (Hrsg.), *Vitamin B17 – Die Revolution in der Krebsmedizin,* BoD-Verlag, 2012
[644] Peter Kern, Krebs bekämpfen mit *Vitamin B17 – Vorbeugen und heilen mit Nitrilen aus Aprikosenkernen,* VAK Verlags GmbH, Kirchzarten bei Freiburg, 2008
[645] G Edward Griffin: *Eine Welt ohne Krebs: Die Geschichte des Vitamin B17 und seiner Unterdrückung,* Kopp Verlag, 2005
[646] https://www.youtube.com/watch?v=CzOl9XtfBJU *"Hilft Methadon gegen Krebs? | Zur Sache Baden-Württemberg!"* veröffentlicht: 12.05.2017
[647] https://www.youtube.com/watch?v=y9zdr8FQTE0 *"Methadon in der Krebstherapie - Pro und Contra - der ganze Talk | stern TV (28.06.2017)"*
[648] as previously
[649] Daniel Prinz, *Wenn das die Menschheit wüsste ...,* Amadeus Verlag GmbH & Do KG, 2017, pages 248f
[650] as previously, pages 237ff und 249f
[651] https://www.youtube.com/watch?v=L2ziG1GKVsg&t=188s „16. AZK: „Digitalisiert in eine strahlende Zukunft – todsicher!" - Anke Kern | www.kla.tv/13437" , veröffentlicht am 01.12.2018

[652] net find

[653]

https://www.facebook.com/dawid.snowden/videos/vb.345142656089183/1274342 572732838/?type=2&theater ||#208| *„Systematische Volksverdummung über die öffentlich rechtlichen Medien|"*, 5.Juni 2019

[654] Joachim Sonntag, *„2025 - Der vorletzte Akt: Warum wir Heimat, Freiheit und Sicherheit verlieren"*, CBX-Verlag München, 2019, Anhang 1, page 228

[655] Joachim Sonntag, *Deutschland im freien Fall – Wie die milliardenschweren Finanzeliten unsere freiheitliche Demokratie zerstören und unsere Politiker und öffentlichen Medien zu deren Werkzeugen wurden,* 2. erweiterte Auflage, BoD-Verlag, 2017, pages 50ff

[656] Alexander Unzicker, *„ Vom Urknall zum Durchknall – Die absurde Jagd nach der Weltformel"*, Springer Verlag Heidelberg Dordrecht London New York, korrigierter Nachdruck 2010, page 119f

[657] https://www.anonymousnews.ru/ , Holger Douglas: *„Biologe vor Gericht: Kritik an Gender-Theorien soll als Volksverhetzung bestraft werden"*

[658] https://www.legitim.ch/home/author/Jan-Walter , Jan Walter: *„Geheime Agenda - Der wahre Grund für 5G ist 1000 Mal schlimmer als die Strahlung!"* , 8. April 2019

[659]

https://www.facebook.com/search/top/?q=www.GMACAG.com&epa=SEARCH_ BOX

[660]

https://www.youtube.com/watch?v=P9dc3Plo7MA&feature=share&fbclid=IwAR 20JzMaRVbxTaTLok4AYCaCROY27ceAYPsbSf7R0h43NLFKTD-PxHZAfHU , *„Der wahre Grund für 5G ist 1000 Mal schlimmer als die Strahlung"*, Am 12.04.2019 veröffentlicht

[661] Joachim Sonntag, *„2025 - Der vorletzte Akt: Warum wir Heimat, Freiheit und Sicherheit verlieren"*, CBX-Verlag München, 2019, pages 14ff und 102ff

[662] https://news-for-friends.de/wie-wird-die-agenda-21-weltweit-umgesetzt/?fbclid=IwAR2uFUSfj_8zESyEV2wn_-OU00kKYJfphcGGxkWOqhD-J-mJq6NYKy_hYYQ , *„Wie wird die Agenda 21 weltweit umgesetzt?"*, 7.April 2019

[663] http://www.wisnewski.ch/rezo-kulturrevolution-2-0/

[664] G. Wisnewski, *Verheimlicht, vertuscht, vergessen,* Kopp Verlag, 2018, pages 46f

[665] https://www.youtube.com/watch?v=_G9GQvwsfT4 , „Grüner Hass: Hetzen Spaß-Youtuber die Jugend auf? - Gerhard Wisnewski im Gespräch", am 05.06.2019 veröffentlicht

[666] F. Fabian, *Die geheim gehaltene Geschichte Deutschlands – Was bis heute von Historikern verschwiegen wird,* Bassermann Verlag (innerhalb der Verlagsgruppe Random House GmbH, München), 2015

[667] https://www.youtube.com/watch?v=pD0t2M2cNc4 , „Das Ende der Parteien. Teil 1. Deutschland vor wunderbarem Neubeginn.", 06.01.2020

[668] https://www.youtube.com/watch?v=TNuhH6arYPw , „Das Ende der Parteien. Teil 2. Deutschland vor wunderbarem Neubeginn.", 06.01.2020

[669] Ulrich Mies (Hg.), *Der Tiefe Staat schlägt zu – Wie die westliche Welt Krisen erzeugt und Kriege vorbereitet*, Promedia Verlag, Wien, 2. Auflage 2019, page 33)

[670] https://www.youtube.com/watch?v=19asrm-S4i0&t=14s
„Horst Seehofer, erklärt warum Wählen sinnlos ist !!! Bei Pelzig 20.5.2010"

[671] Ulrich Mies und Jens Wernicke (Hg.), *Fassadendemokratie und Tiefer Staat – Auf dem Weg in ein autoritäres Zeitalter*, Promedia Verlag, Wien, 6. Auflage 2018, page 10f

[672] Ulrich Mies (Hg.), *Der Tiefe Staat schlägt zu – Wie die westliche Welt Krisen erzeugt und Kriege vorbereitet*, Promedia Verlag, Wien, 2. Auflage 2019, page 123

[673] Rainer Mausfeld, *Warum schweigen die Lämmer? – Wie Elitendemokratie und Neoliberalismus unsere Gesellschaft und unsere Lebensgrundlagen zerstören*, Westend Verlag GmbH, Frankfurt/Main, 2018, page 137

[674] as previously, page 131

[675] Joachim Sonntag, *„2025 - Der vorletzte Akt: Warum wir Heimat, Freiheit und Sicherheit verlieren"*, CBX-Verlag München, 2019, pages 75ff

[676] Ulrich Mies (Hg.), *Der Tiefe Staat schlägt zu– Wie die westliche Welt Krisen erzeugt und Kriege vorbereitet*, Promedia Verlag, Wien, 2. Auflage 2019, pages 17f

[677] as previously, page 13

ISBN 9783945794937
Paperback, 272 pages, 1st edition, 04/2019
CBX Verlag UG Munich,   15 €

The year "2025" is borrowed from the NASA document *"The Future Is Now! NASA Future Strategic Issues and Warfare - Circa 2025"* and is synonymous with the Day X, when the gradual process of globalization (in which we are now) is replaced by the global takeover by the elite. Globalization, which is being pushed forward with all violence, repressive measures against politically different thinkers and the brainwashing by the media, "Germany is colorful", are just smoke candles. It is intended to obscure what it is all about: The transparent person, complete control and total submission of the world under the rule of the financial elite - the New World Order (NWO).

ISBN 9783744809542
Paperback, 229 pages, 2nd extended edition, 09/2017
BoD Verlag Norderstedt, Germany   9,99 €

Germany is developing with giant strides from a free social state to a multi-cultural state dominated by left / green thinking templates and ideologies, supported by the media through the indoctrination of a "politically correct" media sovereignty - described by the author as "Free fall of Germany". This process takes place in close cooperation with the unions, authorities, political bodies, citizens' initiatives, churches, non-governmental organizations (NGOs), the public media and a multi-billion dollar refugee industry that has developed. This development, which is fatal for our homeland, is largely influenced by foreign powers and a consequence of the fact that Germany has not been sovereign since May 8, 1945.